CAMINEMOS CON JESÚS

CAMINEMOS CON JESÚS

Toward a Hispanic/Latino Theology of Accompaniment

Roberto S. Goizueta

Orbis  Books
Maryknoll, New York

Copyright © 1995 by Roberto S. Goizueta.
Published by Orbis Books, Maryknoll, New York.

Some of the ideas in this book have appeared, in different form, in the following articals by the author: "*Nosotros:* Toward a U.S. Hispanic Anthropology," *Listening* 27 (Winter, 1992): 55-69; "Otherness Has a Face . . . and It is Not a Pretty Face," *The Merton Annual* 6 (1993): 92-114; "*La Raza Cósmica?* The Vision of José Vasconcelos," *Journal of Hispanic/Latino Theology* 1 (February, 1994): 5-27; "Rediscovering Praxis: The Significance of U.S. Hispanic Experience for Theological Method," in *We Are a People! Initiatives in U.S. Hispanic Theology,* ed. Roberto S. Goizueta (Minneapolis: Fortress Press, 1992); "Theology as Intellectually Vital Inquiry: The Challenge of/to U.S. Hispanics," *Proceedings of The Catholic Theological Society of America* 46 (1991): 58-69; "U.S. Hispanic *Mestizaje* and Theological Method," *Concilium* 248 (1993): 22-30; "U.S. Hispanic Popular Catholicism as Theopoetics," in *Aliens in the Promised Land,* ed. Ada María Isasi-Díaz and Fernando Segovia (Minneapolis: Fortress Press, 1995); "U.S. Hispanic Theology and the Challenge of Pluralism," in *Frontiers of a United States Hispanic Theology,* ed. Allan Figueroa Deck (Maryknoll, NY: Orbis, 1992).

Library of Congress Cataloging-in-Publication Data

Goizueta, Roberto S.
    Caminemos con Jesús : toward a Hispanic/Latino theology of
accompaniment / Roberto S. Goizueta.
        p.   cm.
    Includes bibliographical references and index.
    ISBN 1-57075-034-3 (alk. paper)
    1. Hispanic American Catholics—Religious life.   2. Hispanic
Americans—Religion.   3. Catholic Church— Doctrines.   4. Christian
life—Catholic authors.   I. Title.
BX1407.H55G65   1995
230'.2'08968073—dc20

                                                    95-30162
                                                         CIP

DEDICATORIA

A Mami, cuyo amor ha sido la cuna de mi propio ser y me ha dado
las alas de la esperanza, la fe, y el sueño, con las cuales quizás
haya podido dejar atrás la cuna pero nunca el amor;

A Papi, quien, por su palabra y ejemplo, me ha enseñado a usar las
alas y a perseguir el sueño;

A Nana y Abuelita Aida, cuya fe en la bondad de la vida y de Dios
me ha enseñado que el amor de la vida y de Dios son el mismo
amor;

A Abuelito Segundito y Abuelito Críspulo, quienes me han enseñado
que la suavidad de carácter es una marca de nobleza, no de de-
bilidad;

A Javier y Olga Mari, cuya paciencia conmigo en nuestra vida fa-
miliar me ha enseñado que la unidad y la diferencia no son in-
conmensurables;

A Carlos Alberto, quien me ha enseñado que el amor nunca será
conquistado por la muerte; es especialmente por él y en su nom-
bre que nunca le concederé a la muerte la última palabra;

A Elizabeth, quien me ha enseñado a buscar la belleza en todo, y
con quien la he encontrado;

A Cristina y Roberto Carlos, quienes han compartido conmigo la
profunda sabiduría de los niños, y por cuyo futuro seguiré
luchando.

Contents

Preface

This book is written as an expression of gratitude to those U.S. Hispanics whose lives have borne witness—and continue to bear witness—to the liberating power of a God who walks with us. Their courageous, passionate affirmation of life in the midst of suffering and death bears witness to a central Christian belief, revealed in the incarnation, even if too-often forgotten: the love of God is inseparable from the love of life itself. It is my conviction that this unwavering affirmation of life has much to teach a U.S. society which, though desperately searching for some modicum of peace and happiness, finds itself increasingly divided, anxious, fearful, and apprehensive about the future.

My hope is that this book will help U.S. Hispanics claim our heritage—especially our popular Catholicism—as a privileged place of God's revelation and, therefore, a privileged source for theological reflection. The book is also written, however, for others in our church, academy, and society who might find in that heritage a goodness, truth, and beauty which are not limited to U.S. Hispanics but transcend any particular culture—and which may, thus, aid all of us as we confront the divisiveness and fear that mark a U.S. society on the threshold of the twenty-first century.

Focusing on theological method, the book asks the question "How might we U.S. Hispanics go about articulating a theology grounded in our historical experience?" It thus represents one U.S. Hispanic theologian's attempt to trace the outlines of a theological method. I take as my *locus theologicus* the popular Catholicism of U.S. Hispanics, more specifically, the popular religious celebrations of the Holy Week triduum and Our Lady of Guadalupe, as well as the religious symbols and narratives surrounding these celebrations. I then suggest what some of the implications of such a starting point might be for our understanding of God, Jesus, Mary, the human person, human action, the theological enterprise, and the preferential option for the poor. In the last chapter, I propose a "theology of accompaniment," *una teología de acompañamiento*, which would appropriate the anthropological and theological wisdom of U.S. Hispanic popular Catholicism.

The book is organized in the form of a "hermeneutical circle." In the first chapter, I discuss salient aspects of the "social location," or historical context, which informs the theological reflections that follow. Though the contents of the discussion would perhaps suggest its inclusion as an

Introduction, I have opted to incorporate it as the first chapter out of re-spect for that history: the biographical, historical, and methodological is-sues addressed are not merely introductory, precursory comments or even a passive "context" extrinsic to the theology; rather, these issues are them-selves intrinsic to and constitutive of the theological analysis. As my fam-ily and my Latino community are all an integral part of me and my own identity, so are they—and many other persons—an integral part of this book.

Chapter Two specifies the historical context even further: first, as the popular Catholicism of U.S. Hispanics and, secondly, and more concretely, as the symbols, narratives, and rituals associated with the triduum cele-brations of Holy Week and devotion to Our Lady of Guadalupe. The re-mainder of the book will seek to make explicit the anthropological ("who we are") and theological ("who God is") insights implicit in, and emerg-ing from, these first two chapters.

In Chapter Three, I articulate a U.S. Hispanic understanding of the self, or the human person, as informed by the experiences delineated in the first two chapters. I suggest that, for Latinos and Latinas, the human per-son is intrinsically communal, or relational. This "organic" anthro-pology—as revealed especially in Latino popular Catholicism—differs from the modern liberal, individualistic anthropology prevalent in the larger U.S. society.

In the fourth and fifth chapters, I develop this anthropology further: if the human person is constituted by communal relationships, the person is defined by her or his *interaction* with others. Thus, a relational an-thropology implies a particular understanding of the nature of human ac-tion or praxis. In Chapter Four, I outline several influential Western interpretations of the nature of praxis—those of Aristotle, Marx, Latin American liberation theologians, and José Vasconcelos—in order to lo-cate a U.S. Hispanic understanding of praxis in relation to this broader discussion. Thus, in the next chapter, I suggest how a U.S. Hispanic un-derstanding of human action might draw upon while nevertheless going beyond these.

The anthropology developed in the above chapters further suggests a holistic, organic understanding of human reason, the intellectual enterprise, and specifically, the theological task. In Chapter Six, I thus examine the *theological rationality* of Latino popular Catholicism. Distinguishing it from both the rational*ism* of modernity and the irrationalism of post-modernity, I suggest that this U.S. Hispanic theological rationality makes possible the theological and cultural pluralism which the former ideologies promise but, on their own, cannot deliver.

Having moved from experience (Chapters One and Two) to an analy-sis of that experience (Chapters Three through Six), I return, in Chapter Seven, to the experience—though now in a new light. Now, the funda-mental character of the historical and religious praxis which informed the analysis, and which will be presupposed in any genuinely pluralistic church or society, is revealed: a theology grounded in that praxis is a theology grounded in a *preferential option for the faith of the poor* understood as a process of *acompañamiento*, or accompaniment. Such an option is both the condition of the possibility and the consequence of the holistic, organic worldview of Latino popular Catholicism. It is also the condition of the possibility of an authentic pluralism. After examining the preferential option for the poor as articulated within Latin American liberation theology, especially in the work of Gustavo Gutiérrez, I suggest how, rooting itself in popular Catholicism, U.S. Hispanic theology might contribute to the understanding of the option for the poor as the foundation of Christian theology.

I should note that translations from the Spanish are mine (unless otherwise cited). I should also call the reader's attention to the fact that, unfortunately, many of the texts I quote directly contain noninclusive language. I have chosen not to note this in every instance since such constant repetition would be distracting for the reader.

I, myself, have been accompanied in the preparation and writing of this book. I am grateful to the Cuban-American community which formed me and the Mexican-American community which adopted me as a fellow Latino. The ongoing support of the Latin American theological community has been a source of empowerment and inspiration. The members of the Academy of Catholic Hispanic Theologians of the United States, many of whose writings are cited in the following pages, have welcomed me with a *cariño* which I also feel for them. The same is true of my colleagues in *La Comunidad* and the Fund for Theological Education.

I am especially grateful to Virgilio Elizondo, the "intellectual father" of our growing number of Catholic Latino theologians. Much more than is commonly known, he has generously given—and continues to give—of his time and wisdom to generations of U.S. Hispanic theologians and theological students. I know that his extraordinary contributions will become increasingly visible in coming years. I am also grateful to him and Tim Matovina for their review of and comments on the manuscript of this book.

I have been blessed with many other supportive mentors and colleagues. My *doktorvater*, Matthew Lamb, instilled in me a profound respect for the intellectual enterprise as a Christian vocation and, therefore, an equally profound sense of my responsibility as a theologian; he has always reminded me that the poor deserve the very best scholarship. I have also benefited from the generous support of my colleagues and friends at the Aquinas Center of Theology and Emory University in Atlanta. I am especially indebted to the theology faculty and the administration of Loyola University of Chicago for their friendship and support. The completion of this book was made possible by a semester's leave of absence which they graciously afforded me.

My research and field work were made possible by the financial support of the Lilly Endowment and the Cushwa Center for the Study of American Catholicism at the University of Notre Dame, which awarded me a summer research stipend in the History of U.S. Hispanic Catholics. This project has also benefited from the unstinting support and patience of Robert Ellsberg and Bill Burrows at Orbis Books.

Finally, I am deeply grateful to Elizabeth, Cristina, and Roberto Carlos. As always, so too during the course of this project, their love has accompanied and sustained me. Their patience, wisdom, and insight have been an inspiration.

CAMINEMOS CON JESÚS

[1]

Learning to Walk in an Alien Land

"*Caminante, no hay camino, se hace camino al andar.*" (Traveller, there is no path, the path is forged as one walks.)[1] These words from a poem by Antonio Machado were taught to me by my father, a Cuban exile. "*Caminemos con Jesús.*" (Let us walk with Jesus.) These words from the Holy Thursday liturgical procession were taught to me by the Mexican-American parishioners of San Fernando Cathedral in San Antonio, Texas, exiles in their own land.

My life has been lived between these two statements, these two communities: one, my own exiled Cuban community and, the other, the predominantly Mexican community which has been the context of much of my work here in the United States. "*No hay camino*" . . . "*caminemos con Jesús.*" One is the cry of the exile, forced into the solitude and loneliness of an alien country. The other is the call of the same person who, though still in exile, has discovered a new home. That home, however, is no longer simply a physical place, with its implied stability and security, but a community of persons who, as exiles themselves, are together "walking with Jesus."

My earliest memory is of something that happened one afternoon in Havana many years ago. I was in my room, having just returned home from school, where I was attending kindergarten. My mother walked into the room and sat down. Fighting back her own anxiety, she proceeded to tell me very calmly that we would soon be moving to Miami, in the United States. The only other memory I have of Cuba is that of sitting in a Miami-bound airplane on the airport tarmac, straining to see my father and paternal grandfather standing on the viewing deck atop the terminal building, and waving goodbye to them through the plane's scratched-up window—not knowing when or if I would see either of them again. Fortunately, I would see my father shortly thereafter. My grandfather, however, would not be allowed to leave the island for seven

---

1. Antonio Machado, *Selected Poems*, translated with an introduction by Alan S. Trueblood (Cambridge, MA: Harvard University Press, 1982), pp. 142–3.

long years, after which he joined his wife, daughters, and their children in Mexico City, where they had all settled.

My earliest memories, then, are not of life in my homeland, Cuba; they are, on the contrary, memories of leaving that life behind. My earliest memories are not of family and community, but of their destruction. They are not memories of home but of homelessness, not of personal growth but of loss, not of life but of death.

Yet the profound pain of those very memories awakened in me the still deeper sense that, somehow, destruction, death, homelessness, and loss are not the fundamental reality of life. More real than the destruction was that which had been destroyed—otherwise, I would not have experienced its loss as so very painful. The remainder of my life has been an attempt to recover what was lost: my connection to a community which, spanning many generations, had given me birth. I bear that community, those men and women, in the deepest recesses of my soul; what I thus seek is not only a connection to those others, both dead and living, but a connection to my very self.

The most dehumanizing aspect of exile is its power to isolate the person from others and, therefore, from him or herself. My life as an exile is irretrievably divided between a "before" (in Cuba) and an "after" (in the United States). What is "in between," the enduring passage itself, is just too heart-wrenching to confront; it was not until two or three years ago that my mother was finally able to share with my siblings and me those memories. Yet it is precisely the struggle to maintain the *connection* between the before and the after—the struggle to live in the "in between"—which has informed my own life as an exile, a Christian, and a theologian. It is there that I have sought God. This book represents an attempt, however partial and incomplete, to articulate the theological significance of a passage still ongoing, a life lived "in between."

My sense of loss was heightened by the fact that, unlike so many other Cuban exiles, I spent most of my youth, not in the large Cuban community of South Florida, but in the middle of the Southern Bible Belt. The Cubans in South Florida could continue to identify with their life "before," in Cuba; indeed, they virtually recreated that life in Miami. Thus, they were sometimes tempted to deny the reality of the passage itself, the reality that, for better or worse, we live between the Cuban past and the North American present. Growing up in Atlanta, Georgia, I too was tempted to resolve the tension. Since, at the time, U.S. Hispanics were a minute minority in Georgia, the danger I faced was the opposite, that of identifying exclusively with life "after" Cuba, becoming thereby a fully-assimilated "*americano.*" This was easy for me, since I spoke English without an accent, am economically privileged, and I am white.[2]

---

2. Ada María Isasi-Díaz notes that "white Americans are willing to accept Latinos who are white enough, as one of them when we become sufficiently middle

That I did not completely succumb to this danger is a testament to the tenacious love of a mother and father who themselves, though successfully integrating into a new country, refused to do so at the expense of their Cuban heritage. In our home, we continued to celebrate traditional Cuban holidays, eat Cuban food, and sing traditional Cuban songs, accompanied by our mother on the guitar. Moreover, the children all knew that, once we set foot in the house, we would be allowed to speak only Spanish (even though both of my parents were fluent in English). We hated this restriction above all, since it, more than any other, separated us from the surrounding Anglo community and our Anglo friends. Today, we consider the Spanish language—passed down to us with such great love and against such stubborn resistance—one of our parents' most important legacies.

The Spanish language is what made it possible for me, in later years, to recover what had been destroyed by exile. Having found myself in Latino communities comprised mostly of Mexicans, however, it has been primarily there—among Mexican Americans—that I have recovered the communal ties of my birth. And it would not have been possible if not for the Spanish language which, wherever U.S. Hispanics meet, forms an instant bond between us; whatever our differences—and there are many—we share a common language and, therefore, a common worldview.

It was in college that, for the first time, I was exposed to Latinos and Latinas who were self-consciously affirming their own identity as distinct from the larger U.S. culture. These Chicano students from the Southwest represented my first real contact with U.S. Hispanics other than Cubans. I realized that the schizophrenic life I had been living, as

---

class and sufficiently 'Anglicized.' " *En la Lucha/In the Struggle: Elaborating a Mujerista Theology* (Minneapolis: Fortress Press, 1993), p. 52. Yet this "acceptance" also reflects certain stereotypes about "Hispanics." I have often been told, for instance, that I don't look or talk like a "Hispanic." Likewise, I have often been insulted by persons who have made ethnic slurs to my face without realizing that I was one of "those people." Consequently, such categories as "people of color" can, when used to categorize Latinos and Latinas, simply perpetuate stereotypes by imposing the dominant culture's own racial self-definition on a people whose self-definition is primarily cultural and linguistic. For Latinos and Latinas generally, self-identity is more closely linked to culture and language than to race; see Jaime Vidal, "Popular Religion among Hispanics in the General Area of the Archdiocese of Newark," in *Presencia Nueva: A Study of Hispanics in the Archdiocese of Newark* (Newark: Archdiocesan Office of Research and Planning, 1988), p. 257 (also cited with approval by Ada María Isasi-Díaz in the above reference). While racism is also present in Latino culture, the particular manifestations of racism are often different; see Isasi-Díaz, *En la Lucha*, p. 52. Thus, to suggest that U.S. Hispanics do not identify *primarily* with race is not, in any way, to suggest that our communities are not seriously divided along racial lines or that racism is not a major form of oppression *within* our own communities (see ibid.).

a Cuban at home and an Anglo everywhere else, could not continue. My college studies—especially numerous courses in Latin American literature—afforded me the opportunity to deepen my appreciation of the community that I had left behind but which, thanks to my parents, was still very much a part of me. Having spent my youth, like so many Latinos and Latinas, trying to be accepted as a full-fledged *americano*, I would now self-consciously affirm my Latin American roots.

Consequently, when it became clear to me, in my mid-twenties, that I had a vocation to study and teach theology, I was instantly attracted to Latin American liberation theologies. What inspired me about the work of theologians like Gustavo Gutiérrez, Jon Sobrino, Juan Luis Segundo, Enrique Dussel, and José Míguez Bonino was their lived commitment to the liberation of their predominantly poor Latin American communities, to the transformation of society, and to the Christian faith—as essential to their theological reflection. For them, there was a deep, intrinsic connection between their Latin American identity, the struggle for social justice, and the Christian faith.

Entering graduate school with the intent of studying the work of these theologians, it became clear to me that, while a number of individual professors strongly encouraged and supported my interest, the world of academic theology as a whole simply did not take seriously the work of Latin American liberation theologians. Liberation theology was not considered "serious theology" and was dismissed as "mere Christian witness," a passing fad which, though perhaps useful pastorally, would have no permanent impact on the discipline of theology.

During my years in graduate study, I gradually came to the conclusion that there were two principal reasons for this lack of appreciation: liberation theology was perceived as a threat to the very foundations of the theological enterprise as understood on this side of the equator, and, since relatively little liberation theology had been translated into English, most of the Latin American scholarship was simply inaccessible to the vast majority of North American theologians, who had no knowledge of the Spanish language. The reason for this latter situation hit home in a very concrete way during my studies: I was informed that, even though most of my dissertation research would be in Spanish, this language would not be accepted as one of the two "scholarly languages" that I, as a Ph.D. student, would be required to learn for graduation. Only French and German would be accepted. The message could not have been clearer: no significant scholarship has been written in Spanish.

Though this particular prohibition has now changed at this and many other graduate schools and seminaries, the North American ignorance of Latin American scholarship has not. It does not occur to people, for example, that the supposed "demise" of liberation theology over the past decade may be more a reflection of changing North American needs and interests than of the actual state of Latin American scholarship. Despite the exceptional work of Orbis Books in bringing Latin American liberation theology to the United States, what has been translated into English is but the very tip of the iceberg. Often those books which have gone untranslated have been precisely the most "sophisticated," since these would have only a limited market.

Having access to both the Latin American and North American theological contexts, I came to see my own vocation as that of trying to build bridges between the two. For my dissertation topic, I chose the work of the Argentine philosopher-historian-theologian, Enrique Dussel. I made this decision for two reasons: first, the breadth and depth of his extensive writings were truly astounding and, secondly, he was the perfect example of an extremely "sophisticated" (as that term is used in North American intellectual circles) Latin American scholar, very little of whose work had been translated into English. I chose, further, to compare the writings of Dussel with those of Bernard Lonergan, long acknowledged as one of the most "sophisticated" North American theologians.

My work in Latin American liberation theology made it possible for me to recover my roots, not only as an essential source of self-identity, but also as an important theological source, that is, as a *locus theologicus*, a place where the God to whom I had committed my life was and is revealed. As that process of recovery remained at a primarily intellectual level, however, I made plans to live in Latin America, with a group of sociologists and theologians working among the poor in Chile. Such a practical grounding was, after all, essential to both my Christian faith commitment and my understanding of the theological task.

At about that time, however, my road took another turn—again common for Latinos and Latinas in the United States. Having come to know Father Virgilio Elizondo, the founder of the Mexican American Cultural Center in San Antonio, I began to realize that, if I wanted to do theology out of the lived experience of my community, I would find that community not in Latin America but in the United States, among the Latin Americans who, like myself, had adopted this country as their home. *This* was now my *locus theologicus*.[3] After years of trying to become "American,"[4] and, then, trying to become Latin American, I realized that I was not and could never be either: instead, I was *both*, I was *in between*.

---

3. The ongoing dialogue with Latin American liberation theologies would continue, however, to provide a rich source of insight and inspiration to myself, as well as to other U.S. Hispanic theologians.

4. Justo González has noted the arrogance underlying the United States' appropriation of the term "America"—or "American"—for itself. "Even the name 'America' raises the question: What preposterous conceit allows the inhabitants of a single country to take for themselves the name of an entire hemisphere? What does this say about that country's view of those other nations who share the hemisphere with it?" *Mañana: Christian Theology from a Hispanic Perspective* (Nashville: Abingdon Press, 1990), p. 37.

Having initially seen my theological vocation as that of building bridges, I now came to realize that, like all Latinos and Latinas, I *am* a bridge. I would now identify with the New York-born Puerto Rican writer who, when asked whether she felt more at home in New York or in Puerto Rico, responded "I feel most at home on the airplane." As Justo González observes, "we are no longer Latin Americans living in exile in the United States but Hispanic Americans, people who have no other land than this, but who nevertheless remain exiles."[5]

This revelation was both liberating and frightening. It was liberating because it forced me to confront a truth that I had not previously seen. Like the contact lenses on my eyes, it was too close for me to see. It was, also, frightening because, while I knew what an *americano* and a *latinoamericano* were, I did not have the foggiest idea what a *hispano* was—except, of course, as an inchoate awareness with which I had lived all my life. Indeed, the very term Hispanic was foreign to me. At that time, Cuban Americans simply referred to ourselves as "*cubanos*" or, in a broader sense, as "*latinos*."

I knew the U.S. God of manifest destiny and the Latin American God of the poor, but who was the God revealed among this people, a people neither "American" nor Latin American? For so long, I had been trying to resolve my cultural schizophrenia; now I had set for myself the task of finding a God who, somehow, is revealed in the very midst of that schizophrenia!

This revelation did not occur all at once, however, but has been supported and aided by my experience raising my own family and working with Latino communities over the past twelve years. My home life is still lived "in between," though now I do so not only as a son but as a husband and father. I see my children, Cristina and Roberto Carlos, reliving my own childhood struggles—and my wife, Elizabeth, and I reliving those of my own parents.

As an Irish American woman with a graduate degree in Spanish, an unaccented command of the language, and the special resolve of a "convert" to Spanish, Elizabeth has accompanied me in our common desire to pass the language down to our children. Unlike my own parents, however, we experience in our own relationship the tensions particular to an intercultural marriage. Though at times very painful, these tensions have also brought us closer together and enriched our mutual love—in the process giving birth to a family that is neither "American" nor Latin American, but both. Through the common struggle and mutual love of this U.S. Hispanic family I continue to be born and reborn. It is here that I know the living God most intimately and, thus, here that my theology finds its deepest meaning, in the seemingly insignificant activity of our shared, everyday life.

---

5. Ibid., p. 41.

My family, however, extends beyond the boundaries of the home. In New Orleans, Atlanta, San Antonio, and Chicago I have had the privilege of working with and getting to know many Latinos and Latinas whose lives and witness are an inspiring testament to the vital presence of a liberating God. They too have taught me that this schizophrenic, "in between" life of ours is not something to be resolved, solved, or transcended; it is, instead, something to be cherished and nurtured, for it is indeed the revelation of God. They too are my family.

I have also learned something else: in finding this community of faithful *caminantes*, I have found my very self. The intuition which, from the beginning, had motivated me has indeed been confirmed: only as I learn who *we are*, can I learn who I am—and we are a richly diverse people, of many nations, colors, and classes. What unites us is language and culture. Though both of these are also quite varied among us, the variations are always recognizable. When I ask one of my Cuban cousins visiting from Miami when he will be arriving at our house and he says "*ahorita*," I know to expect him in a short while; when I ask one of my Mexican cousins visiting from Mexico City the same question, and get the same response, I know to expect her immediately. In both cases, however, I know I am among family.[6]

As we live together in this alien land, moreover, the differences are in many cases becoming increasingly attenuated. The reality of U.S. Hispanics is increasingly becoming a *mestizaje*—or racial and cultural mixture—not only between European and indigenous or African cultures, and not only between Latin American and Anglo American cultures, but an intermixing among the various U.S. Hispanic communities themselves.[7] "Increasingly," writes Justo González, "Hispanics in the United States, and the new generations that are being born are no longer merely Mexican or Cuban. They are this new reality, the 'Hispanic' or

---

6. Though there is certainly a tremendous diversity *within* U.S. Hispanic culture, e.g., between Cuban Americans and Mexican Americans, I will suggest in the following chapters that there is also a fundamental commonality of worldview, cosmology, anthropology, and, indeed, theology: the differences "often are very great but yet not sufficient to break the essential unity that causes a Colombian and Uruguayan to meet the same situation in much the same way." William Lytle Schurz quoted in Lawrence S. Graham, "Latin America: Illusion or Reality? A Case for a New Analytic Framework for the Region," in *Politics and Social Change in Latin America: The Distinct Tradition*, ed. Howard J. Wiarda (Amherst, MA: University of Massachusetts Press, 1974), 232.

7. Technically, the term "*mestizaje*" has traditionally referred specifically to the mixture of European and Native American races and cultures, and the term "*mulataje*," or "*mulatez*" to European-African mixture. Among U.S. Hispanic theologians, however, "*mestizaje*" is now generally used as a broader, umbrella term that encompasses any type of racial-cultural mixture: among U.S. Hispanics, primarily Native American and Spanish or African and Spanish. It is in this lat-

'Latino' reality, this new way of being human."[8] If the confluence of European and indigenous or African cultures marked our first mestizaje, and the confluence of Latin American and U.S. cultures marks our second mestizaje, then we might begin to speak of a third mestizaje taking place *between and among* Latino cultures in the United States.

I now live not only in between Latin American and Anglo American cultures but also in between Cuban and Mexican cultures. If, historically, the terms "Hispanic" or "Latino" have been artificial categories imposed on what are, in fact, distinct national groups, the increased contact and intermarriage among these groups in the United States will, over the coming decades, make the categories less and less artificial. If Virgilio Elizondo's Mexican-American experience of mestizaje is specific to his particular community's history, and Justo González's Cuban-American experience of exile specific to his, both terms nevertheless reflect our common experience of living "in between" different worlds.

As a Latino, I am also Catholic: first, because one cannot be Latino without having a Catholic background (as distinct from explicitly professing Catholic doctrine) and, secondly, because I have made a conscious commitment to the Catholic Church. González, a Cuban Methodist theologian, contends that "the Spanish-American Roman Catholic Church is part of the common background of all Hispanics—if not personally, then at least in our ancestry."[9] Thus, while about three-fourths of U.S. Hispanics belong to the Roman Catholic Church, all Hispanics have Catholic roots: Latino culture and Catholicism have deep, historical links. González provides a humorous illustration:

When I was growing up [as a Methodist], I was taught to think of such things as the Virgin of Guadalupe as pure superstition. Therefore, I remember how surprised I was at the reaction of a Mexican professor in seminary when one of my classmates made some disparaging remarks about Guadalupe. The professor, who was as Protestant as they come and who often stooped because he was then elderly, drew himself up, looked my friend in the eye, and said: "Young man, in this class you are free to say anything you please. You may say anything about me. You certainly are welcome to say anything you wish about the pope and the priests. But don't you touch my little Virgin!"[10]

ter, broader sense that I use the term. On the concept of *mestizaje*, see Virgilio Elizondo, *Mestizaje: The Dialectic of Cultural Birth and the Gospel* (San Antonio: Mexican American Cultural Center, 1978). See also the works by José Vasconcelos cited and discussed in chapter 4.

8. Justo González, "Hispanics in the United States," *Listening: Journal of Religion and Culture* 27: 1 (Winter, 1992):13.

9. González, *Mañana*, p. 55.

10. Ibid., p. 61.

If all Latinos and Latinas have common religious roots, those common roots inform and color our faith, whether Catholic or Protestant. The neat distinctions that are so often made between Catholics and Protestants—for example, that the faith of Catholics is based on sacrament while that of Protestants is based on the word—prove not nearly so neat when used to understand Latino Catholicism and Protestantism. One of the most important lessons I have learned in my work among Hispanics in the United States is, in fact, how much we have in common. Whether Catholic, Protestant, or non-Christian, we are a people who view the world as essentially suffused with Spirit and view ourselves as essentially interrelated with each other. We are a people defined by relationship, with each other, the world, and God. Thus, while it is important to always bear in mind our great diversity, we should not underestimate our common heritage. It is that heritage which makes us all exiles in a land that, whatever its original claims or intentions, today finds its people divided, segregated, alienated, and isolated from each other.

I am not only a Latino and a Catholic; I am also a theologian. It is primarily as a theologian that I seek to serve the church and my U.S. Hispanic community. At a time when the intellectual enterprise is increasingly seen as irrelevant to people's lives, I continue to be convinced of the wisdom of the Cuban poet and revolutionary, José Martí, who maintained that *"pensar es servir"* (to think is to serve).[11] If the best, most sophisticated scholarship is not placed in the service of our communities, then it will continue to be used against them. We will only be able to make our voices heard and our experience appreciated in the church and the academy which continue to legitimate our suppression if we achieve credibility in their eyes. As a Catholic Latino theologian, I must also live "in between" my fundamental commitment to the historical experience of our Latino communities and my responsibility to bring that experience to bear on the oppressive institutional practices and attitudes prevalent in the dominant culture, the academy, and the church. If my privileged education and profession have necessarily distanced me from the everyday lives of Latinos and Latinas, so much greater is my personal and intellectual responsibility.

That responsibility includes, at its very core, a preferential option for the poor. Though, as a Latino, I have known the dehumanizing effects of cultural marginalization, as a white, economically privileged male I have participated in and benefited from the dehumanization of others—in my own Latino community as well as outside that community. My responsibility, as a Christian and theologian, includes, therefore, an identification with the poorest of the poor within my own community and, from within the context of that identification, a practical solidarity with other marginalized groups, especially African Americans and Native Americans. To

---

11. José Martí, "Nuestra América," in *José Martí: Sus mejores páginas*, ed. Raimundo Lazo (México: Editorial Porrúa, 1978), 92.

the extent that we allow our own suffering to be used as a pretext for perpetuating the suffering of others, we will simply be doing the bidding of the dominant culture.

My socio-historical context and self-understanding, as briefly outlined above, will necessarily inform the remainder of this book and specify its content. It is intended as a theological work from a Catholic Latino perspective. Which is to say that, for reasons discussed in chapter six, this is not intended as a work in "U.S. Hispanic theology," as distinct from what is usually referred to as, simply, "theology." Though I (and other U.S. Hispanic theologians) commonly use the former term, I do so only as a convenient, short-hand way of saying "theology done from a self-consciously U.S. Hispanic perspective."

This book is intended, more specifically, as a work in *Catholic* Hispanic theology. Its context is thus limited to those aspects of U.S. Hispanic life that are explicitly and self-consciously understood by the participants to include a historical relationship to the Catholic tradition. Having said that, however, one must bear in mind that the line between our everyday lives and religion is very vague and Roman Catholicism is by no means the only religious framework within which Hispanics relate to the Sacred in our lives:

> The religious universe of Hispanic Americans is *not* homogeneous, easily identifiable with the Roman Catholic tradition. It is complex and varied, even if we could classify the diversity in two basic categories: "popular Catholicism" and "marginal religions" (the first including those elements more or less acceptable—even if peripherally—to the Catholic Church; and the second including those faith expressions which would be unacceptable at any level to the Catholic Church and which probably can be traced back to non-Christian origins [this second category would also cover the explicit non-Christian, Hispanic-Amerindian or Afro-Hispanic religions]).[12]

Yet, as González noted, Catholicism has had a pervasive and profound influence on Latino *culture per se*, in much the same way as Protestantism has had a pervasive and profound influence on U.S. culture. In a culture that has historically been predominantly Catholic, the boundary between religion and culture is as fuzzy as is the boundary between Protestantism and U.S. culture.[13]

---

12. Orlando O. Espín and Sixto J. García, "Hispanic-American Theology," *Proceedings of the Catholic Theological Society of America*, 42 (1987) 115.

13. As John Wilson has noted: "Evidence that Protestant Christianity became the functional common religion of the [U.S.] society would overwhelm us if we sought it out." "Common Religion in American Society," in *Civil Religion and Political Theology*, Leroy S. Rouner, ed. (Notre Dame, IN: University of Notre Dame Press, 1986) 113. Consequently, to Euro-American Protestantism, U.S.

Nevertheless, it would be a mistake to simply identify Latino culture with Catholicism. Such an identification would distort the historical reality and exclude large numbers of U.S. Hispanics and important elements of our culture from the definition of the U.S. Hispanic socio-historical context. Such an oversimplification would be especially ironic since one of the characteristics of Catholicism as practiced in our communities is precisely its openness to and appropriation of indigenous and African religious symbolism within an explicitly Christian context.[14]

As a self-consciously Catholic theologian, however, I theologize from within the context of the larger Roman Catholic tradition as this is lived out in our U.S. Hispanic communities. Indeed, as I will contend in chapter six, only by rooting ourselves in *particular* religious traditions can we make possible a genuinely ecumenical dialogue *among* traditions; just as only by rooting ourselves in our U.S. Hispanic identity can we make possible genuine inter-cultural dialogue with Anglos. Far from implying a close-mindedness or prejudice with respect to other particular traditions, such a rootedness—if profoundly and authentically lived—presupposes and demands an openness to other particular traditions. Moreover, only as a Catholic theologian can I hope to engage critically the larger Catholic tradition from the perspective of U.S. Hispanic Catholicism.

As representing but one U.S. Hispanic perspective, this book in no way pretends to speak for all U.S. Hispanics, Catholic or otherwise. It is merely one interpretation of U.S. Hispanic Catholicism as this has been intentionally and self-consciously lived, experienced, and reflected upon by one theologian. The term "U.S. Hispanic popular Catholicism" necessarily overlooks and thus distorts the amazing diversity of both U.S. Hispanics and popular Catholicism. The tendency toward premature generalization of a particular perspective is an occupational hazard of scholars. It is also, however, an unavoidable necessity: we all work in the realm of words and concepts, which, by definition, are abstractions from, or generalizations of particular, concrete experience. All words and concepts are distortions. Nevertheless, words and concepts are necessary for communication—and U.S. Hispanics must speak; we must write. Yet we do so with the hum-

---

Hispanic Protestants "often appear to think and act like Catholics." Glen Caudill Dealy, *The Public Man: An Interpretation of Latin American and Other Catholic Countries* (Amherst, MA: University of Massachusetts Press, 1977), p. 87. (Though Dealy refers to the Catholic roots of Latin American culture, the statement would also apply to U.S. Hispanic culture.)

14. The openness of U.S. Hispanic popular Catholicism to other, non-Catholic forms of popular religion, is reflected in the ease and freedom with which U.S. Hispanics often move between Catholic, Protestant, and non-Christian symbolic and ritual worlds. In some cases, the same persons who identify themselves primarily with Catholic rituals and beliefs may also participate in Protestant Bible studies and prayer groups, or more explicitly Native American or African rituals. By so doing, they would not necessarily consider themselves any less Catholic.

bling knowledge that, as we speak and write, we may be obscuring as much as we are disclosing. For this, we—and I—must ask, in advance, the forgiveness of the reader and, above all, the U.S. Hispanic community itself. At the same time, I hope that this reflection on my own experience will contribute to the faith life and self-understanding of others, particularly other U.S. Hispanics, with whom I share this life of mestizaje and exile.

Finally, it is incumbent on me to make a few remarks concerning the issue of language in this book. Reflective of the many differences characterizing our U.S. Hispanic communities are the different terms which we use to refer to ourselves: Hispanic, Hispanic American, U.S. Hispanic, Latino, or Latina. None of these terms is indigenous to our communities; we have historically preferred to identify ourselves by country of origin: e.g., Cuban, Puerto Rican, Mexican. Yet, as mentioned above, we do share a great deal (and, with the increased contact among groups in the United States, increasingly so), including a common language that, like all language, not only reflects but also shapes our world. Consequently, these descriptive terms are not altogether artificial. Each has strengths and weaknesses.

The term "Hispanic," given to us by the U.S. government, emphasizes our Spanish heritage while ignoring our Native American and African heritage. If understood as a linguistic rather than a cultural category, however, this problem is alleviated; while indigenous languages such as Quiché are still the primary languages of many Latin Americans in Latin America, the same cannot be said for Latin Americans in the United States (with a few possible exceptions, e.g., recently-arrived Guatemalan farm workers in Florida). Thus, the term Hispanic refers, above all, to our common language; just as the term Anglo refers, not to the English culture, but to the English language shared by North Americans with Irish, Polish, German, Scottish, French, and Swedish heritage, as well as by those with specifically English roots. For Hispanics, language is "the prime identifier"; consequently, "the 'Anglo' is not the Anglo-Saxon, but the Anglophone."[15]

As I will suggest later, language is not merely a superficial reflection of our culture and worldview; it helps construct and shape that culture and worldview. Language is not simply an instrument for communicating human experience; it is, to some extent, that experience itself. Language forms and defines us as much as we form and define it. Ada María Isasi-Díaz notes the significance of this fact for U.S. Hispanics:

The Spanish language functions for Latinas not only as a means of communication but as a means of identification. Spanish has become "the incarnation and symbol" of our whole culture, making

_____

15. Vidal, "Popular Religion among Hispanics," 257; quoted also in Isasi-Díaz, *En la Lucha*, pp. 52–3.

us feel that here in the U.S.A. we are one people, no matter what our country of origin is. The Spanish language identifies us by distinguishing us from the rest of society. It gives us a specificity that we need to be a certain kind of people within a culture not our own. . . . The Spanish language for us Latinos here in the U.S.A. has become "the bearer of identity and values." Our attachment to it is such that even those Latinos born and raised in the U.S.A. who understand a little Spanish and can speak only a few words insist on saying that they do know Spanish. Since the importance of Spanish for Latinas is not so much to be able to communicate but to be able to identify each other, grammatical and pronunciation correctness is totally secondary. For us Spanish is indeed a social construct and, therefore, we do not use Spanish to exclude from our communities those who know little Spanish or use it improperly.[16]

The term "Hispanic," or "U.S. Hispanic," underscores this linguistic basis of our identity.

The term "Latino" also has strengths and weaknesses. It emphasizes our Latin American, as opposed to Spanish heritage, thereby more accurately reflecting our cultural mestizaje. Yet the very term "*Latin* America" is itself not ours, having been coined in France. Consequently, this term may be fairly interpreted as referring to all Latin cultures (*culturas latinas*), not only the Spanish but also the French, Italian, and Portuguese. Unlike "Hispanic," "Latino" is a gender specific term: e.g., "Latino communities" are by no means exclusively masculine, indeed, in Spanish they are feminine, *las comunidades latinas*. Thus, "U.S. Hispanic" has the advantage of gender inclusiveness.

Further complicating the linguistic conundrum is the fact that each of these terms has political connotations which themselves differ according to the particular community and region of the United States. Often, for example, the mere use of the term "Hispanic" to define oneself will be interpreted by Latinos and Latinas as a sign that one has not yet been conscientized and has not yet self-consciously appropriated one's indigenous or African heritage. While the use of the term "Latino/a" may be interpreted as a sign that one is a conscientized political activist.

This is complicated even more by the fact that the terms have different histories within different U.S. Hispanic communities. As I mentioned above, I and other Cuban Americans grew up referring to

---

16. Isasi-Díaz, *En la Lucha*, pp. 52–3. The fundamentally inclusive function of the Spanish language in our communities does not, however, obviate the need for sensitivity to those Latinos and Latinas who do not speak Spanish: "let us not so idolize our culture that we oppress another Hispanic who does not speak as we do, or even one who never learned how to speak Spanish, because the pressures of society were too great." González, *Mañana*, p. 38.

ourselves as Latinos. When I entered college in the 1970s and began to be conscientized, I learned from my activist Chicano friends to call myself a Hispanic. In the 1980s, however, those same friends rejected the European connotation of that term and began calling themselves Latinos and Latinas—which is what we Cubans had called ourselves initially and had rejected in favor of "Hispanic." Thus, the experience of living "in between" extends even to our very self-definitions! I am *both* a Latino *and* a U.S. Hispanic, or Hispanic American.

In any case, it is very unfortunate that any U.S. Hispanic, Latina, or Latino should ever be considered less "Hispanic" by virtue of her or his language or vocabulary. To establish a set of criteria as a litmus test for "Hispanicness" is to subject other Latinos and Latinas to the same unjust stereotyping for which we so strongly criticize the dominant culture. Consequently, I have preferred not to take sides in this debate, acknowledging the strengths and weaknesses of each term, and using them randomly and interchangeably—indeed, as in the *Journal of Hispanic/Latino Theology* and the title of this book, even in conjunction. I do believe that "Hispanic" ought to be preceded by "U.S." to distinguish us from other Spanish-speaking peoples, in Latin America or Spain for instance. When I do refer to "Hispanics," therefore, the adjective "U.S." is implied.

An arguably more serious and complicated linguistic issue is that of the language in which the text itself is written. Like so many U.S. Hispanics, though Spanish was my first language and the one spoken at home, I was formally educated almost exclusively in English. Consequently, my first professional language is English. This, furthermore, is still the dominant language of the society, church, and academy in the United States and, thus, the main language in which U.S. Hispanic theologians not only dialogue with but, indeed, confront these institutions. After all, as I will suggest, effective critique of oppressive institutions is impossible unless we can speak to them in their language and categories—precisely in order to challenge the dominance of their language and categories. Indeed, it is my desire that this book will be read not only by my own Latino communities, but also by Anglos—otherwise our own internal discussions will have little impact on the larger, dominant culture.

There is, however, a second, even more important reason for writing this book in English. This second rationale is the one so eloquently articulated by Justo González for having written his book *Mañana: Christian Theology from a Hispanic Perspective* in English:

> What will be most important in our attempts to rediscover the original liberating gospel will not be our participation in Spanish culture but our participation, jointly with the early church, with Jesus and the apostles, and with Afro-Americans and Asian Americans, in the condition of a dispossessed minority whom God is calling to new life. It is from this perspective that Christian theology must be rewritten.

While the cultural focus of Hispanic identity is exclusively our own, the social focus is something we share with many others in this country. It is for this reason that I have decided to write this essay in English. Written in Spanish, it would have addressed the Hispanic community almost exclusively. It would thus have run the risk of contributing to the distance among minorities . . . that is one of the main reasons why the ruling minority is seldom challenged in its power and prejudice. Written in English, I hope that it may serve to surface some of the common concerns and perspectives that Hispanics share with blacks, women, and other underrepresented groups.[17]

As important as it is to retain the Spanish language as a principal symbol of our identity and as a means of constructing our reality, it is also important to communicate in English in order to make it possible for our reality to engage the rest of U.S. society, especially those other groups which share in our experience of marginalization and exclusion. So it is with very mixed feelings that, for both practical and ethical reasons, I have chosen to write this book in English.

Indeed, one of the most painful consequences of our exile/mestizaje is this very linguistic problem. For an exile to survive in a foreign country, he or she must learn to speak that country's language. As a people living "in between," U.S. Hispanics are constantly forced to make compromises. Let us, at least, know the nature of those compromises and recognize them as the injustice they are. Let our hearts and minds be firmly grounded in the struggle to confront that injustice, while acknowledging the pain which that struggle entails for all of us.

This problem, moreover, is created not by the exiled person but by the *historical reality* of exile, by "the pressures of society."[18] The injustice is especially grave in the case of Mexican Americans, who are not exiles in a foreign land, but exiles in *their own* land. As Virgilio Elizondo points out, Mexican Americans did not cross the border, the border crossed them: the Anglos who insisted that "if the 'Mexicans' did not like it here, let them go back home . . . forgot that this was our home and that we had always been here."[19] A similarly painful process of colonization has marked the unique historical reality of Puerto Rico and Puerto Ricans. "Actually," writes Justo González, "the first Hispanics to become part of this country did not do so by migration but were rather engulfed by the United States in its process of expansion—sometimes by purchase, sometimes by military conquest, and sometimes by simple annexation of territories no one was strong enough to defend. . . . Thus in the beginning

---

17. González, *Mañana*, p. 38.
18. Ibid.
19. Virgilio Elizondo, *The Future is Mestizo: Life Where Cultures Meet* (Bloomington, IN: Meyer-Stone, 1988), pp. 44–5.

it was not Hispanics who migrated to this nation, but this nation that migrated to Hispanic lands."[20]

This history of expansion and conquest conditions the gratitude that many U.S. Hispanics feel toward our adoptive country. Though grateful,

> we are angry because we are becoming increasingly aware of the degree to which the United States, the land of our refuge, is also the land that created our need for exile in the first place. Political exiles discover the complicity of North American vested interests in the events that led to the need to abandon their countries. Economic exiles eventually learn that the poverty of their native lands is the result of the wealth of their adoptive land. Ideological exiles discover that the talk of freedom and equality, constantly heard overseas when it was a matter of opposing enemies of the United States, is less heard in the very land from which it comes when it is a matter of justice for ethnic minorities and for the poor.[21]

To be a mestizo/a and an exile is, thus, to live not only in between Latin America and the United States, not only in between Spanish and English, but also in between gratitude and anger.

One of the underlying theses of this book is that it is our very identity as mestizos/as and exiles, a people living in between, that, indeed, makes us ultimately unacceptable to the dominant U.S. culture. For that culture cannot accept what is "in between," what is "both/and"; it is a culture whose reality is comprised of oppositions and dichotomies. In a world of dichotomies, in a world of black or white, the mestizo/a can only be a nobody, since the mestizo/a cannot, by definition, fit within those categories.

---

20. González, *Mañana*, pp. 31–2. "Even without turning back to history," observes the author, "this is clear when one looks at a map of the United States and finds in it such names as Florida, California, Nevada, Colorado, Los Angeles, San Francisco, San Diego, Sacramento, and Key West (a corruption of 'Cayo Hueso')" (ibid., p. 31).

21. González, *Mañana*, pp. 41–2. As a Cuban American, for instance, I remain grateful to the United States for welcoming us and providing economic opportunity and freedoms often unheard of in other countries. At the same time, this appreciation is conditioned by the knowledge that the Batista dictatorship, whose corruption paved the way for the totalitarian revolution of Fidel Castro, received much U.S. political and economic support. As has too often been the case, the very need for Latin Americans to migrate to the United States was itself at least partially created by U.S. policies vis-à-vis those countries. At the same time, I do not mean to suggest that Latin Americans are not also responsible for the social problems of Latin American countries. The point, however, is that the U.S. must also share that responsibility and that, thus, the willingness to accept immigrants and exiles is not so much an act of charity (over and above the call of duty) as an act of strict justice.

The mestizo/a and exile is a person who, by definition, inhabits the in-between world of "both/and." Indeed, this world is more than a habitat, it is our very identity.

For this exile and mestizo/a, however, the everyday struggle to live this "in between" existence becomes the seedbed of liberation. Here, in the struggle against the destructive consequences of individual*ism*, we discover our freedom as individuals. Here, in the struggle against the dehumanizing consequences of reducing human life to *nothing but* work, we discover the liberating power of human work and social transformation. Here, in the struggle against the oppressive consequences of identifying salvation with human power and privilege, we discover the saving power of the crucified Jesus. Here, in the struggle against the oppressive consequences of the way in which the American dream has so often been interpreted and put into practice, we discover the true promise of our adoptive land, with its deeply-held belief in individual freedom, pluralism, and progress.

As, literally, marginal to this society, we are in a position to recognize its great values while, at the same time, perceiving the dark underside of those very values. Living on the margins of "civilized society," we know that "every great work of civilization is at the same time a work of barbarism."[22] Yet, within our own histories as Latinos and Latinas, we discover rich sources for challenging the "barbarism" of contemporary U.S. society while, nevertheless, helping this extraordinary nation realize its historical promise, its "great work of civilization."

What we offer to our adoptive country is, above all, the hope of a freedom grounded in community. From within our own histories as Latinos and Latinas, we offer the possibility of an individual freedom based in relationship. For, though we are aliens in both our countries of origin and in our adopted country, we U.S. Hispanics know that we are not alone. We walk with each other and with Jesus. We walk with our forebears, with those who died at the end of a rifle, in the heat of an *encomienda*, in a *balsa* crossing the Caribbean, or in the wilds of the Southwestern borderlands. They were like Machado's poet: "*Murió el poeta lejos del hogar. Le cubre el polvo de un país vecino.*"[23] ("The poet died far from home. The dust of a neighboring country covers him.") But their deaths were not in vain. Their homelessness has become our home, a home shared by a carpenter's son who also has nowhere to lay his head. It is shared by his father and mother. It is shared by all Latinos and Latinas. Walking together, then, we *do* have a home, a home constructed not out of bricks and mortar but out of our common struggle: "*no hay camino . . . caminemos con Jesús.*"

---

22. Walter Benjamin, quoted in David Tracy, *Plurality and Ambiguity: Hermeneutics, Religion, Hope* (San Francisco: Harper and Row, 1987), p. 69.
23. Machado, *Selected Poems*, pp. 142–3.

[2]

Caminemos con Jesús

U.S. Hispanic Popular Catholicism

[handwritten margin notes: "This question, it strikes me, is a bit Tendentious to begin with b/c we can find God's presence in all cultural contexts," with arrow pointing to title; "much better question" with arrow]

If we are to find God's presence in our U.S. Hispanic socio-historical context, U.S. Hispanic theologians must begin our theological task with the question, "What is the particular socio-historical context in which we, as Latinos and Latinas, do our theology?" or, more specifically for Catholic Latinos and Latinas, "What is the particular socio-historical context in which we, as Catholic Latinos and Latinas, do our theology?" These questions have occupied U.S. Hispanic theologians for a number of years, now, as we have struggled for answers which, in any case, must always remain partial, transitional, temporary, and open to further development. When focusing on one aspect of U.S. Hispanic experience, for example, we remain cognizant of the fact that this is indeed but *one* aspect of an infinitely varied historical reality: there are a multiplicity of U.S. Hispanic experiences, contexts, histories, etc. Yet this multiplicity should not *ipso facto* prevent us from uncovering similarities and commonalities any more than the existence of different cultures, or differences within a particular culture, should prevent us from uncovering commonalities and similarities within those differences.[1]

Certain common trends have emerged in U.S. Hispanic attempts to define more precisely the particular features of "the U.S. Hispanic experience." Perhaps the most common characteristic of our attempts to define the socio-historical context of Latinos and Latinas has been the central role ascribed to popular religion in any interpretation of that context.[2] While popular religion is itself defined in various ways, at least two claims

---

1. The issue of the relationship between universality and particularity will be treated more extensively in chapters 6 and 7.

2. Orlando Espín contends that "popular religion seems to be an omnipresent phenomenon among U.S. Latinos," while adding the following clarification: "Although I will insist on the importance of popular religion for understanding

18

of recent U.S. Hispanic theological scholarship seem to be beyond question. What remains unchallenged and often taken for granted is, first, the fundamentally sacramental character of the U.S. Hispanic way of life, wherein physical existence is seen as intrinsically related to the supernatural, transcendent realm of the sacred.[3] Secondly, U.S. Hispanic theologians assume the crucial significance of this sacramentality for the theological task, i.e., any theology done from the perspective of U.S. Hispanics cannot ignore this fact and still remain rooted in the experience of U.S. Hispanics. Among Catholic Hispanic theologians in particular, popular religion has come to be seen as an essential element of our *locus theologicus*, the place in and from which we must do our theological reflection.[4] Indeed, Protestant Hispanic theologians are also examining the popular religious practices of Protestant Latinas and Latinos as a theological resource.[5] In the future, this promises to be a fertile area for ecumenical collaboration.

Latinos, the reader should realize that not all Hispanic Catholics participate in the rites or hold the beliefs of this religious universe. However, an argument can be made on the enduring cultural importance of the symbols of popular Catholicism for all Latinos (including Protestant and agnostic ones)." "Popular Catholicism among Latinos," in *Hispanic Catholic Culture in the U.S.: Issues and Concerns*, ed. Jay P. Dolan and Allan Figueroa Deck (Notre Dame, IN: University of Notre Dame Press, 1994), 308–309.

3. On sacramentality, see note 26 below.

4. Espín, for example, makes the following specific claims: "It can be argued that, first of all, popular Catholicism is the manner in and through which most U.S. Latinos are Catholic; and secondly, that this popular Catholicism is a key matrix of all Hispanic cultures. If this is the case, and I believe it is, then the importance of the study of this religion is crucial for an adequate understanding of all Hispanics, whether they currently participate in this type of Catholicism or not." "Popular Catholicism among Latinos," 313. See this same essay by Espín for an excellent analysis of the historical development of Latino popular Catholicism. See also his "Popular Catholicism: Alienation or Hope?" in *Aliens in the Promised Land*, ed. Ada María Isasi-Díaz and Fernando Segovia (Minneapolis: Fortress Press, 1995).

5. See, for example, Edwin David Aponte, "Coritos as Active Symbol in Latino Protestant Popular Religion," *Journal of Hispanic/Latino Theology*, 2:3. (February 1995): 57–66 See also Orlando O. Espín, "Popular Catholicism among Latinos," 343–45, and "Pentecostalism and Popular Catholicism: Preservers of Hispanic Catholic Tradition?" Presidential Address at the Fourth Annual Colloquium of the Academy of Catholic Hispanic Theologians of the United States (San Diego, 1992). Text in: *ACHTUS Newsletter* 4 (1993). In these essays, Espín makes fascinating connections between the pre-Tridentine Spanish Catholicism that lies at the heart of Latino popular Catholicism and the growth of Latino Protestant pentecostalism, which he sees as preserving the pre-Reformation "sacra-

Popular religion among U.S. Hispanics takes numerous and diverse forms, not always expressly Christian.[6] This entire scope of popular religion merits study from not only anthropological and sociological but also theological perspectives.[7] However, for the reasons adduced in the foregoing chapter, I will limit my discussion to U.S. Hispanic popular Catholicism, or those forms of popular religion with the closest historical ties to expressly Catholic Christian religiosity. Neither can I pretend to interpret the Protestant forms of popular religion becoming increasingly important within Hispanic communities in the United States. The aim here, then, is by no means to provide an exhaustive treatment of U.S. Hispanic popular religion, nor of the full range of its implications for systematic theology, but rather to offer a *methodological model* for doing theology from a particular socio-historical

---

mental, symbolic ethos and worldview" over against a Euro-American Catholicism that has abandoned them in favor of a modern, individualistic, rationalist ethos and worldview. It is with no small irony, he suggests, that contemporary Euro-American Catholicism uses the same arguments against Latino popular Catholicism (e.g., it is mere superstition, it is idolatrous in its use of statues, it divinizes Mary, it is irrational) that were once made by Protestant reformers against Catholicism ("Popular Catholicism among Latinos," 343–44). Thus, the potential for ecumenical cooperation and understanding among U.S. Hispanics has important historical roots.

6. On this diversity, see Espín, "Popular Catholicism among Latinos," 310–312. Beyond the question of popular religion, there emerges the question of what, in fact, constitutes religion *as such*—if, indeed, one can even speak of religion "as such." This question is much broader than the scope of this book (as is the question of what constitutes Catholicism "as such"). Like definitions of culture, any definition of religion is necessarily limited. On the difficulties in defining religion, and for examples of interdisciplinary, multicultural approaches to a definition of religion, see Mircea Eliade and David Tracy, eds., *What is Religion? An Enquiry for Christian Theology* (Edinburgh: T. & T. Clark, 1980). Among U.S. Hispanic theologians, Orlando Espín has defined religion, in a broad sense, as "the socialization of the experience of the divine." "Popular Catholicism: Alienation or Hope?" forthcoming. For a U.S. Hispanic theologian's analysis of the phenomenon of religion "as such," and an examination of U.S. Hispanic popular religion as "religion," I would refer the reader to the above articles by Espín.

7. This statement applies, moreover, not only to popular religion but to religions such as Santería. As a Catholic theologian rooted in the Catholic Christian community and seeking to speak from within and to that community, my interest is not primarily anthropological or sociological but theological; that is, I am speaking *from within* a particular faith community. Consequently, I cannot pretend to speak *theologically* from within, say, the Santería religion. Indeed, one of the challenges facing U.S. Hispanics remains that of promoting not only the social scientific study of religions such as Santería, but also the articulation of their theological significance *from within* the context of those communities themselves.

context, namely, that of U.S. Hispanic popular Catholicism.[8] What are the implications of U.S. Hispanic popular Catholicism for theological method?

Definitions of popular religion abound.[9] In my use of this term, the adjective "popular" does not primarily mean "common," "widespread," or "well-liked" though popular religion is, indeed, all of these. Rather the adjective refers to the socio-historical fact that these religious symbols, practices, and narratives are *of the people*: "Popular religion is 'popular' not because it is widespread but because its creators and practitioners are the people, and more concretely, the marginalized people in

---

8. Though there is, indeed, much diversity within U.S. Hispanic popular Catholicism itself (e.g., among Mexican-American, Cuban-American, and Puerto Rican communities), "a closer look would clearly indicate a basic similarity in the fundamental structures and functions of the popular religious universe in all three communities." Espín, "Popular Catholicism among Latinos," 313.

9. These can be found throughout the extensive literature on popular religion. In addition to the works cited elsewhere below, see: in the U.S. Hispanic context, Orlando O. Espín, "Tradition and Popular Religion: An Understanding of the *Sensus Fidelium*," *Frontiers of Hispanic Theology in the United States* (Maryknoll, NY; Orbis, 1992); idem, "Popular Catholicism among Latinos," in *Hispanic Catholicism in the United States: Issues and Concerns*, ed. Jay P. Dolan and Allan Figueroa Deck (Notre Dame, IN: University of Notre Dame Press, 1994); Jaime Vidal, "Popular Religion among Hispanics in the General Area of the Archdiocese of Newark," in *Presencia Nueva: A Study of Hispanics in the Archdiocese of Newark* (Newark: Archdiocesan Office of Research and Planning, 1988), 235–352; in the closely-related Latin American context, C. J. Friedemann, *Religiosidad popular entre Medellín y Puebla: Antecedentes y desarrollo* (Santiago de Chile: Pontificia Universidad Católica, 1990); Segundo Galilea, *Religiosidad popular y pastoral* (Madrid: Ediciones Cristiandad, 1979); idem, "The Theology of Liberation and the Place of Folk Religion," in *What is Religion? An Inquiry for Christian Theology*, ed. Mircea Eliade and David Tracy (Edinburgh: T. and T. Clark, 1980) 40–45; Pablo Richard and Diego Irarrazaval, *Religión y Política en América Central: hacia una nueva interpretación de la religiosidad popular* (San José, Costa Rica: DEI, 1981); Aldo Büntig et al., *Catolicismo popular* (Quito: IPLA, 1970); Equipo Seladoc, *Religiosidad popular* (Salamanca: Sígueme, 1976); Diego Irarrazaval, "Religión popular," in *Mysterium Liberationis: Conceptos fundamentales de la teologia de la liberación*, vol. II (Madrid: Editorial Trotta, 1990); Ricardo Falla, *Esa muerte que nos hace vivir: estudio de la religión popular* (San Salvador: UCA, 1984); Juan Carlos Scannone, "Enfoques teológico-pastorales latinoamericanos de la religiosidad popular," *Stromata* 40 (1984): 33–47; John A. McCoy, "Popular Religion in Latin America," *America*, 31 December 1988, 533–36. For insightful comparative analyses of the divergent interpretations of popular religion, see Orlando O. Espín, "Religiosidad popular: un aporte para su definición y hermenéutica," *Estudios Sociales* 58 (1984): 41–56 and Robert J. Schreiter, *Constructing Local Theologies* (Maryknoll, NY: Orbis, 1985), pp. 122–43.

society (i.e., those social sectors pushed against their will to the 'dispensable' or 'disposable' margins of society)."[10] The Catholicism which, as Justo González averred, lies at the heart of U.S. Hispanic culture as such[11] is not so much the hierarchical Catholicism as the Catholicism

---

10. Orlando Espín, "Popular Religion as an Epistemology (of Suffering)," *Journal of Hispanic/Latino Theology*, 2:2 (November 1994):66. Espín adverts to and takes issue with some scholars' definition of popular religion as that religion which is widespread and, therefore, "popular." Here, what is perceived as popular about these religious practices and worldviews is their commonality, or "popularity." I would agree with Espín's rejection of this interpretation, while nevertheless noting that the two interpretations are not necessarily mutually exclusive. The religion of the people, i.e., popular religion, might *also* be widespread and common, especially when, as in Latin America, the marginalized sectors include the vast majority of the population.

For example, from within a Latin American context, Diego Irarrazaval includes both the prophetic character of popular religion and its majoritarian character in his definition of the term "popular." ("Religión popular," p. 346). Also within a Latin American context, Juan Carlos Scannone sees the two interpretations as interrelated. He defines the term *"el pueblo,"* or "the people" as the "communitarian subject of a history and a culture," which subject is preferentially incarnated "among the poor and those who become like them." "Religión, lenguaje y sabiduría de los pueblos: Aporte filosófico a la problemática," *Stromata* 34 (1978): 41–2. He thus notes two interrelated meanings of *el pueblo*: "as organic community and as the underprivileged majoritarian sectors" (ibid., p. 42). Thus, for Scannone, the underprivileged *are* the majority.

However, I would concur with Espín's assertion that this latter, majoritarian dimension is not and cannot be the *defining* characteristic of popular religion, since, if strictly applied, it would exclude underprivileged *minorities*—such as U.S. Hispanics—from the definitions of *"el pueblo"* and *"religión popular."* Consequently, to thus define popular religion would, indeed, be to "deprive this term of its existential, socio-analytic and historical roots in the *pueblo* (. . . a precise socio-analytic category)" and "to dismiss them [the marginalized people] and their religious universe as ultimately insignificant for theology and society" (ibid.).

In the context of literary theory, Jon Thompson draws a helpful distinction between popular culture as "all the cultural practices produced for a mass audience for the purposes of entertainment" and as "those largely localized practices whose ideological function is to affirm the identity of a subculture or marginalized group." *Fiction, Crime, and Empire: Clues to Modernity and Postmodernism* (Urbana and Chicago: University of Illinois Press, 1993), p. 5. Thus stated, this distinction suggests how, in the U.S. context, what is majoritarian may legitimate (as mere "entertainment") rather than counter the oppression of minoritarian, marginalized groups.

11. I am not suggesting that there is such a "thing" as U.S. Hispanic culture—or, for that matter, U.S. culture—"as such." This would be to mistake a living, ever-changing reality for a static, inert object. In addition to the tremendous diversity *within* any given culture (see my discussion of U.S. Hispanic diversity, in the preceding chapter), culture, like popular religion, is not a static

it doesn't

which manifests itself in the faith and religious practices of the people: " 'soy *católico, pero no creo en los curas*' (I am a Catholic, but I don't believe in priests)."[12] Popular religion is "popular" because it emerges from and constitutes us as a people. "Its specificity," suggests Diego Irarrazaval, "is given by its *collective and believing subject*, whose practices are different, though dialectically linked to those of the elites and ecclesial organizations."[13]

The adjective "popular" does not, then, imply an *opposition* between popular religion and "official" or "institutional" religion. González warns that the U.S. Hispanic understanding of faith ought not to be interpreted as a form of modern liberal anti-institutionalism:

This is not, as is often thought, a blanket anticlericalism, after the fashion of the French Revolution. It is rather a statement that only those priests who live up to their vocation . . . are believable priests.

but this is true of most any "popular" religion.

"thing" but a dynamic, living, ever-changing historical process. These are abstract categories that are helpful for analyzing and understanding human life, which is a living reality that cannot be fully encapsulated by any such category.

but how helpful can they be if they're static?

Culture has been defined in many different ways, all of them necessarily limited. Orlando Espín has defined culture as "the dynamic sum of all that a human group does and materially and symbolically creates in order to prolong its life in history within geographical contexts." "Grace and Humanness: A Hispanic Perspective," in *We Are a People! Initiatives in Hispanic American Theology*, ed. Roberto S. Goizueta (Minneapolis: Fortress Press, 1992) 143. In their classic work, *Habits of the Heart: Individualism and Commitment in American Life* (New York: Harper and Row, 1985), Robert N. Bellah et al. define culture in a broad sense as: "Those patterns of meaning that any group or society uses to interpret and evaluate itself and its situation. Language . . . is an important part of culture. Since culture always has a history, it frequently takes the form of tradition. . . . We take culture to be a constitutive dimension of all human action. It is not an epiphenomenon to be explained by economic or political factors" (p. 333). John Francis Kavanaugh notes the etymological connection between "culture" and "cult," or ritual: "A culture is a cult. It is a revelation system. It is the entire range of corporate ritual, of symbolic forms, human expressions, and productive systems." *Following Christ in a Consumer Society: The Spirituality of Cultural Resistance* (Maryknoll, NY: Orbis, 1981), p. 56.

12. González, *Mañana*, p. 63.

13. Irarrazaval, "Religión popular," p. 346. As indicated in note 10 above, the notion of "the people" (*el pueblo*) as a collective subject of history has been systematically developed by Juan Carlos Scannone. See especially his "Religión, lenguaje, y sabiduría de los pueblos: aporte filosófico a la problemática," *Stromata* 34 (1978): 27–42; and idem, "Un nuevo punto de partida en la filosofía latinoamericana," *Stromata* 36 (1980): 25–47. See also Michael Candelaria, *Popular Religion and Liberation* (Albany, NY: SUNY Press, 1990), pp. 56–9.

Authority does not reside in priesthood in the hierarchical sense but rather in Catholicism—in Catholicism understood as the faith of the people and not as the monopoly of the hierarchy.[14]

Indeed, our Hispanic communities have been fortunate to have had a number of courageous priests who, in the face of seemingly insurmountable obstacles, have truly lived up to their vocations, identifying themselves with the lived faith of the people against attempts to crush it from outside.[15]

In Latino popular Catholicism, there is an intrinsic relationship between popular religion and "official" religion, between what Orlando Espín and Sixto García have called the "two visions of Christian Tradition":

If the contents of the two visions of Tradition were to be synoptically compared, we would find significant differences in the symbolic, cultural and analogical use of language, in liturgical expressions and in doctrinal emphases. . . . We do not believe, however, that significant differences will be found in the *essential* elements of the faith (keeping in mind the role that culture plays in always contextualizing the faith and every expression of it). In other words, when careful examination is made of the "official" and "popular" versions of Tradition, the two will be found to be *essentially* the same, though culturally and symbolically expressed in different manners, and with doctrinal and praxical emphases that deeply reveal the socio-historical realities and interests of the holders of either vision of the Tradition. We further believe that it is these socio-historical realities and interests that ultimately create the significant distinctions between these two strands of Christian Tradition.[16]

The tendency to read popular religion, whether explicitly Catholic or not, as *by definition anti*-institutional is, I will suggest in the next chapter,

---

14. p. 63. On this understanding of Catholicism, see also Espín, "Tradition and Popular Religion."

15. González, *Mañana*, pp. 61–63.

16. Sixto J. García and Orlando Espín, " 'Lilies of the Field': A Hispanic Theology of Providence and Human Responsibility," *Proceedings of The Catholic Theological Society of America*, 44 (1989): 75. Leonardo Boff makes a similar point from within a Latin American context (especially ironic and powerful in his case, given the persecution he suffered at the hands of the "institutional church"): "we should not view the grassroots church as a church running parallel to that of the larger institution. . . . The antagonism does not lie between institution and community. It lies between a Christendom system (a church tied to the classes exercising hegemony in civil society) and a people's church. In Brazil, and in Latin America in general, one can see a noticeable convergence between

more a reflection of modern Western intellectual biases than of the reality itself. As Irarrazaval maintains, "the people's way of living and thinking is integrative; it embraces different dimensions, but they all comprise a whole. . . . The people think in terms of complementary relations and oppositions."[17]

Popular religious practices and beliefs are themselves an ancient Christian phenomenon, extending back to "at least the post-apostolic church (and some might claim, not without reasonable arguments and evidence, that even the apostolic generation had created its own brand—or brands—of popular religion)."[18] As long as human beings desire to make contact with the transcendent dimension of everyday life, as long as we seek to find meaning in life and death, as long as we strive to express the ineffable and to relate religious belief to everyday life—which is to say, always—there will be popular religion.[19] Indeed, because of the intrinsic relationship between popular religion and dogma, "some of today's official dogmas were yesterday's popular beliefs, often the subject of heated debate by theologians and bishops of the time."[20]

Yet, as indicated above, we should be careful not to simply equate popular religion with any and all religious practices that have become widespread and thus, in this sense of the word, "popular." Popular Catholicism is not simply coextensive with those forms of Catholicism which have become popular over time. Such an interpretation ignores the particular socio-his-

Convenient qualification

---

the larger church, structured as a network of institutional services, and the church as a network of grassroots communities. From the larger church the latter gets the symbolic capital of the faith, its links with apostolic tradition, and the dimension of universality. The larger church, in turn, benefits from the grassroots church. From the latter it gets concrete embodiment on the local and personal level, insertion among the common people, and links with the most urgent human causes revolving around justice, dignity, and participation. The two are geared toward each other, in mutual consideration and acceptance." "Theological Characteristics of a Grassroots Church," in *The Challenge of Basic Christian Communities*, ed. Sergio Torres and John Eagleson (Maryknoll, NY: Orbis, 1981), 139.

17. Irarrazaval, "Religión popular," 345.

18. García and Espín, "Lilies of the Field," pp. 73–74. On the historical origins and development of popular religion, see Luis Maldonado, *Génesis del catolicismo popular* (Madrid: Ediciones Cristiandad, 1979) and *Introducción a la religiosidad popular* (Santander: Sal Terrae, 1985).

19. Popular religion emerges at the grass roots as the answers provided by the religious experts, or "religious virtuosi," to these fundamental human questions become disconnected from the people's own everyday lives. Espín, "Popular Catholicism among Latinos," 309. Yet, as Espín noted with respect to the two versions of Tradition, popular religion itself remains "somehow still connected with the normative version of the religion." Ibid.

20. García and Espín, "Lilies of the Field," p. 74.

torical context of popular religion—on the margins of society—and thus results in a cooptation of popular religion.[21]

For instance, an analogy is sometimes drawn between U.S. Hispanic popular Catholicism and Euro-American Catholic devotionalism to argue that both are forms of popular Catholicism. It is, however, its very *socio-historical context*—not its popularity—that makes U.S. Hispanic popular Catholicism different from Euro-American popular Catholicism. The liturgical scholar Mark Francis has insightfully elaborated some of the differences:

> . . . while many of these practices appear similar, it would be a pastoral error to assume that they always "mean" exactly the same thing. The popular religion of many Hispanics, for example, while based in part on the same medieval matrix as Euro-American devotionalism, includes elements indigenous to the "New World." These elements express deeply held convictions about one's place in the universe, access to the sacred, and how human beings experience time. These convictions were formed from experiences of life that are different from those of Europeans.[22]

In a comparative historical analysis of Latino popular religion and Euro-American devotionalism, Francis notes that the latter became widespread especially in the 19th century, as "a means of evangelizing the faithful and of encouraging identification with the Catholic church in the midst of the often hostile Protestant culture. An important aspect of this 'devotional revolution' was the fact that it was officially sanctioned by the hierarchy of the church and went hand in hand with . . . the 'Romanization' of Catholicism—especially Irish Catholicism—during the 19th century."[23]

U.S. Hispanic popular religion, on the other hand, emerges in a socio-historical context that is virtually the opposite: far from enjoying the support and encouragement of the hierarchy, the indigenous people of the Americas were "systematically excluded from full participation in the official religion."[24] Thus, "while not rejecting the official liturgy and clerical leadership, the poor and marginalized often developed popular religion as a way of expressing cultural and religious identity when their access to the holy was denied through 'official channels.' "[25] This history helps

---

21. See note 10 above.

22. Mark R. Francis, "Building Bridges Between Liturgy, Devotionalism, and Popular Religion," *Assembly* 20:2 (April, 1994): 636.

23. Ibid., p. 637.

24. Ibid.

25. Ibid.

explain the central role played by popular religion in the U.S. Hispanic community; the symbols, rituals, and narratives[26] of popular religion are, in the words of Justo González, "one of the ways—probably the most

---

26. As I use the term, a popular religious symbol is an object, image, or action that reveals, mediates, and makes present what may be called the ineffable, the holy, the sacred, or the supernatural. A symbol is not univocal, but multivocal, or polysemous, that is, it is "pregnant with a plenitude of meaning which is evoked rather than explicitly stated." Avery Dulles quoted in C. Gilbert Romero, *Hispanic Devotional Piety: Tracing the Biblical Roots* (Maryknoll, NY: Orbis, 1991), p. 51. This "plenitude of meaning" is conveyed not primarily explicitly and logically, but implicitly and affectively, by attracting and drawing us into its world (ibid.). Symbols make present here and now what they re-present. Though the ultimate referent of the symbol is beyond itself (e.g., God), the symbol draws us to itself so that we may first encounter this "beyond" *within* the symbol itself. The symbol thus effects a *relationship* between its transcendent, ultimate referent and ourselves—and *among* all of us who *together* participate in and share that relationship. Because the symbol communicates primarily through affect rather than through logic, it "has the power of recognizing and expressing what logical discourse abhors: the existence of internal tensions, incompatibilities, conflicts, struggles, destructions." Bernard Lonergan, *Method in Theology* (New York: Crossroad/Seabury, 1972), p. 66.

In Catholic theology, symbol is usually identified with sacrament: "The teaching on the sacraments is the classic place in which a theology of the symbol is put forward in general in Catholic theology. The sacraments make concrete and actual, for the life of the individual, the symbolic reality of the church as the primary ['in relation to the single sacraments, not to Christ'] sacrament and therefore constitute at once, in keeping with the nature of this church, a symbolic reality." Karl Rahner, "The Theology of the Symbol," *Theological Investigations*, Vol. IV (Baltimore: Helicon Press, 1966), p. 241.

A symbol differs from a mere sign. The symbol reveals its transcendent meaning by first drawing us *to* itself; in order to communicate its meaning, a sign immediately directs our attention *away* from itself. When we see an "exit" sign, we immediately look elsewhere, i.e., for the exit door to which the sign points us. When we see the bread and wine on the altar, we are attracted by and drawn to the objects themselves—and only in the context of that attraction are we opened up to their meaning and truth. Signs communicate information; symbols effect relationships. If we lose a symbol, we feel as if we have lost a part of ourselves (e.g., a wedding band, the photograph of a loved one). If we lose a sign, all we have lost is information—however important it may be (e.g., we are unable to find the exit door). As this example also illustrates, a sign is not multivocal. On the nature and function of symbols, see also Roger Haight, *Dynamics of Theology* (New York: Paulist Press, 1990), pp. 129–66. In a more general context, see the following classic works on symbol: Paul Ricoeur, *The Symbolism of Evil* (Boston: Beacon, 1967); Mircea Eliade, *Images and Symbols* (New York: Sheed and Ward, 1969); Mary Douglas, *Purity and Danger* (London: Routledge and Kegan Paul, 1966).

Narratives, or stories, and rituals are the primary ways in which a community generates and identifies with its symbols, by explicitly locating them within the

important way—in which the church of the dispossessed continues its existence. . . ."[27]

Because of its origins in our own communities, at the margins of society, popular religion thus remains "one of the ways—probably the most important way" in which Latinos and Latinas can maintain our own

---

community's own ongoing history. Narrative is symbolic discourse; ritual is symbolic action (see Victor Turner's books cited below). When part of a story, the crucifix is no longer merely a static object but is now the life, passion, and death of a person, Jesus Christ, and his community; the bread and wine are no longer merely "species" but are the relationships among Jesus and his disciples as lived out in the Last Supper and as these relationships continue to be lived out today in the Christian community, which continues to break bread and share the cup; the image of Guadalupe is not only a static picture but is the birth and ongoing life of the Mexican people and their relationship with God; the photograph of a deceased parent is now the memory of that parent's joys and struggles, and, therefore, the ongoing relationship between the deceased person and those of us who continue to retell his or her story; the wedding band brings to life a couple's many years together. Like all symbols and rituals, narratives are able to convey the contradictions, ambiguities, and conflicts of life in a way that logical discourse cannot. On the significance of narrative for theology, especially political and liberation theologies, see Johann Baptist Metz, *Faith in History and Society: Toward a Practical Fundamental Theology* (New York: Seabury/Crossroad, 1980), esp. pp. 184–227. Like symbols and rituals, narratives are at the same time disclosive and transformative. They help us understand ourselves and the world around us; they also help transform us and our world. Cf. Thompson, *Fiction, Crime, and Empire*, pp. 117–21, 174–80.

The most fundamental form in which communities disclose and create meaning is in ritual. Like all relationships, the relationship between God and ourselves which is mediated by symbolic objects (e.g., the crucifix) and narratives (e.g., the gospels) demands more than simply affective participation; it also demands inter-*action*, or performance. It is this interaction which defines and constitutes relationship: e.g., the sacrament (or symbol) of the eucharist is defined and constituted not only by the eucharistic bread and wine, and not only by the eucharistic narrative, but, first and foremost, by the ritual act of *breaking* the bread together and *sharing* the cup, which act is *mediated* by the symbolic objects and narrative. The foundation of symbol and narrative is ritual, just as the foundation of belief, or theory, is praxis, or human action. See Catherine Bell, *Ritual Theory, Ritual Practice* (New York: Oxford University Press, 1992), and chapter 5 below.

For analyses of the nature and function of ritual, see Bell's recent work, ibid., Victor Turner, *The Ritual Process: Structure and Anti-Structure* (Ithaca: Cornell University Press, 1977); idem, *Dramas, Fields and Metaphors: Symbolic Action in Human Society* (Ithaca: Cornell University Press, 1974); Clifford Geertz, *The Interpretation of Cultures* (New York: Basic Books, 1973); Jonathan Z. Smith, *To Take Place: Toward Theory in Ritual* (Chicago: University of Chicago Press, 1987); Claude Lévi-Strauss, *The Naked Man* (New York: Harper and Row, 1981). On symbol, narrative, and ritual in popular religion, see especially Maldonado, *Introducción a la religiosidad popular*, and Irarrazaval, "Religión popular."

27. González, *Mañana*, p. 61.

It is interesting, however, that Xty, no matter how you cut it, is a European import.

identity and history alive in the face of the dominant culture. U.S. Hispanic identity and U.S. Hispanic popular religion are so closely intertwined because, as Espín and García suggest, this latter "is probably the least 'invaded' area of any of the Hispanic cultures, one of the most 'popular' of our peoples' creations, and the more deeply 'ours.' It can be seen as a font of Hispanic worldviews and self-concepts."[28] Indeed, in their very definition of popular religion, Espín and García note the close relationship between popular religion and the self-identity of historically marginalized communities:

> In general terms, popular religiosity can be defined as the set of experiences, beliefs and rituals which more-or-less peripheral human groups create, assume and develop (within concrete socio-cultural and historical contexts, and as a response to these contexts) and which to a greater or lesser degree distance themselves from what is recognized as normative by church and society, striving (through rituals, experiences and beliefs) to find an access to God and salvation which they feel they cannot find in what the church and society present as normative.[29]

yes

is This as cohesive as we think?

U.S. Hispanic popular Catholicism thus fosters the internal cohesion of U.S. Hispanic communities while, at the same time, maintaining links—"to a greater or lesser degree"—with the larger church and society. Those links make it possible for U.S. Hispanic communities to draw on the riches of the larger Christian tradition, interpreting that tradition from within our own particular histories, thereby discovering its liberating power. Consequently, those very links also make it possible to *critique* persons, groups, and institutional structures which misuse and abuse the Christian tradition, turning the "good news to the poor" into a weapon of oppression.

If popular Catholicism plays a key role in defining the U.S. Hispanic socio-historical context, two particular religious figures or symbols in turn play a key role in defining popular Catholicism among U.S. Hispanics: these are the symbols of Jesus and Mary so prevalent in every aspect of U.S. Hispanic life, from explicitly religious rituals to everyday "*dichos*,"

---

28. García and Espín, "Lilies of the Field," 73.

29. Espín and García, "Hispanic-American Theology," 115. Espín defines Latino popular Catholicism, specifically, as "an effort by the subaltern to explain, justify and somehow control a social reality that appears too dangerous to confront in terms and through means other than the mainly symbolic. However, this popular religion is founded on the claim that the divine (identified by the people as the Christian divine) has been and is encountered by them in and through the symbols (ritual, ethical and doctrinal) of popular Catholicism." "Popular Catholicism: Alienation or Hope?" forthcoming.

or sayings.[30] Jesus and Mary are "the two core devotions of Hispanic popular religion."[31] Virgilio Elizondo recalls that "from my earliest memories, it was in Jesus and in *Nuestra Señora de Guadalupe* that our people found comfort and strength."[32] One might even go so far as to say that, for many Latinas and Latinos, religious faith is virtually indistinguishable from our everyday relationship with Jesus and Mary, lived out in everything from the most highly "institutional" liturgical services to the most intimate, personal devotions—and every aspect of life in between. If this insight—so common in the theologies being developed by U.S. Hispanics—is true, then it will be impossible to articulate a theology grounded in the particularity of U.S. Hispanic experience without attending, specifically, to these central symbols which so suffuse the everyday lives of so many Latinos and Latinas. In short, Jesus and Mary function as more than explicitly religious symbols; for us, they are identified with life itself.[33]

Consequently, to know who we are, to understand our socio-historical experience, to identify us, we should try to identify who this Jesus and Mary are. We must inquire about the *particular* embodiment of Jesus and Mary in U.S. Hispanic communities: Who are *this* Jesus and *this* Mary? What are their particular characteristics? What are they like—not in general, but in their particular relationship to *us* as Latinos and Latinas, as U.S. Hispanic communities? As we attempt to define the *locus theologicus* of a Catholic U.S. Hispanic theology, the remainder of this chapter, as well as the next, will address these specific questions.

Since Latino popular Catholicism is itself a variegated, dynamic phenomenon, any attempt to provide an exhaustive understanding of the Jesus and Mary of popular Catholicism will confront a multiplicity of Jesuses and Marys. Again, however, it is not my intention to provide such an exhaustive treatment but, instead, to outline a model for uncovering and articulating the theological significance of U.S. Hispanic popular Catholicism. I will thus focus primarily on one U.S. Hispanic religious community, that of San Fernando Cathedral in San Antonio, Texas. This cathedral parish is unique for several reasons: 1) it is the

---

30. E.g., a common exclamation after one sneezes, equivalent to the English "God bless you!" is "*¡Jesús!*" after a second consecutive sneeze, "*María!*" and after a third, "*José!*"

31. Orlando Espín, "Tradition and Popular Religion," 76.

32. Elizondo, *The Future is Mestizo*, p. 68.

33. The intimate connection between popular religion and the people's common life is underscored by Virgilio Elizondo, who maintains that "were it not for Our Lady of Guadalupe there would be no Mexican or Mexican American people today." "Popular Religion as Support of Identity: A Pastoral-Psychological Case-Study Based on the Mexican American Experience in the U.S.A.," in *Popular Religion*, ed. Norbert Greinacher and Norbert Mette (Edinburgh: T. & T. Clark, 1986), p. 39.

No all These "unique" characteristics actually serve to separate it, or at least distinguish it, from its counterparts.

only U.S. cathedral which has always been predominantly Latino in character, 2) it is the oldest, continuously active Latino worship center in the United States, 3) it is one of the very few "cathedrals of the poor" in the United States, yet it draws parishioners from a broad cultural and economic range, from the poorest Mexican immigrants to the wealthy Hispanic elite, including primarily Mexican Americans but also Cubans and other Hispanics, 4) it is the episcopal seat of the first U.S. Hispanic bishop, 5) it is the oldest canonically-erected U.S. parish in continuous service in the same location, and 6) the parish has, over the past several years, intentionally set for itself the task of developing theological analyses of their own popular religion, a ground-breaking project initiated by San Fernando's rector, Father Virgilio Elizondo, participated in by a number of scholars, including myself, and funded by the Lilly Endowment. This project has thus already begun the process of developing a collaborative theology ("*teología de conjunto*") which will take seriously the everyday religious faith of our communities as a rich source for theological reflection. *So This book becomes a study of a very unique* — *US Hispanic popular Catholicism*

If popular religion is the dimension of Latino culture most deeply "ours," there are aspects of particular symbols, narratives, and rituals that are more deeply ours than others. While the Holy Week celebrations are, of course, framed and formed by the Christian gospel narratives, especially the narrative of Jesus' passion, what is most "ours" about the Holy Week celebrations is the *particular way* in which those narratives are embodied and reenacted in ritual. For that reason, I will focus on the image of Jesus presented not only in the narratives but, especially, in the *rituals*, or celebrations of the triduum. The opposite is, arguably, the case with respect to Mary, or Our Lady of Guadalupe. Here, it is the *narrative* itself which is most "ours," since it emerges from within the Mexican people. The association of Guadalupe with the Virgin Mary, already present in the narrative, made it easy for ritual devotion to Guadalupe, however, to be identified with the church's broader tradition of Marian devotionalism (as exemplified in, for example, May crownings). This process of integration into the larger liturgical tradition began very early on in the Guadalupan tradition.[34] Nevertheless, to the extent that the particular narrative of Guadalupe (as opposed to other Marian apparitions) remains central to Mexican popular Catholicism, that process of assimilation has never been completely successful. In the case of Jesus, the people have taken from the larger Christian tradition a narrative by adapting and interpreting the narrative through their own ritual; in the case of Guadalupe, the people have taken from the larger Christian tradition a ritual devotion by adapting it and interpreting the ritual through their own narrative. In neither case is there by any means a dichotomy, since

34. Clodomiro L. Siller Acuña, *Para comprender el mensaje de María de Guadalupe* (Buenos Aires: Editorial Guadalupe, 1989), p. 94.

the people's tradition and the broader Christian tradition are always interrelated, but there are differences in emphasis.

The Jesus of the Triduum

It is possible to speak of the plural Jesus*es* of U.S. Hispanic popular Catholicism, since, in fact, U.S. Hispanics relate to Jesus not as an abstract, other-worldly spirit but as "*el niño Jesús,*" or "*Jesús, hijo de María,*" or "*Jesús, mi hermano,*" or "*Cristo, nuestro Rey,*" or "*el Sagrado Corazón,*" or "*Jesús, el peregrino.*" Yet from among all these Jesuses, one stands out by virtue of both its pervasiveness throughout Latino communities and the centrality of its role in those communities. That centrality is most visible precisely during the culmination of the liturgical year in Holy Week. During Holy Week, the Jesus of U.S. Hispanic popular Catholicism is revealed as, above all, the crucified Jesus. This fact is evident to even the most casual observer. The highpoint of the triduum celebration is Good Friday, beginning with the vigil on Holy Thursday night: the entire day—literally—is spent in communal religious celebrations. For each of the principal celebrations of the day, the church is packed to overflowing. (To underscore the significance of Good Friday, one might note that the only day which rivals Good Friday in the number of people attracted to San Fernando Cathedral is the related feast of Ash Wednesday.) The Easter Vigil cannot compare either in the time devoted to the celebration, the sheer number of participants, or the extent and intensity of their participation.

Since, at no time is the figure of Jesus a more important focal point for the Latino community than during the celebration of Holy Week, especially on Good Friday, or *Viernes Santo*, it would thus be helpful, here, to describe in greater detail a "typical" Hispanic celebration of the Holy Week triduum, from Holy Thursday through the Easter Vigil. By examining, in this case, the triduum celebration at San Fernando Cathedral we can gain greater insight into the particular place from which a U.S. Hispanic theological reflection might emerge. This beautiful, 260 year old cathedral is located in downtown San Antonio, on the city's main plaza. Its congregation is predominantly poor and of Mexican descent, though it includes persons from all classes, races, and walks of life.

The triduum begins at San Fernando, with the Holy Thursday celebration: the celebration of the Lord's Last Supper and Agony in the Garden. It is important to note that this is itself a two-part celebration, with each of equal significance: not just the Last Supper, or just the Agony in the Garden, but both. The celebration begins with the congregation's procession to the cenacle, followed by the eucharistic liturgy. Yet this general description cannot truly convey the sensual character of the experience. All one's senses are drawn in: the sanctuary has been arranged and decorated in the form of a real dining room, the people gathered around the table have donned clothing which they imagine the people in Jesus' time may have worn, the Archbishop—surrounded by the many children who have run onto the sanctuary to witness the scene—washes the feet of the "apostles," the sermon commands the congregation to go out into their homes and workplaces to re-enact there this example of service. The end of the mass is not the end of the Holy Thursday celebration. Rather, when the eucharistic liturgy is completed, the congregation rises and walks out of the church, into the evening, in a candlelight eucharistic procession. During the procession, which circles the main plaza, a litany is sung to which the people respond: "*Caminemos con Jesús*" (let us walk with Jesus). The people are walking with Jesus to Gethsemane. It is again an experience that stirs all one's senses: the hundreds of flickering candles under a darkening sky, the loud horns of impatient drivers, the wide-eyed stares of curious onlookers, the angry insults of fundamentalist hecklers, and the incense-like fragrance of the smoke wafting from the multitude of candles . . . and always: "*Caminemos con Jesús.*"

As the procession wends its way back into the church, the people find that the sanctuary has been transformed from a dining room to the garden of Gethsemane. A huge painting of Jesus at prayer hangs from the back wall of the sanctuary, and, in front of it, numerous kneelers surrounded by hundreds, maybe even thousands of devotional candles bursting forth in a cacophony of light. The eucharist is reposed to the poignant sound of traditional Mexican hymns. After a few moments of silent prayer, the people are invited to remain here at Gethsemane with Jesus during the night, accompanying him in his agony. Until midnight, the traditional hour of Jesus' arrest, the scene at the cathedral sanctuary will be one of solemn silence, yet also a paradoxical activity, as people come forward to accompany and pray with Jesus. Before leaving the evening's liturgical celebration, each person is given a small piece of bread which he or she can take home to share with family and friends.

At midnight, the sanctuary is again transformed, this time from the garden of Gethsemane to the hill of Calvary. This is the responsibility of the men of the parish, who take a special pride in this work. As they hoist the life-size crucifix onto its pedestal at the entrance to the sanctuary and carefully place the statues of Mary and Mary Magdalen at the foot of the crucifix, it is clear that this process is for these men much more than mere physical labor. The love and reverence so evident on their faces makes it seem that this time "between" the Holy Thursday and Good Friday celebrations is really itself a part of the triduum liturgical celebration. These men are not simply "setting up" the church for the subsequent liturgical celebration; this pre-dawn labor in the earliest hours of Good Friday morning is itself a liturgical celebration.

Only a few hours later, at 8:00 A.M., those members of the parish who will be participating in the morning's procession and re-enactment of

Jesus' passion and death gather to put on their colorful attire. Again, the reverence on the people's faces indicates that this is more than just a "suiting up" or a "preparation" for some important event; the preparation is itself a part of the religious celebration. After they are ready, the group leaves for San Antonio's old *mercado*, or market square, where the Good Friday services will begin.

A stage has been erected at the entrance to the *mercado*; there Jesus will be confronted by Herod and Pilate. Across from and all around the stage, thousands of people are mingling, standing quietly, praying, and, at times, breaking into song—people of every age, race, class, and nationality have joined the parishioners to take part in the morning's festivities. Religious and civic leaders from the San Antonio area eventually take the podium to lead prayers and make introductory speeches to the assembled crowd.

At 10:00 A.M., a loud trumpet signals the entrance of Pilate onto the stage to confront Jesus of Nazareth. From this point on, the words and actions follow the gospel passion narratives, with San Fernando parishioners playing the parts of the different characters in the passion story. Pilate sends Jesus to Herod, who in turn returns him to Pilate for judgment. After the crowd calls for the release of Barabbas, Jesus is flogged and crowned with thorns. Pilate presents the beaten and broken Nazarene to the people—that is, to the assembled crowd in San Antonio/Jerusalem—who cry out for his crucifixion. The scene can only be described as eerie: this is not an event that happened two thousand years ago, but an event taking place today and in which we are actively participating. With the crack of the Roman soldier's whip echoing through the crowd, one can hear a young woman at the back instinctively let out a half-muffled shriek, or see an old man not far from her wincing in pain, as if he himself were feeling the sting of the whip.

His face and body covered with blood from this torturous abuse, Jesus is given his cross and led out onto the street to carry the cross along his Via Dolorosa to Calvary (ironically, the San Antonio street which he will walk along is named Dolorosa Street, perhaps after similar processions which may have taken place on the street many years ago). Accompanying Jesus on the way to his crucifixion, the crowd sings the traditional song, *"Perdona a tu pueblo, Señor"* (Lord, forgive your people). During this procession, it becomes clearer than ever that this is not so much San Fernando's celebration as that of the entire community. Lawyers on their way to the San Antonio courthouse only a few blocks away stop to observe and become a part of the procession. Shopkeepers along the route take time out from business to step outside their stores and join in the singing. Newspaper and television reporters, unable to remain mere observers, become participants in the procession. One of the most moving points in the procession occurs when Jesus falls for the first time, in front of one of San Antonio's most famous Mexican restaurants. A woman in very colorful garments comes out onto a second-story balcony to sing to Jesus the song "I don't know how to love him." The deep sense of anguish and love reflected in her beautiful voice is felt by the entire crowd, who stand motionless as the mournful eyes of this woman, looking down at the fallen Jesus, meet his glassy, bloodshot eyes, glancing up at her.

When the procession continues, the Roman soldiers become increasingly vehement in their taunting of Jesus: bellowing condemnations, mocking him sarcastically, and flogging him as he struggles to stay on his feet under the heavy cross. Unable to do so, Jesus falls for a second time. At this point, something unplanned and unexpected happens, another indication that this is no mere staged theatrical event. A young boy, about eight years old, breaks away from his mother in the crowd and runs to the fallen Jesus. The boy wipes Jesus' face with a handkerchief and spontaneously starts to kiss the wounds on Jesus' head and face. As the procession continues, Simon of Cyrene enters the scene in the person of the Archbishop of San Antonio, who himself has been following along. Simon then takes Jesus' cross upon his own shoulders.

Finally the procession arrives at the main plaza, where the crucifixion will take place. The people who had been accompanying Jesus in the procession meet another equally large crowd of people who have been waiting at the plaza and the cathedral for Jesus' arrival. Even with police blocking the streets around the plaza, it hardly seems possible that these thousands of people could fit into this two-block area . . . but they do . . . cramming shoulder to shoulder into the plaza, the cathedral entrance, and the surrounding streets. The cross is laid down on the sidewalk in front of the cathedral, Jesus is stripped, and he is placed on the cross. Now takes place what many participants describe as the most powerful moment of the passion. Jesus is nailed to the cross. Yet such a simple, matter-of-fact description cannot possibly convey what transpires in these few minutes. The Roman soldiers begin to hammer huge nails into Jesus' hands and feet. The scene is numbing and hair-raising at the same time. Above the heads of the multitude, the soldiers' hammers rise menacingly into the air only to come down with a terrible force. The ear-splitting sound of the hammers hitting the nails reverberates through the crowd over and over again. Each sharp sound of iron hitting iron is accompanied by the condemned man's agonizing screams. Though this process takes only a few minutes, these terrifying sounds seem to last forever, as if suspended in time. One can hear gasps coming from the crowd and see hundreds of tear-stained faces.

At high noon, the cross is raised up, with Jesus hanging from its beam. Mary and the women approach the cross. Together with the rest of the crowd, they are sobbing, crying tears of anguish at the sight of Jesus on the cross. At the same time, the soldiers continue to shout their mocking insults. The soldiers eventually fall silent and Jesus' voice is heard: "Father, forgive them for they know not what they do." "My God, my God, why have you abandoned me?" And finally: "Father, into your hands I commend my spirit." The only sound heard now is a tolling bell. Then, all of a sudden, one of the previously insulting soldiers proclaims: "Truly this was the Son of God," and the crowd begins to disperse in silence, with heads bowed in reverence and sorrow.

The sanctuary of the church, transformed into Calvary the night before, now becomes the center of the people's attention. In the early afternoon, to the sound of song, the clergy file down the cathedral's aisle to the foot of the cross in the sanctuary. There they fall prostrate on the floor for a few minutes of prayer. With this begins the service of *Las Siete Palabras* (the seven last words of Jesus on the cross). The clergy then stand up and walk over to the side walls of the sanctuary, where they sit down on a simple wooden bench. Each of the seven Scripture readings is followed by a short sermon, a collective prayer, and a song. Different members of the community take turns reading the scriptural texts. The church is absolutely packed; people are crammed into every pew, squeezed into every aisle, and jammed into every entrance. The service ends with communion and the veneration of the cross to the sound of the song: "*Venid, o cristianos, la cruz adoremos*" (Come, oh Christians, let us adore the cross). The people now file to the foot of the cross to be with Jesus. They kneel before him, touch and kiss his feet, caress his wounds. Several persons, holding smaller crucifixes, are stationed at various areas of the church, where the people may also go to touch and kiss the Crucified. Parents can be seen carrying their tiny babies to Jesus, and putting their babies' lips up to his feet—so that the infants too may be with him. The procession of people to the cross continues for the entire afternoon.

At dusk, the community participates in the *Santo Entierro*, or Holy Burial, of Jesus. The service begins as a group of gypsies, draped in black dresses, *mantillas*, and hoods, process to the sanctuary to take Jesus down from the cross. This procession is accompanied by the shrill tones of gypsy lamentation songs: "Why, oh why did I drive the nails through your hands . . . ?" The entire congregation joins the singers in their songs of lamentation. Carrying Jesus' corpse on a litter, the gypsies lead the congregation in a procession out the church doors and around the plaza. With candles and torches, they all accompany Jesus and Mary (the statue of *la Soledad*, or Mary in her solitude) on the way to the grave. Once again bystanders look on in amazement and the whole city is drawn into the solemn celebration as the black night sky is dotted with thousands of small, flickering candle lights.

Gradually, the procession wends its way around the plaza and back into the church, which will now become the holy sepulchre. Jesus' body is laid down on a bier in the sanctuary and the people begin to process up to the body to pay their final respects, each person laying a flower on the corpse as a sign of love. Again, the people kneel beside Jesus, hold his hands, touch his face, kiss his feet. By the end of the procession, Jesus' body is completely covered by a mountain of flowers.

Yet this is still not the end of the community's celebration of Good Friday. Having accompanied Jesus, it is now time to accompany Mary in her suffering, in her solitude. Mary is *la Soledad*; she is *la Dolorosa* (the sorrowful or suffering one). During the evening service of the *Pésames a la Virgen* (condolences to the Virgin) the congregation assures Mary that she is not alone; they are with her in her pain. One by one, members of the congregation who have had some particularly painful or difficult experience during the previous year walk up to *la Soledad*, and, in front of the entire congregation, share their pain with her: the father whose son committed suicide, the young woman who has just been diagnosed with cancer, the mother whose son was killed in a drive-by gang shooting. This collective grieving, shared by Jesus, Mary, and the entire community, ends the Good Friday celebration. While certainly a very sorrowful ending to the day, it is also strangely empowering and hope-filled. There is an abiding sense that we are strengthened and given new life even in the midst of our common suffering, perhaps precisely because it is a suffering undertaken in common. When we stand alongside Mary in her pain, she is no longer *la Soledad*—and neither are any of us.

Saturday is a day of rest, reflecting the stillness and quiet of Jesus' tomb after he had been laid to rest. Moreover, the people are simply exhausted—physically and, even more, emotionally—from the previous day's events. On Saturday night, however, the church again comes to life. People begin to file into the cathedral, many dressed in their Sunday best. The Easter Vigil begins as a fire is lit and blessed, and each person in the congregation lights her or his own candle from this fire. As the light spreads from one candle to another, gradually filling the whole church, the congregation sings "*La luz de Jesús ha venido al mundo*" (the light of Jesus has come into the world). The great events of salvation history are read from the scriptural texts and, when the resurrection is proclaimed, the church explodes in joy: a curtain which had been covering the sanctuary is pulled open, the lights are turned on throughout the church, organ music resounds, and dozens of children come running and skipping up the center aisle from the sanctuary, singing "He has risen, *ha resucitado*," and tossing flower petals into the air as they skip down the aisle—petals from the flowers that had earlier lain on Jesus' corpse. The Easter Vigil mass then proceeds, a glorious culmination to the week's celebrations.

Our Lady of Guadalupe

Depending on our Latin American countries of origin, or even on the particular region to which we trace our roots, U.S. Hispanics might have a personal or family devotion to any of over a dozen patronal Marys. What is common to all forms of U.S. Hispanic popular Catholicism, however, is the central place of Mary: "It is difficult to find, besides the

crucified Christ, another more powerful religious symbol."[35] For historical reasons, however, there is one Mary who stands out as unique among
the Hispanic Marys, and that is *la Morenita*, Our Lady of Guadalupe. No
other popular religious devotion is as closely linked to a people's self-identity, or socio-historical context, as is the Mexican devotion to Our Lady
of Guadalupe; none other is more deeply "ours."[36] Precisely because the
link between popular religion and self-identity is so strong here, it would
be virtually impossible to develop a U.S. Hispanic theology which did not
somehow take seriously, in systematic fashion, the Mexican devotion to
Guadalupe. So strong is this link, in fact, that, as we have increasingly
come in contact with Mexicans in the United States, U.S. Hispanics from
other Latin American countries have also begun to develop a devotion to
Our Lady of Guadalupe.[37]

Before looking more closely at Our Lady of Guadalupe, however, we
should note that, like almost any feast in a Latino parish, the Holy Week
celebration discussed above is not just a celebration of Jesus but it is also
a celebration of Mary. Jesus is never just Jesus; he is always also the son
of Mary. And Mary is never just Mary; she is always also the mother of
Jesus. As *la Madre Dolorosa* (the Sorrowful Mother), Mary accompanies
Jesus in his passion. At the end of Good Friday, she herself takes center
stage as *la Soledad*, whom we accompany in her mourning.

Just as the Holy Week celebrations are based on a narrative, that of the
gospels, so too is the people's celebration of Our Lady of Guadalupe based
on a narrative, that of the *Nican Mopohua*, written in Náhuatl, the language of the indigenous Nahua people, who were part of the Aztec empire.[38] (The title comes from the first two words of the text, which roughly
mean "here is told.")[39] It recounts the story of the encounter between the

---

35. Espín, "Tradition and Popular Religion," 71–2.

36. Andrés Guerrero, for example, asserts that "to understand the symbol of
Guadalupe is to understand the essence of being Mexican." *A Chicano Theology*
(Maryknoll, NY: Orbis, 1987), p. 96.

37. A moving example of the influence of Guadalupe among non-Mexican
Latinos and Latinas is the work of Jeanette Rodríguez, *Our Lady of Guadalupe:
Faith and Empowerment among Mexican American Women* (Austin, TX:
University of Texas Press, 1994). In the Preface (pp. xvii–xxii), she recounts how
the faith of the Mexican-American women with whom she worked brought her,
an Ecuadoran, to a deep appreciation of and love for Our Lady of Guadalupe:
"At first I thought her message was especially and possibly exclusively for
Mexicans and Mexican Americans. My research and personal reflection now tell
me that Our Lady of Guadalupe truly comes to show her love, compassion, help,
and defense to all the inhabitants of the Americas. . . . Guadalupe again offers
God's loving embrace for the rejected people of the Americas" (p. xxii).

38. For an explanation of the relationship between the Nahuas and the Aztecs,
see ibid., p. 2.

39. Siller, *Para comprender el mensaje de María de Guadalupe*, p. 12.

poor indigenous man, Juan Diego, and "the Lady" of Mt. Tepeyac in the year 1531. The word "Guadalupe" is not Náhuatl, but a homophonic Spanish mispronunciation of an unknown Náhuatl word, perhaps *Tlecuauhtlacupeuh*—translated as "she who comes flying out of the Light like the Eagle of Fire" or, alternatively, "she will crush the serpent of stone."[40] The Spanish associated this "Guadalupe" with their own shrine in Estremadura, Spain.[41] The original text of the narrative was possibly composed by Don Antonio Valeriano, an indigenous scholar, teacher, and translator who was "Governor of the Indians" in Mexico for forty years.[42] One cannot understand the significance of Guadalupe for popular religion—and for U.S. Hispanic self-understanding—without understanding how this narrative reveals to us who God is and, simultaneously, who we are. The following brief analysis of the Guadalupe narrative (a full analysis would require another book) is based on the scholarship and follows the interpretations of Clodomiro L. Siller Acuña, Virgilio Elizondo, and Jeanette Rodríguez.[43]

The narrative begins shortly after the Nahuas have surrendered to the invading Spanish *conquistadores*, "ten years after the conquest of Mexico City."[44] It then goes on to describe the wondrous events through which "the knowledge of Him by Whom we live, the true God [*Dios*], *Téotl*, flowered and burst forth."[45] It is interesting to note that the word used for God is the Spanish "*Dios*," suggesting already an identification between the Christian God and the Aztec *Ipalnemohuani*, "Him through whom we live," the true God, *nelli Téotl*. The events to be retold took place "a few days into the month of December," on a Saturday, "while it was still night." In Náhuatl mythology, the creation of the world began

---

40. Ibid., p. 94; Siller opts for the first translation, while Espín opts for the second ("Tradition and Popular Religion," 72).

41. Rodríguez, *Our Lady of Guadalupe*, p. 16; Jacques Lafaye, *Quetzalcóatl and Guadalupe: The Formation of Mexican National Consciousness, 1531–1813* (Chicago: University of Chicago Press, 1976), pp. 217–30.

42. Siller, *Para comprender el mensaje de María de Guadalupe*, p. 13.

43. In addition to the works cited elsewhere in this chapter, see also: Clodomiro L. Siller Acuña, *Flor y canto del Tepeyac: Historia de las apariciones de Santa María de Guadalupe, texto y comentario* (Xalapa, Veracruz, México: Servir, 1981); idem, "Anotaciones y comentarios al *Nican Mopohua*," *Estudios Indígenas* 8:2 (1981): 217–74; Virgilio Elizondo, *Galilean Journey: The Mexican-American Promise* (Maryknoll, NY: Orbis, 1983).

44. Siller, *Para comprender el mensaje de María de Guadalupe*, p. 58. While the following account is primarily dependent on Siller's book, which provides the complete text of the story together with his commentary, more synoptic versions of the story may be found in Virgilio Elizondo, *La Morenita: Evangelizer of the Americas* (San Antonio, TX: Mexican American Cultural Center, 1980), pp. 75–81, and Rodríguez, *Our Lady of Guadalupe*, pp. 31–46.

45. Siller, *Para comprender el mensaje de María de Guadalupe*, p. 59.

"*huel oc yohuatzinco*," while it was still night. Thus, the events which would take place on that day would themselves signal a new creation.[46]

The first person we are introduced to in the story is Juan Diego, described as a *macehual*, a "low class but dignified Indian."[47] "While it was still night," Juan Diego left his home and, on the way to Tlatelolco "in pursuit of the things of God and his teachings," came to the hill of Tepeyac in the dawn hours: this hill "was well known to the Mexican world as the site where the goddess virgin-mother of the gods [*Tonantzín*] was venerated."[48] There he heard the beautiful sound of birds singing. In the Náhuatl world, the symbol of truth was "*flor y canto*," or flowers and song (*in xochitl in cuicatl*). In that world, truth was always mediated by and represented as "the union of two words or two symbols to express or refer to one single meaning."[49] Consequently, the singing of the birds indicates the beginning of a revelation of truth—though still incomplete, since the second element of the requisite pair, the flowers, has not yet appeared.[50]

So gorgeous was this music that he thought he must be in paradise. He wondered where he was: "[Perhaps] there in the Land of the Flower, in the Land of our flesh?"[51] Here Mt. Tepeyac is identified as the place where truth is revealed and where a people are born.[52]

Juan Diego felt compelled to seek out the source of the music, thus interrupting his journey to Tlatelolco. As he searched, he heard a soft voice call out to him in his native tongue: "*Quihuia; Iuantzin Iuan Diegotzin.*" These words have been translated as "*Juanito, Juan Dieguito*" or "*digno Juan, digno Juan Diego.*" The first translation, using the diminutive form of the name, suggests the special intimacy and nurturing concern with which the speaker views Juan Diego. The second translation emphasizes the speaker's recognition of Juan Diego's dignity and worthiness. In Náhuatl, "*tzin* is a suffix which indicates respect, dignity and also familial affection."[53] The diminutive *tzin* conveys all of the following: the most dignified, the smallest, the dearest, the most abandoned, the most forsaken.[54]

The text goes on to say that Juan Diego: "dared to go where he was being called. His heart was not at all disturbed, nor did he have any fear. . . ."[55] Following the sound of the voice, he came to the top of the

---

46. Ibid., pp. 58–61.

47. Virgilio Elizondo, *The Third Creation: A Woman Clothed with the Sun* (Maryknoll, NY: Orbis, forthcoming), p. 40.

48. Elizondo, *La Morenita*, p. 72.

49. Siller, *Para comprender el mensaje de María de Guadalupe*, pp. 13, 61–62.

50. Ibid., p. 61–62.

51. Ibid., p. 62.

52. Ibid., p. 63.

53. Ibid.

54. Ibid., pp. 66–67.

55. Ibid., p. 64.

hill, where he saw a beautiful Lady, radiantly dressed. She asked him to come to her side. Looking lovingly at him, she asked: "Juanito, the dearest [or alternatively, the smallest, the most abandoned, the most dignified, or the most forsaken] of my children, where are you going?"[56] Juan Diego told the Lady that he was on his way to "her house in Mexico/Tlatelolco to hear about the divine things which are given and taught to us by our priests, the images [or delegates] of Our Lord." She then identified herself as the Virgin Mary: "Know and rest assured in your heart, my dearest [or smallest, most forsaken, etc.] child, that I am the Ever Virgin Mary, Mother of the God of Great Truth, *Téotl*, of Him by Whom we live, of the Creator of Persons, of the Master [literally, Owner] of what is Close and Together, of the Lord of Heaven and Earth."[57] Mary and the Christian God are again identified with *Téotl*. The Lady then told Juan Diego to go to the palace of the bishop to ask him to build a temple on this hill, so that there she would "show and give all her love, compassion, assistance, and protection to the people." Juan Diego had informed her that he was going to "her house" in Mexico (the seat of the bishop and center of the Spanish evangelizing efforts); she, in turn, replied that her house should be built here, on Mt. Tepeyac.[58]

Arriving at the bishop's palace, Juan Diego had to wait a long time before being allowed to see the bishop, "Lord of the priests."[59] The prelate was kind to Juan Diego but, upon receiving the message from the Lady, cut short the poor man's visit, asking him to return some other day when there was more time to hear the entire story. Juan Diego left very disappointed. Returning to Tepeyac, he told the Lady how the bishop had received him: "My Mistress, my Lady, the dearest [or smallest, most forsaken, etc.] of my Daughters, my Girl, I went where you sent me to tell your thoughts and words. Although with great difficulty I entered the place of the Lord of the priests, I saw him, and before him expressed your thoughts and words, just as you ordered. . . . But, I could tell by the way he responded that his heart did not accept it, he did not believe."[60] Juan Diego then asked her to send someone else to the bishop, someone of higher social standing who would, thus, be a more effective messenger: "Because, for sure, I am a meager peasant, a cord, a little ladder, the people's dung, I am a leaf. . . ."[61] Addressing him as "the dearest [or smallest, most forsaken, etc.] of my children," she continued to insist that Juan Diego be her messenger and commanded him to return to the bishop.

---

56. Ibid., pp. 66–67.
57. Ibid., p. 68.
58. Ibid., pp. 68–69.
59. Ibid., p. 71.
60. Ibid., p. 73; Elizondo, *La Morenita*, p. 77.
61. Siller, *Para comprender el mensaje de María de Guadalupe*, p. 74.

The next day he returned to the bishop's palace. This time the bishop asked Juan Diego many detailed questions about his story but, once again, turned Juan Diego away. The bishop refused to believe the story unless, he said, Juan Diego could bring him a sign that the Virgin Mary had indeed appeared to him. Returning to Tepeyac, Juan Diego told the Lady the bishop's response: "But even though he was told everything, how she looked, and everything he had seen and admired, through which she was rightly revealed as the beloved, Ever Virgin, the wondrous Mother of Our Savior and Our Lord Jesus Christ, yet still he did not believe."[62] She then asked Juan Diego to come back to Tepeyac the next day, at which time she would give him a sign to take to the bishop.

However, Juan Diego did not return the next day. After arriving home the night before, he had discovered that his uncle, Juan Bernardino, was ill. Consequently, Juan Diego "went to call a doctor, and he helped him, but he could no longer do anything, since he was very seriously ill."[63] At the urgent request of his uncle, Juan Diego had rushed back to Tlatelolco to find a priest who could prepare Juan Bernardino for death. On December 12, 1531, then, Juan Diego left in a hurry for Tlatelolco and, coming to Tepeyac, tried to sneak around the back of the hill so that the Lady would not see him and delay his important trip. Yet the Lady spied him, came down the hill, and asked him why he was so anxious and in such a hurry. Juan Diego was not embarrassed or scared, but, instead, "greeted her and told her: 'My Girl, my dearest [or smallest, most forsaken, etc.] Daughter, Lady, I hope you are happy, how did you sleep? . . .' "[64] Juan Diego then told the Lady about his uncle's illness and his need to find a priest. He continued: "the moment I get back, I will return to take your words and thoughts. My Mistress and Girl, forgive me and, for now, have a little patience, I don't want to deceive you, my dearest [or smallest, most forsaken, etc.] Daughter, my Girl. Tomorrow, for sure, I will come in all haste."[65] Consoling him, she told Juan Diego not to worry, for she would cure his uncle. Juan Diego was very relieved and "pleaded very much with her to send him immediately to see the Lord of the priests to take him her sign. . . ."[66]

At that point, the Lady commanded Juan Diego to go to the top of a nearby hill, where he would find some flowers; these he should cut and bring to her. When Juan Diego arrived at the top of the hill he discovered, to his amazement, beautiful roses blooming (something inconceivable and miraculous in the middle of December). After cutting them, he returned

---

62. Ibid., p. 78; Rodríguez, *Our Lady of Guadalupe*, p. 42.

63. Siller, *Para comprender el mensaje de María de Guadalupe*, p. 80.

64. Ibid., p. 82.

65. Ibid., p. 83.

66. Elizondo, *La Morenita*, p. 78; Siller, *Para comprender el mensaje de María de Guadalupe*, pp. 84–85.

with the roses to the Lady. She then took the flowers, placed them in his *tilma*, or mantle, and commanded him to take the roses to the bishop as the proof he had demanded. The revelation is now complete: "*flor y canto.*"

Juan Diego once again made the trip to the bishop's palace, this time certain that, upon seeing these miraculous roses, the bishop would have to believe his story. The Lady ordered Juan Diego to open his mantle and show the flowers "only in the presence of the bishop."[67] The bishop's servants, however, insisted on seeing what the Indian was carrying in his mantle, so Juan Diego gave them a peek at the flowers. After entering to see the bishop this third time, Juan Diego unfolded his *tilma*, from which cascaded to the floor the many beautiful roses he had picked. At that moment, the "beautiful image of the Ever Virgin Mary, Mother of the God Téotl" suddenly appeared on the *tilma*, visible to all present. They all fell to their knees in homage. The bishop was converted; he invited Juan Diego to stay overnight in the palace and ordered the construction of the temple on Tepeyac.

Many people were gathered together to build the temple. But, before starting construction, Juan Diego wanted to pay his uncle a visit. Arriving at Juan Bernardino's house with his many co-workers, Juan Diego found that—just as the Lady had said—his uncle had been cured. Juan Bernardino was "very astonished that his nephew would come so well-accompanied and honored; and he asked him why they honored him so much" (in the Spanish translation, the original Náhuatl is rendered as "*muy acompañado y muy honrado,*" which literally means "very accompanied and very honored").[68] The temple was constructed on Tepeyac and the image of the Lady is still visible today on Juan Diego's *tilma*.

Interestingly, the story of Guadalupe that has come down to us ends, not with the construction of the temple on Tepeyac, but with the transferral of the Lady's image from the bishop's palace to the cathedral in Mexico City. Though she had, from the beginning, insisted that her place was with the poor people themselves, on Tepeyac, her home now became the cathedral in Mexico City, "so that all would see and admire her precious image."[69] Upon seeing her image in the church, "the whole city was moved; they came to admire her precious image as a divine object, they came to pray to her."[70]

The emphasis is no longer on the *story* of Juan Diego and the Lady of Tepeyac, but on the *miraculous image as a divine object*. According to Clodomiro Siller Acuña, this development has important ramifications: the Lady's historical commitment to and identification with the poor is subordinated to the *whole* people's devotion to a spiritualized, univer-

---

67. Ibid., p. 86.
68. Ibid., p. 93.
69. Ibid., p. 94.
70. Ibid.

salized Mary. In short, the intrinsic relationship between faith and justice is attenuated as the unique Guadalupe story becomes assimilated into the larger Marian tradition of the church. Consequently, Siller argues against the authenticity of the last two paragraphs of the Guadalupe text:

> It appears to us that, given the structure of the *Nican Mopohua*, our text should have ended with verse 121 [the construction of the temple on Tepeyac]. What follows (verses 122–123) appears to have a different framework, a different concern, a different spirituality. . . . These lines, the last in the *Nican Mopohua*, which are not clearly Guadalupan, are the ones which have, to a large degree, determined the official Guadalupan religiosity and the pastoral orientation taken toward those devoted to the Queen of Heaven. Fortunately, Juan Diego, concealed at the end of our text, is present everywhere, devoted in his repeated walking toward the little hill of Tepeyac which is called Guadalupe.[71]

Among the people, the poor Juan Diego is never far from Our Lady of Guadalupe.

The image itself is, nevertheless, of immense significance because of the many beautiful and powerful symbols it contains. These are both Christian and Náhuatl. Many are symbols of new life, a new beginning, and a new birth: e.g., she is pictured as pregnant, she is wearing a "maternity band" around her waist, and she bears on her womb the symbol which, for the Nahuas, represented the "reconciliation of opposites."[72] Perhaps the most

---

71. Ibid. Orlando Espín argues against both a simple and exclusive identification of Guadalupe with Tonantzín and against a simple and exclusive identification of Guadalupe with Mary: "The Virgin of Guadalupe cannot be simply identified with Tonantzín—not even at the very beginning. But I do not see either how the natives could have simply identified Guadalupe with the Catholic Mary. From the start it seems that there was an effort (on the part of the Native Americans) at speaking a religious language, through culturally understandable religious categories, that would interpret for them the Christian message about God. And just as there had been much said to the natives about the conquering might of God, much had also been said to them about the compassionate mercy and care of that same God. These latter attributes or dimensions of the divine are the ones that were interpreted as the feminine form of the Christian high god, symbolized through the acceptable Catholic imagery of Mary." "Popular Catholicism among Latinos," 329. For a more extended argument against either identification, see Espín, "Tradition and Popular Religion," 72–5. He suggests, for example, that, while the figures of Tonantzín and Guadalupe share a great deal of symbolism, the former had a destructive side that is absent from the latter (ibid.). We thus seem to have here an example of genuine religious *mestizaje*. On Guadalupe as "the feminine face of God," see Rodríguez, *Our Lady of Guadalupe*, pp. 152–58.

72. Elizondo, *La Morenita*, p. 83; Rodríguez, *Our Lady of Guadalupe*, pp. 22–30; Espín, "Tradition and Popular Religion," 72–5.

obvious symbol, however, is the very color of the Lady's skin. To Western Christians accustomed to images of a blonde and blue-eyed Mary, this Lady must surely appear incongruous; her olive skin tells the indigenous people of Mexico that she, *la Morenita*, is one of them. It tells all Latinos and Latinas that she is one of us. This identity between the Lady and her children is powerfully symbolized by her eyes, in which are reflected the image of Juan Diego.[73]

Thus, despite attempts to coopt Guadalupe by severing the image from its historical roots in the story of a poor indigenous man, the story of Juan Diego remains present today in the image itself: "The devotion to Our Lady of Guadalupe, especially among Mexicans and Mexican Americans, has remained central throughout the centuries since Juan Diego's visions. The Guadalupe symbol was immediately judged to belong to the poor, since the educated and the wealthy had their Virgin of Remedies. And for over four centuries Guadalupe has belonged to the vast majority of the people."[74]

Like the gospel narratives, this story is not past history; it is taking place today and is relived each year, especially on December 12. This is true of the San Fernando community and many others throughout the United States, where the annual celebration, like the Guadalupe story itself, begins with beautiful music. The night before the feast, the community gathers to serenade Our Lady, usually led by some of the most popular musicians and singers from the Mexican-American community. Shortly before midnight, the Mariachi choirs and all the members of the community gather around Our Lady for the *serenata* (serenade). The next morning, the community gathers before sunrise for the singing of *Las Mañanitas*, the traditional Mexican song that, recalling the encounter on Tepeyac, celebrates the birth of new life. The Lady's mantle has been covered with ribbons, which are now tossed into the crowd so that each person will be holding a part of the mantle. This, "the Easter sunrise service of the people," is a spectacular scene that proclaims, in glorious music, the dawn of a new day—in many more ways than one.[75]

The rest of the day the church is abuzz with activity. People stream into church all day long, as individuals but, especially, as families to visit

73. Rodríguez, *Our Lady of Guadalupe*, p. 27

74. Espín, "Tradition and Popular Religion," 73–4. The author here cites the work of Lafaye, *Quetzalcóatl and Guadalupe*, pp. 238–300, and Robert Ricard, *The Spiritual Conquest of Mexico* (Berkeley: University of California Press, 1966), p. 188: "As Lafaye points out, the Virgin of Guadalupe became the symbol of Mexican nationality and independence. Ricard explains the devotion of the Spaniards to Our Lady of Remedies almost as in conscious opposition to the natives' and mestizos' devotion to Our Lady of Guadalupe. In the United States today César Chávez and his followers have explicitly evoked the symbol of Guadalupe in their struggle for farm workers' rights" (ibid., p. 85 n. 46).

75. Elizondo, *Galilean Journey*, p. 44.

with Our Lady, often touching her tenderly, kissing her feet, and presenting her with flowers from their homes. At the end of the day, the children of the parish take turns leading the entire community in praying a "living rosary." Once again, the people walk up to Our Lady to present flowers to her, this time in between the mysteries of the rosary. And again, the people kiss, touch, and caress Our Lady. Some have gentle smiles on their faces, others a tear in their eye—though, their facial expression indicates, probably from joy rather than sorrow. This is as poignant and powerful a statement of a people's intimate relationship with Mary as is the celebration of the *Pésames* on Good Friday. And as fitting an end to the day.[76]

---

76. See Virgilio Elizondo, Timothy Matovina, and the People of San Fernando, *Mestizo God*, to be published as part of the Lilly-funded study of San Fernando Cathedral.

[3]

Nosotros

Community as the Birthplace of the Self

In U.S. Hispanic popular Catholicism, the identities of Jesus and Mary reveal our own identity as Latinos and Latinas. If Jesus and Mary reveal who God is, they also reveal who *we* are. As Juan Diego saw himself reflected in the eyes of *la Morenita* on Tepeyac, so too do we see ourselves reflected in her eyes, and in the eyes of *el Divino Rostro de Jesús*.

In this chapter, we will examine the connection between U.S. Hispanic popular Catholicism and our self-understanding, or identity as Latinos and Latinas. What is the anthropology[1] which is implicit in and generated by the stories, symbols, and rituals of popular Catholicism? Who are the Jesus and Mary whom we accompany on Calvary and Tepeyac? And what do this Jesus and this Mary tell us about who *we* are, as U.S. Hispanics and as human beings? What can we learn from this Jesus and this Mary about the particular socio-historical context of Latinos and Latinas, and hence, about the interpretative horizon[2] of U.S. Hispanic theology?

---

1. By "anthropology" I mean a particular view or understanding of the human person, what it means to be a human being.

2. By "interpretative horizon," I mean that presupposed, implicit world view (including all our social, cultural, political, and psychological presuppositions) which functions as the "field of vision" or background against which we understand and interpret ourselves and our world, including all concepts or ideas. A horizon both makes vision possible (without a horizon, we would be unable to make distinctions among different objects within the horizon or understand them in relation to each other) and, at the same time, limits that vision (we cannot see objects that lie beyond the horizon). Bernard Lonergan defines a horizon in the following manner: "In its literal sense, the word horizon denotes the bounding circle, the line at which earth and sky appear to meet. As one moves about, it recedes in front and closes in behind so that, for different standpoints, there are different horizons. Moreover, for each different standpoint and horizon, there are different divisions of the totality of visible objects. Beyond the horizon lie the

In other words, before proceeding to examine what popular Catholicism can contribute to our understanding of the theological task itself, we should stop to consider what popular Catholicism can contribute to our understanding of the persons and communities undertaking that task. Before asking, "What can popular Catholicism say to U.S. Hispanic theology?" we should stop to ask, "What does popular Catholicism say about U.S. Hispanics and, therefore, about U.S. Hispanic theologians?" Before moving on to a U.S. Hispanic theological method, we should address the issue of a U.S. Hispanic anthropology, or understanding of the human person.

The Person as Sacrament

As noted in the previous chapter, one of the central aspects of Latino popular Catholicism is its incarnational character. When, at San Fernando, an elderly Mexican woman approaches the Crucified Jesus to plant a gentle kiss on his feet, or reaches to touch Mary's veil during a procession, there is little doubt that, for this elderly woman, Jesus and Mary are truly present *here*. These religious statues or figures are not mere representations of a reality completely external to them, rather they are the concrete embodiment, in time and space, of Jesus and Mary. These are, in short, sacramental images: natural, particular entities that mediate, embody, and reveal a supernatural, universal, absolute reality.[3]

Implicit in the definition of sacrament is the presupposition that the concrete, particular object or entity that embodies the universal reality is *in fact* historically concrete and particular. Consequently, an indispensable prerequisite of any sacramental relationship with a particular entity, i.e., a relationship in which the supernatural Absolute is revealed, is that one affirm both the particularity and the historical concreteness of that particular entity. Only then, and only as a "byproduct" or "side-effect" of one's affirmation of that particularity and concreteness, does the object or entity reveal its universal significance.

The eucharist, for example, is a true sacrament only if the bread is *real* bread and the wine *real* wine—capable of being eaten and drunk. A

---

objects that, at least for the moment, cannot be seen. Within the horizon lie the objects that can now be seen. . . . Horizons, finally, are the structured resultant of past achievement and, as well, both the condition and the limitation of further development. They are structured. . . . Within such contexts must be fitted each new item of knowledge and each new factor in our attitudes. What does not fit, will not be noticed or, if forced on our attention, it will seem irrelevant or unimportant. Horizons then are the sweep of our interests and of our knowledge; they are the fertile source of further knowledge and care; but they also are the boundaries that limit our capacities for assimilating more than we already have attained." *Method in Theology*, pp. 235-37.

3. See chapter 2, note 26.

sacramental *relationship* exists where one affirms that concrete, particular reality, not only through the assent of faith, but also through the physiological, material act of taking and eating the bread, and taking and drinking from the cup.

One can make virtually identical statements with respect to the roles of Jesus and Mary in U.S. Hispanic popular Catholicism. The genuine love with which the Mexican woman relates to the crucified Jesus or Mary is not a universal love of some purely spiritual reality, whether Christ or Mary; it is, on the contrary, a very particular love of this Jesus, whose feet she is kissing, or this Mary, whose veil she is holding. Paradoxically, it is the very concreteness, physicality, and particularity of the statues that makes them capable of revealing a spiritual, universal and absolute reality. Only if, by one's actions of kissing and touching, one affirms the *intrinsic* value of the statues—as natural, created objects—can one recognize, in and through them, the real presence of a supernatural reality. Only if, by one's actions of eating and drinking, one affirms the *intrinsic* value of the bread and wine—as "fruit of the earth and work of human hands"—can one recognize, in and through them, the real presence of Jesus Christ. In both cases, the merely relative value of the particular material objects—as mediations of a deeper, supernatural reality—is revealed only if and when one first recognizes and affirms their intrinsic value as natural, material objects.

One cannot love the universal and supernatural if one cannot love the particular and natural—and love these precisely *as* particular and natural. One cannot love the Creator if one cannot love the creature—and love him, her, or it precisely *as* creature. In the well-known story of the Last Judgment (Mt 25:31–46), where the sheep are divided from the goats, the ones saved are the ones who fed the hungry, clothed the naked, visited the infirm, etc., *without even knowing* that, in so doing, they were ministering to Christ; only afterwards, in retrospect, did they find out the religious significance of their actions. The "sheep" were saved because they responded to the *particular, material, human* needs of the "least of these." By loving the creature, as a particular creature, through the satisfaction of his or her physical, material needs, they were implicitly loving the Creator.

The relationship between popular Catholicism and a U.S. Hispanic anthropology now begins to emerge. If a central aspect of Good Friday and Guadalupe—and, by extension, other forms of popular Catholicism—is the affirmation of the intrinsic value of the concrete and particular as a prerequisite for an encounter with the spiritual and universal, this affirmation reflects an underlying understanding of the human person and human relationships. To suggest that the particular mediates the universal is to suggest that there is no such thing as an isolated, individual entity that is not intrinsically related to others: every human person is a concrete, particular, and unique mediation of the universal. In other words, every "individual" is a particular, unique mediation of universal

humanity, universal creation, and, in the last analysis, a unique mediation of the Absolute. Each person (precisely *as a* person) is defined and
constituted by his or her relationships, both personal and impersonal,
natural and supernatural, material and spiritual.

For U.S. Hispanics, there is no such thing as an isolated individual
who is not intrinsically defined by his or her relationship to others.
"Community," writes Ada María Isasi-Díaz, "is not something added on,
but a web of relationships constitutive of who we are."[4] The assertion
that personal identity is intrinsically relational, or given by others from
"outside," is thus the corollary of a sacramental worldview which asserts
that the identity of every concrete, particular entity is relational, or given
by an Other from "outside." In both cases, the particular is the place
where and the material through which the universal is encountered.

For U.S. Hispanics, the entire cosmos—including the earth below and
the heavens above—is an intrinsically relational reality where, as in an
organism, each member is necessarily related to every other member.[5] The
person, therefore, is always *intrinsically* relational. Indeed, the individual
is, quite literally, given birth by and through the parents' relationship to
each other and to the newborn. (The Spanish word "*criar*," which means
to nurse or rear children, comes from the same root as "*crear*," which
means to create.) This is not merely a biological statement; it is also an
anthropological statement, i.e., a statement about what it means to be a
human being. My identity is given me by my parents, relatives, friends,
and many other relationships and communities; there is no "I" without
all these others. I am a particular, concrete, and unique embodiment of
all those relationships; when someone encounters me, they also encounter
my parents, relatives, friends, community, my people, as well as the God
who created me and the earth which nourishes me.[6]

To be an isolated, autonomous individual is, literally, to have no
humanity, no identity, no self, it is to be no-thing, a no-body. For, if
personhood presupposes relationality, my humanity is defined by my

---

4. Ada María Isasi-Díaz, *En la Lucha/In the Struggle: Elaborating a Mujerista
Theology* (Minneapolis: Fortress Press, 1993), p. 171. In the words of Bernard
Lonergan, "none of us is an Adam living at the origin of human affairs, becom-
ing all that he is by his own decisions, and learning all that he knows by personal
experience, personal insight, personal discernment." "The Ongoing Genesis of
Methods," *Studies in Religion* 6 (1977): 348.

5. The theological analogue is, of course, the Pauline concept of the Body of
Christ (1 Cor 12:12–31).

6. "Man is essentially social and cultural," asserts Juan Carlos Scannone, "but
that society is not immediately that of humanity, rather it is human society through
the mediation of historical-cultural communities, that is, *the peoples* [*los pueblos*]. . . . knowledge of the Origin or the Holy is indeed universal, but, as a situated universal, it is given analogically in the historical wisdom of the peoples and
their languages, which, in turn, are creatively appropriated by individual

relationships with others; I recognize myself as a self, as a person, only when I encounter—or, more accurately, am encountered by—another person. When first born, a child has no personal identity, or "self," apart from the child's immediate environment. The newborn experiences the mother as merely an extension of him or herself, and him or herself as an extension of the mother. Self-consciousness emerges only when the child is able to recognize the mother as "mother," that is, as another.[7] Thus, the possibility of relating to another beyond the self presupposes an affirmation of the other's own particularity. Paradoxically, only by affirming the uniqueness of *this* or *that particular* person (e.g., the mother) can one encounter his or her relationship to oneself. Again, the affirmation of the particular *as* particular is what reveals its intrinsic relationship to other particulars.

Ada María Isasi-Díaz notes that the term "*individuo*" in Spanish often carries a pejorative connotation: "Commonly, when one says *ese individuo* (that individual), one is talking about someone who is selfish, who is despicable in some way or other, someone who for some reason or other is outside the Latino community."[8] When two U.S. Hispanics meet each other, the initial discussion after the introductions will likely involve family and relationships: Who are your parents? What town is your family from? I knew your mother's second cousin twice removed! I had a friend who must have known your sister. It is thus quite disconcerting for Hispanics to meet an Anglo whose initial discussion will, instead, likely involve career and work: What do you do for a living? Oh, that must be very interesting work! Where did you do your training? These latter questions, reflecting an emphasis on individual, "achieved" and chosen identity over organic, received identity, are often perceived by U.S. Hispanics as insultingly dismissive of these relationships. This organic anthropology is reflected, moreover, in the very definition of family. For U.S. Hispanics, one's family is comprised, first and foremost, of those relationships intrinsic to one's inherited identity, namely, blood relatives. For Anglos, one's family is comprised, first and foremost, of those relationships which one *chooses* to have, namely, one's spouse and children. Thus, when a U.S. Hispanic asks "How is your family?" he or she will likely mean something very different from an Anglo who asks the same question.

Another linguistic difference illustrates the fact that, for Latinos and Latinas, relationship exists prior to individuality. The verb "reunite" in English means "to come together *again*." In Spanish, however, the verb

---

persons." Juan Carlos Scannone, "Religión, lenguaje y sabiduría de los pueblos: Aporte filosófico a la problemática," *Stromata* 34 (1978): 30. See also Scannone, "Filosofía primera e intersubjetividad: El a priori de la comunidad de comunicación y el nosotros ètico-histórico," *Stromata* 42 (1986): 367–86.

7. See Martin Buber, *I and Thou* (New York: Scribner's/MacMillan, 1970), pp. 76–9.

8. Isasi-Díaz, *En la Lucha*, p. 171.

"*reunir*" means, simply, "to come together," or "get together." ("*Vamos a reunirnos*" means "Let's get together.") In English, then, one's first meeting with another person is the first time one comes together with that person; only in the second meeting is there a "*reunion*." However, in Spanish, there is a reunion ("*una reunión*") the *first* time we come together, or meet each other. Why the difference? I do not think it far-fetched to suggest that, in this latter case, there is a presupposition that, before we ever meet each other physically, we are already "united." We are organically related to each other even before we actually meet, so our first meeting is, indeed, a re-union.

The community to which I belong extends beyond me not only spatially but also temporally: that community includes my ancestors as well as my progeny and their progeny. The stories, symbols, and rituals of popular religion mediate these intergenerational bonds, thereby strengthening communal identity and self-identity. This trans-generational understanding of community also explains why U.S. Hispanic popular Catholicism and culture are not intrinsically anti-institutional. Despite their tendency to ossification and corruption, institutions, like the family or church, are essentially structures which perpetuate a community, its identity, and values over time. Without some form of institutionalization, that identity and those values would die after one generation. Thus, an organic anthropology cannot be *intrinsically* anti-institutional. Institutions are in constant need of criticism, reformation, and transformation but they are, at least, a necessary evil; they are by definition an extension of community, a "patterned way of living together" not only here and now but through time.[9]

Finally, the organic anthropology underlying U.S. Hispanic popular Catholicism and culture helps explain the importance which U.S. Hispanics attach to the Spanish language—and our consequent fear of losing our language. Perhaps more than any other aspect of culture, language symbolizes the communal origins of the individual person. None of us creates our own language; each of us is *born into* a language which, from childhood, not only reflects but, indeed, shapes our reality. We are "born already *in* culture and language, what is more, in the bosom of *one* people, *one* culture and *one* language."[10]

An example of how language shapes one's reality is an experience which is common to many bilingual Latinos and Latinas who grew up speaking Spanish in the home and English in our public, professional lives. At a very deep level, the Spanish language has shaped our interpersonal,

---

9. Robert N. Bellah et al., *The Good Society* (New York: Alfred A. Knopf, 1991), p. 4. See also note 16 in chapter 2.

10. Scannone, "Religión, lenguaje y sabiduría," 30. One might argue that, among U.S. Hispanics, that common language is increasingly becoming "Spanglish."

affective lives. Spanish is thus the language to which we instinctively turn when we want to express deep personal feelings, for it is the language which, from our childhood, has mediated and shaped those feelings.

I am constitutionally incapable, for example, of presenting the same lecture in English that I present in Spanish. The content of the words may be the same, but the "person" delivering them will be different. Consequently, the message conveyed will be different: the Spanish lecture (in my "interpersonal" language) will likely involve an affective dimension, an affective engagement with the materials and the audience which will likely not be conveyed as directly in the English lecture (in my "professional" language), which will tend to be delivered in a more dispassionate, disengaged manner. Yet the difference in manner is not merely incidental to the content; it alters the content itself (hence, as expressed in the first chapter above, the painfulness of a socio-historical context which necessitates that the content of a U.S. Hispanic theology be conveyed in English). The language is not incidental to the individual person's self-understanding and worldview; it shapes and informs these. If community is prior to individuality, language is prior to self-understanding. As family, community, and culture give birth to self-identity, language gives birth to self-understanding.

The centrality of language as an integral part of one's self becomes especially evident when that language is threatened, marginalized, or stripped away by the dominant culture. When, as a theology graduate student, I received the implicit message that Spanish is not the equivalent of French and German as a scholarly language, what was rejected was not simply my ability to use some linguistic tool of expression—i.e., some mere technical communication "skill." I experienced that rejection, instead, as a denigration of my self and, therefore, of my family, my community, my culture, and my entire history as a Latino. These, among whom have been accomplished writers, lawyers, doctors, college professors, engineers, etc., were simply dismissed as intellectually inadequate. What was dismissed, then, was much more than just my language and more, even, than just my individual self.

Modern Liberal Individualism

The organic anthropology of U.S. Hispanics conflicts dramatically with the individualistic anthropology of the dominant U.S. culture. As Robert Bellah et al. have observed, "individualism lies at the very core of American culture" and "is deeply rooted in America's social history."[11]

---

11. Robert N. Bellah et al., *Habits of the Heart: Individualism and Commitment in American Life* (New York: Harper and Row, 1985), pp. 142, 147.

The U.S. tradition of modern liberal individualism[12] manifests itself in three distinct, though interrelated areas of our lives: 1) the political, 2) the religious, and 3) the economic.[13]

The political variant of modern liberal individualism is best expressed in that well-known axiom of U.S.-style democracy, "one person, one

---

12. As I am using the terms, "liberal" and "liberalism" denote a broad range of philosophical and political perspectives and thinkers that, in the words of Kenneth Schmitz, "tend to merge with the more general movement of thought associated with the Enlightenment and its antecedents." "Is Liberalism Good Enough?" in *Liberalism and the Good*, ed. R. Bruce Douglass, Gerald M. Mara, and Henry S. Richardson (New York: Routledge, 1990), p. 87. As he notes, liberalism is not a static but a dynamic tradition that has evolved and developed over time (ibid.). Liberalism recognizes "the primacy of the individual self": "an *elector* self in the root sense of the Latin term. For, as far as possible, and in some sense prior to other individuals and society, it would select the terms under which it relates to them; let us say, then, in shorthand: a *selective* self. It is in some sense a law unto itself: hence we might call it an *autonomous* self, since even Kant's law-obligated moral ego is self-governed. Again it is in some sense a *pre-institutional* self, since the institutions to which it subscribes are in principle its own product and derive their legitimacy in some way from its consent. It is in some sense an *independent self*, since it holds itself in reserve and apart." Ibid., p. 95.

Michael Sandel explains that this liberal tradition, which he calls deontological liberalism, reflects a particular conception of justice, or the nature of "the good": "'Deontological liberalism' is above all theory about justice, and in particular about the primacy of justice among moral and political ideals. Its core thesis can be stated as follows: society, being composed of a plurality of persons, each with his own aims, interests, and conceptions of the good, is best arranged when it is governed by principles that do not *themselves* presuppose any particular conception of the good; what justifies these regulative principles above all is not that they maximize the social welfare or otherwise promote the good, but rather that they conform to the concept of *right*, a moral category given prior to the good and independent of it. This is the liberalism of Kant and of much contemporary moral and political philosophy. . . ." *Liberalism and the Limits of Justice* (London: Cambridge University Press, 1982), p. 1.

This liberal tradition is at the heart of *both* contemporary U. S. liberalism and contemporary conservatism. It functions as the presupposed and implicit interpretative horizon against which *all* political debates take place in the United States: "so-called conservatism and so-called radicalism in these contemporary debates within modern political systems are almost exclusively between conservative liberals, liberal liberals, and radical liberals. There is little place in such political systems for the criticism of the system itself, that is, for putting liberalism in question." Alasdair MacIntyre, *Whose Justice? Which Rationality?* (University of Notre Dame Press, 1988), p. 392. In chapter 6, I will suggest that the most recent variant of the modern liberal autonomous self, and its logical outcome, is the "deconstructed" self of postmodernism.

13. See my "U.S. Hispanic Theology and the Challenge of Pluralism," in *Frontiers of Hispanic Theology in the United States*, ed. Allan Figueroa Deck (Maryknoll, NY: Orbis, 1992).

vote." This axiom reflects an important underlying assumption concerning the nature of society, namely, that the fundamental building block of society is the autonomous individual,[14] whose values and vote are thus equal to those of any other individual human being (though, tragically, not always practiced in reality, this ideology continues to guide our perception, and thus interpretation, of that reality).[15] Though the principle of one person, one vote safeguards the fundamental ideals of human equality and individual rights, it does so only at a price: the reduction of each person to a mere number, "1" vote, whose identity, life, and values are thus indistinguishable from those of any other person, or any other "1." Moreover, each of these "1's" is conceived as autonomous and separate vis-à-vis every other "1."[16]

Society, then, is little more than the composite, or collection, of these discrete individuals; society itself has no intrinsic political value except as the collection of individual political values. Hence, for example, the way we make political decisions is by, literally, counting up the individual votes. As a society, we accept the decisions of the majority because, as individual citizens, we have entered into a "social contract" wherein we implicitly agree, for the good of the whole, to bind ourselves by the decisions of the majority of the citizens.[17] Again, society is not a political reality—it has no value in and of itself.[18] The term "society" is merely an artificial, shorthand way of referring to a sum of individuals. Indeed, in the words of Ralph Waldo Emerson, "society is everywhere in conspiracy against the manhood of everyone of its members."[19]

This political individualism also has important ramifications for our understanding of, not only society as a whole, but also the intermediate groups and communities to which all of us belong and which form such an important part of our lives. If society is little more than a collection of individuals, so too is *any* group or community. Within the interpretative horizon of modern liberal individualism, community is understood to be a "temporary and voluntary association of separate individuals."[20]

---

14. On the notion of the "autonomous individual" in U.S. politics, see David Milligan and William Watts Miller, eds., *Liberalism, Citizenship and Autonomy* (Aldershot, England: Avebury, 1992).

15. It is important, of course, to acknowledge that the criteria for determining who is a "human being" have historically been used to deny certain groups the very equality and vote which this axiom purports to uphold. But what I am addressing in this section is not the socio-historical reality so much as the interpretative horizon which frames anthropological and theological questions.

16. See Richard Norman, "Citizenship, Politics and Autonomy," in Milligan and Miller, eds., *Liberalism, Citizenship, and Autonomy*.

17. Bellah et al., *Habits of the Heart*, p. 143.

18. See Sandel, *Liberalism and the Limits of Justice*, pp. 145–46.

19. Quoted in Bellah et al., *Habits of the Heart*, pp. 55–6.

20. Paul Wachtel, *The Poverty of Affluence* (New York: Free Press, 1983), p. 118.

A particular type of community is, of course, the religious community. Political individualism readily lends itself to an analogous and symbiotic religious individualism.[21] The religious community, e.g., church, comes to be viewed as a collection of individual believers who have freely chosen to join and who, therefore, could freely choose to leave when their religious needs are no longer being met:

> One cannot defend one's views by saying that they are simply the views of one's parents. On the contrary, they must be particularly and peculiarly one's own. Traditionally, Protestant piety demanded that a young person experience a unique conversion experience of his or her own, even while specifying more or less clearly the content of that experience. More recently we have come to expect even greater autonomy. . . . The American understanding of the autonomy of the self places the burden of one's own deepest self-definitions on one's own individual choice. For some Americans, . . . tradition and a tradition-bearing community still exist. But the notion that one discovers one's deepest beliefs in, and through, tradition and community is not very congenial to Americans. Most of us imagine an autonomous self existing independently, entirely outside any tradition and community, and then perhaps choosing one.[22]

Religious belief precedes, and can—indeed, must—exist independently of participation in a religious community. When questioned about their religious faith, Anglo Americans are often wont to respond, "I'm religious, but I don't belong to a church," or "I have my own spirituality, though I don't ascribe to any particular religion." The assumption underlying such responses is that participation in a religious community is in no way intrinsic or essential to religious belief; one relates to God as an individual, not as part of a community. The locus of religious faith is the individual believer, not the community of faith. The latter is but an extension of the former.[23] Church membership is thus seen as freely chosen and open to mobility, so that, to acquire members, churches must compete with each other in the marketplace.

The notion of competition in the marketplace already suggests, of course, the third form of liberal individualism, economic individualism.[24] If the axiom of political individualism is "one person, one vote," the

---

21. See Bellah et al., *Habits of the Heart*, pp. 62–5, 142ff., 232–35.

22. Ibid., pp. 62–3.

23. See ibid., pp. 142ff, and especially their discussion of religious individualism, pp. 232–35.

24. I use this term, "economic individualism," to emphasize the specifically economic dimension of what Bellah et al. call "utilitarian individualism" (ibid., pp. 55–84).

axiom of economic individualism is "one dollar, one vote." If the individual citizen is the foundation of the former, the individual consumer is the foundation of the latter. In political individualism, the individual citizen is free to choose between the Democratic Party and the Republican Party—or no party at all. In religious individualism, the individual believer is free to choose between the Methodist and Presbyterian Churches—or no church at all. In economic individualism, the individual consumer is free to choose between Listerine or Scope—or no mouthwash at all. As opposed to political individualism, however, here the locus of value is not in the individual person, with each person and vote having theoretically equal value, rather the locus of value is in the individual dollar, the economic analogue of the political vote. Consequently, while the consumer is the foundation of economic individualism, the locus of value is not the consumer as such but the number of dollars that consumer has available to purchase commodities in the marketplace.

As is already evident, these three forms of individualism have a great deal in common. What they have in common is the anthropology that underlies all three. This anthropology has its historical roots in the Enlightenment, with its exaltation of the rights of the autonomous individual over against the state, the church, and all other collective entities, which were perceived as threats to individual autonomy. The fifteenth through the eighteenth centuries were the centuries of Christopher Columbus, René Descartes, Martin Luther, John Calvin, Adam Smith, John Locke, Voltaire, and Immanuel Kant; all, in one way or another, exponents of the rights of the individual.[25]

Bellah at al. speak of the *"socially unsituated self"* as the foundation of U.S. liberal individualism and the arbiter of all values, from the political (who is the best candidate) to the religious and moral (which is the right religion and the moral course of action) to the economic (which is the best brand of mouthwash). Thus, not only matters of taste but also matters of truth and morality come to be decided on the basis of quantitative criteria: that which the majority believes is accepted as *ipso facto* true, and the behavior of the majority is accepted as *ipso facto* moral.

---

25. The connections among these three forms of individualism have been the subject of numerous studies. One of the most famous and influential is Max Weber's *The Protestant Ethic and the Spirit of Capitalism*, which, as the title indicates, traces the historical relationship between the rise of capitalism and Protestantism in northern Europe during the age of Enlightenment. More recent works include John Hall, *Liberalism: Politics, Ideology and the Market* (Chapel Hill, NC: University of North Carolina Press, 1988); Paul Wachtel, *The Poverty of Affluence* (New York: Free Press, 1983); and especially, and abovementioned works of Robert Bellah and his colleagues, *Habits of the Heart* and *The Good Society*. The role of Columbus as a "father" of modern individualism has only recently begun to be explored; see especially Enrique Dussel, *El Encubrimiento del Indio* (México, DF: Editorial Cambio XXI, 1992).

Once all corporate arbiters of truth or morality, with their qualitative guidelines for making judgments, are rejected in favor of the autonomous, individual decision-maker, left to his or her own isolated judgment, the only remaining criteria on which to base judgments of truth and value are quantitative.[26]

The ironic result is, not a society of unique individuals, but a society of conformists:

> As Tocqueville observed, when one can no longer rely on tradition or authority, one inevitably looks to others for confirmation of one's judgments. Refusal to accept established opinion and anxious conformity to the opinions of one's peers turn out to be two sides of the same coin.[27]

The exaltation of the individual over against corporate authority, both contemporary and traditional, thus results in the very conformity which the Enlightenment had so despised. Ironically, the socially unsituated self is perennially susceptible to manipulation and coercion: ". . . Tocqueville was probably right in believing that it was isolation, not social involvement, that led to conformism and the larger danger of authoritarian manipulation. There are authoritarian groups in the United States, sometimes devoted to destructive ends. . . . A radically isolating individualism is not a defense against such coercive groups. On the contrary, the loneliness that results from isolation may precipitate the 'hunger for authority' on which such groups feed."[28]

The socially unsituated self has, moreover, another important consequence: the subordination of the political and religious dimensions of individualism to the demands and criteria of economic individualism, the demands and criteria of the marketplace:

> In the absence of any objectifiable criteria of right and wrong, good or evil, the self and its feelings become our only moral guide. . . . But while everyone may be entitled to his or her own private space, only those who have enough money can, in fact, afford to purchase the private property required to do their own thing.[29]

---

26. E.g., *because* surveys show that a majority of Catholics use artificial contraception and oppose the Catholic Church's ban on artificial contraception *therefore* the ban on artificial contraception *must* be wrong and ought to be lifted. (The problem I point to here is not the morality or immorality of artificial contraception, but the assumption that quantitative criteria can be *ipso facto* morally determinative.)

27. Bellah et al., *Habits of the Heart*, p. 148.

28. Ibid., p. 162.

29. Ibid., p. 76.

The inexorable logic of any anthropology that unites political, religious, and economic individualism thus leads to the triumph of the economic over the first two. In the political sphere, "one person, one vote" becomes "one P.A.C. dollar, one vote," while in the religious sphere the quantitative criteria of tithing and church membership (the number of religious "consumers" who choose to "buy" this particular religion or church) become the determinants of religious value.

In the end, the individual is bound by the dictates of the marketplace and, with the emergence of a society where the absolute value of the individual is replaced by the absolute value of the commodity, the rights of the individual are undermined. Notions of value, rights, truth, and freedom are defined *by* the wealthy, and are defined *as* the acquisition of wealth, or purchasing power—whether what is purchased is mouthwash, political influence, or ecclesiastical influence.

As distinct interpretative horizons, political individualism, religious individualism, and economic individualism each preserves important values, especially the absolute value of the person vis-à-vis the political state, the corporate religious authority, or the planned economic system. Yet, together, these reinforce each other and engender, in their conjunction, a type of thoroughgoing *cultural*, anthropological individualism that characterizes the U.S. and differs from, say, the political individualism one might find in Canada, or the religious individualism one might find in France, or the economic individualism one might find in Japan. It is by virtue of this conjunction that individualism defines and "lies at the very core" of the dominant U.S. culture.

For modern liberal individualism, then, the individual (or "socially unsituated self") exists prior to his or her relationships with others, which relationships the particular individual may or may not choose to enter. Relationality is thus not essential to the individual person, but only a secondary, optional choice available to each person: I remain a complete person whether or not I choose to enter into relationships with others. Furthermore, since each individual is an essentially self-enclosed entity with no intrinsic relationship to others, there is no necessary relationship between one individual's life, or experience, and that of another individual: my experience is only mine, and yours is only yours. Personal identity is thus created through individual improvisation: "The improvisational self chooses values to express itself; but it is not constituted by them as if from a pre-existing source."[30]

If relationships with others might in some instances be advisable, they are never necessary. Indeed, the cultural ideal becomes the rugged individual, self-made man, or the self-made woman. Even if individuals turn to family and friends as an antidote to the emotional and intellectual aridity of rugged individualism, these newly-discovered relationships are

---

30. Ibid., p. 80.

always viewed as intentionally chosen, i.e., as extrinsic to and, hence, optional for each individual person. The point is, not that the modern liberal individual has no community ties, but that those community ties—however important they may be deemed—are assumed to be voluntarily chosen and, therefore, secondary, ancillary, or accidental characteristics of "the human being."[31] If an individual can choose relationship to others, he or she may likewise choose isolation; relationality is optional.

As a "voluntary association of separate individuals," a community is nothing more than a collection of individuals who have chosen to enter into a contractual relationship with each other for some common purpose: e.g., to worship, to share living quarters, to create a social order, to study a topic of common interest, to do business, to socialize, to promote a political ideology, or, for that matter, to engage in inter-cultural dialogue. The individual can and does exist as a distinct entity prior to any involvement in society or community, which involvement is, in any case, an option which he or she is "free to choose" or, presumably, not choose. Likewise, once an individual opts for one particular community he or she is always free to leave that community when it no longer satisfies his or her needs. For the modern liberal individual, human relationships are not constitutive of the self; they are voluntarily chosen and "possessed" by the self.[32] Like any possession, relationships can be discarded when they no longer meet the needs of the individual.[33]

Presupposed in this modern liberal anthropology is a dichotomy between the individual and community. That is, community is always extrinsic to individuality. Community is, at best, an addition or supplement to the individual and, at worst, a threat to and limitation of the individual. One of the many cultural assumptions that reflect such an anthropology is the assumption that, to become a full-fledged person, one must at some point (usually in adolescence) leave one's familial relationships behind in order to "discover oneself," undergo an "identity crisis," "become one's own person," and "achieve one's own identity":

> In a culture that emphasizes the autonomy and self-reliance of the individual, the primary problems of childhood are what some psychoanalysts call separation and individuation—indeed, childhood is chiefly preparation for the all-important event of leaving home. . . . Separation and individuation are issues that must be faced by all human beings, but leaving home in its American sense is not. In many peasant societies, the problem is staying home—living with one's parents until their death and worshipping parents and ancestors

---

31. Wachtel, *The Poverty of Affluence*, p. 61.

32. Brian Lee Crowley, *The Self, The Individual, and the Community* (Oxford: Clarendon Press, 1987), p. 218.

33. See Kavanaugh, *Following Christ in a Consumer Society*.

all one's life. In traditional Japan, the expression "leaving home" was reserved for those entering monastic life, who abandoned all ties of ordinary existence. For us, leaving home is the normal expectation, and childhood is in many ways a preparation for it.[34]

The Mexican American author Richard Rodriguez makes a similar observation:

In the United States, we show how much we love our children by raising them to leave home. We do not expect our kids to hang around. We don't like a mama's boy. We like our daughter to stand on her own two feet. . . . All over the world, from Peruvian villages to Chinese cities, the siren call from America is the first-person singular pronoun, "I." Leave your parents behind; leave your home; come to America and become someone new. No greater glamor do we offer the world than the first-person singular pronoun. The price we pay for our famous individualism is loneliness. Eighteenth-century Protestants who fled the tyranny of the British crown used to gather in New England to share the experience of being alone before God. Now we talk on the "Oprah Winfrey Show" about our solitary lives. We have grown dangerously homesick. We think we remember our leafy hometown—the way people greeted each other; how polite children were. Of course, we conveniently forget the individual reasons we left home.[35]

The U.S. Hispanic experience of exile, whether in an alien land—as in my case—or in one's own land—as in the case of Mexican Americans—is thus itself foreign and incomprehensible to a dominant culture which not only does not fear the loss of communal ties but, indeed, presupposes and demands that one leave one's parents and home behind. Though itself constructed by immigrants, the U.S. has romanticized the immigrant experience and the life of the frontier, thereby denying the profound loss implicit in any experience of exile or immigration. (Ironically, this romanticization is today accompanied by an increasing hostility toward flesh-and-blood immigrants themselves.)[36] Latinos and Latinas are caught between our own experience of loss, on the one hand, and a dominant culture which encourages us to deny and repress that pain: we must forget the past, we are told, "pull ourselves up by our bootstraps" and forge our own future. Such a culture will never understand the feelings I experienced years ago while

---

34. Ibid., pp. 56–7.

35. Richard Rodriguez, "When Did Americans Ever Embrace Family Values?" *Chicago Tribune*, January 5, 1995, sec 1, p. 23.

36. On the connection between romanticization and oppression, see chapter 6 below.

sitting in that airplane at the Havana Airport. But I refuse to forget those feelings, for to do so would be to deny the past, to deny my community, and thus to deny my very self.

As suggested above, the religious variant of the expectation that one will "leave home," "stand on one's own two feet," and "pull oneself up by one's own bootstraps" is the expectation that, at some point, one will leave his or her religious "home," church, or faith community behind, undergo a "faith crisis," and make a "personal decision" for one's beliefs. Such an understanding of religious faith as a private, individual decision reflects the underlying assumption that faith is "the experience of being *alone* before God." Consequently, authentic belief implies a personal choice to stand alone before God.[37]

In each of these cases, the individual person's relationships, whether familial or ecclesial, are viewed as extrinsic to and thus optional for the person: they can be rejected as easily as they can be chosen. Moreover, the achievement of full maturity, whether personal or religious, is predicated upon precisely such a rejection (at least temporary) of those relationships: to be a fully mature human being is to leave community behind. This understanding of the person ignores the simple fact that many of our most important relationships are preexistent and involuntary:

> In ordinary life we are bound to one another not merely by obligations which we have voluntarily chosen but also, and pervasively, by obligations which are simply given. The relationship between siblings is precisely such a case. My responsibilities to (and for) my brother are not responsibilities which I have freely chosen (or chosen at all). They are responsibilities which arise simply from the fact that this is my brother. And similar considerations apply to responsibilities to parents, to colleagues and to neighbours. In all these cases my obligations are not, or not wholly, voluntarily undertaken. They are, nevertheless, obligations, and in so far as autonomy is construed as a matter of choice, they are therefore restrictions on autonomy, since they specify areas in which choice is inappropriate or limited. They specify the unchosen background against which choice must be made.[38]

Again, community is not simply some reality extrinsic to the individual, which he or she is "free to choose."

Also presupposed in the dichotomy between individual and community is a dichotomy between community and institution, where community

---

37. On the connection between leaving home and leaving church, see Kavanaugh, *Following Christ in a Consumer Society*, pp. 62–5.

38. Susan Mendus, "Strangers and Brothers: Liberalism, Socialism and the Concept of Autonomy," in *Liberalism, Citizenship and Autonomy*, ed. Milligan and Watts Miller, p. 8.

is defined as face-to-face relationships among individuals and institution is defined as an impersonal, faceless, inhuman, and bureaucratic organizational structure.[39] Thus, when the modern liberal individual does recognize the need for community, this community will typically be "understood as connoting a heavy patina of 'emotional warmth' and general *Gemütlichkeit*."[40] The broader "cultural and institutional requirements" that, in fact, make possible the survival of these communities will tend to be either ignored or perceived as antithetical to the "emotional warmth" of the community.[41]

This *sentimental* (and still ultimately individualistic) notion of community is very different from a *constitutive* notion of community:

> For on the sentimental conception, the good of community was limited to the communitarian aims and sentiments of antecedently individuated subjects, while on the constitutive conception, the good of community was seen to penetrate the person more profoundly so as to describe not just his *feeling* but a mode of self-understanding partly constitutive of his identity, partly definitive of who he was.[42]

Though the community which is constitutive of the self certainly includes "emotional warmth," it is not *defined* by its ability to generate these feelings but, rather, by its ability to partially constitute the very identity of each individual member:

> And insofar as our constitutive self-understandings comprehend a wider subject than the individual alone, whether a family or tribe or city or class or nation or people, to this extent they define a community in the constitutive sense. And what marks such a community is not merely a spirit of benevolence, or the prevalence of communitarian values, or even certain "shared final ends" alone, but a common vocabulary of discourse and a background of implicit

---

39. Again, this is not to suggest that institutions are not impersonal and bureaucratic. The point is, rather, that in modern liberal individualism, community and institution are understood as mutually exclusive and incommensurable realities: a community is not in any way an institution, and an institution is not in any way a community. A variant of this is the community-society dichotomy, where "society" is viewed as nothing but a network of impersonal, faceless, bureaucratic institutions. On the community-society dichotomy, see the classic work of Ferdinand Tönnies, *Community and Society* (East Lansing, MI: Michigan State University Press, 1957).

40. William M. Sullivan, "Bringing the Good Back In," in *Liberalism and the Good*, R. Bruce Douglass et al., eds., 151.

41. Ibid.

42. Sandel, *Liberalism and the Limits of Justice*, p. 161.

practices and understandings within which the opacity of the participants is reduced if never finally dissolved. . . . For a society to be a community in this strong sense, community must be constitutive of the shared self-understandings of the participants and embodied in their institutional arrangements, not simply an attribute of certain of the participants' plans of life.[43]

The sentimental notion of community as an unstructured, deinstitutionalized, face-to-face, emotionally warm, and voluntary association implies, furthermore, a dichotomy between community and tradition: as a "voluntary association," a community cannot include those persons, past and future, who, because they are not present today, cannot intentionally choose, or "volunteer" to join our community. Thus, for modern liberal individualism, community bonds cannot extend beyond this particular time and place; insofar as, through its structures and traditions, an institution extends communal bonds beyond and between generations, it can only do so illegitimately. If community is limited by space and time, then all institutions, all tradition, and all forms of institutionalization will necessarily be viewed as intrinsically coercive, that is, as a former, dead community's attempt to impose its identity and values (by definition obsolete, since that community no longer exists) on the only real community, that *voluntary* community which exists here and now. We have no responsibility to the past or to the future, since neither exists nor participates in our voluntary community.

Where there is no strong, constitutive sense of community, then, the relationship between the particular (individual) and the universal (family, church, community, tradition, institution) will be viewed as intrinsically dichotomous: i.e., the particular is in no way constituted by the universal; the universal is *ipso facto* oppressive because it limits individual autonomy. What defines an individualistic anthropology is this *dichotomy* between the particular and the universal, the individual and the community. Within this dichotomy, modern liberal individualism opts for the individual against community. However, the opposite is also possible: an option for the universal, or community, *against* the particular, or individual. The most obvious examples of this latter are all the various forms of authoritarian and totalitarian ideologies and systems. Though these appear, on the surface, as the opposite of individualism, they are "opposite" only inasmuch as they are, in fact, the other side of the individualist coin. Implicit in any anthropology that views the good of the whole as incommensurable with individuality is a view of the human person as an autonomous individual who is not essentially related—and in this case is, indeed, opposed—to the whole. Both the modern liberal individual and the totalitarian dictator view persons as

---

43. Ibid, pp. 172–3.

autonomous individuals. The only difference is that the former celebrates the individual, while the latter fears him or her. As Alasdair MacIntyre contends, "the essence of individualism is not so much to emphasize the individual rather than the collective . . . as to frame all questions according to an ostensible antithesis between the individual and the collective."[44]

The Anthropology of Jesus

The anthropology implicit in U.S. Hispanic popular Catholicism is altogether different. Here, community is understood to be fundamentally *preexistent* (therefore involuntary) and *constitutive*. Therefore, the universal is not merely the sum of the particulars; rather, the universal is mediated by the particulars.

Within an individualistic anthropology, the type of popular religion witnessed at San Fernando Cathedral is inconceivable. If the particular has no intrinsic relationship to the universal, and an individual entity is, in itself, nothing but an individual entity, then devotions to statues can only be seen as pantheistic or idolatrous: when the elderly Mexican woman kisses the feet of the crucified Jesus she is only kissing *this* (particular) piece of wood, which has no intrinsic relationship to the (universal) Christ of our faith. If this piece of wood merely "points to" some external supernatural reality, not itself revealed in and through the wood, then to kiss the wood is to commit an act of idolatry.

But, if this piece of wood, shaped into Jesus' crucified body, is itself the particular and concrete manifestation of a universal, supernatural reality revealed in and through this object, then to kiss the wood is to make the *only* appropriate Christian response. The difference between the two interpretations of this act is not the difference between a "mature" faith, which would relativize the particular (wooden statue), and an "immature" faith, which would absolutize the particular. Rather, the disparate interpretations stem from a fundamental, anthropological and epistemological difference: that between an individualistic worldview, which would deny any necessary, intrinsic connection between the particular (e.g., *this* autonomous individual, or *this* statue of Jesus Christ) and the universal (e.g., the community, or the Jesus Christ of Christian faith and tradition), and an *organic* worldview, which would presuppose an essential, intrinsic, or "organic" relationship between the particular and the universal. In popular Catholicism, for example, Jesus and Mary are defined relationally, by their relationship to each other and to us. Jesus and Mary are thus the primordial religious symbols of the U.S. Hispanic organic

---

44. "Durkheim's Call to Order," *The New York Review of Books*, March 7, 1974, 26.

anthropology. Jesus is never just Jesus; he is always also our brother, father, co-sufferer, friend, and, above all, son of Mary. Jesus is defined and constituted by his relationships; these are not merely accidental or tangential to his identity. As a flesh-and-blood person, Jesus, like us, is the unique, particular mediation of the preexistent communities which define him.

Hence, the importance of Mary in U.S. Hispanic popular Catholicism. Mary is not merely another autonomous individual who happened to have a relationship with Jesus; she is, rather, the symbol of the preexistent, involuntary community which defines and constitutes the individual person we call Jesus. If community is indeed constitutive of the person, then to know Mary, the mother of Jesus, *is* (at least partially) to know Jesus. Conversely, one *cannot* know Jesus without also knowing Mary. To suppose otherwise is to suppose that Jesus is an autonomous individual whose identity can essentially be defined in isolation from those preexistent relationships which partially constitute that identity.

What is common to virtually all the depictions of Jesus one finds in Latino homes or churches is that each implies a concrete, physical historicity *and* concrete, physical relationship. Jesus is identified and known as a flesh-and-blood, historical reality which, precisely as such, is identified and defined by his concrete, personal relationships—to his mother, to his brothers and sisters, to his subjects, to his beloved, to his fellow pilgrims, to us. (The Trinity is, after all, the theological symbol for the intrinsically and constitutively communal character of God.)[45] Indeed, what enables Jesus to relate to us is the fact that he, like us, knows what it is to be part of a family and community.[46]

In further specifying the Jesus of U.S. Hispanic popular Catholicism, one must note again that the snapshots of Holy Week and Guadalupe

---

45. As Mary Ann Fatula writes, " . . . the divine persons *are* their relations to one another; their relationship to one another defines each person's entire identity and *is who* each one is." *The Triune God of Christian Faith* (Collegeville, MN: The Liturgical Press, 1990), p. 71. The inherent difficulty in any attempt to understand the Trinity within the interpretive horizon of modern liberal individualism, and the implications of trinitarian doctrine for expressing the essential, constitutive character of God's relationality vis-à-vis creation, are articulated and developed in Catherine Mowry LaCugna, *God for Us: The Trinity and Christian Life* (San Francisco: Harper, 1991). On the anthropological implications and trinitarian doctrine, see also Leonardo Boff, *Trinity and Society* (Maryknoll, NY: Orbis, 1988); Juan Luis Segundo, *Our Idea of God* (Maryknoll, NY: Orbis, 1974); and Sixto J. García, "A Hispanic Approach to Trinitarian Theology: The Dynamics of Celebration, Reflection, and Praxis," in *We Are a People! Initiatives in Hispanic American Theology*, ed. Roberto S. Goizueta (Minneapolis: Fortress, 1992).

46. See Rodríguez, *Our Lady of Guadalupe*, p. 60.

presented in the last chapter are hardly exhaustive.[47] With that caveat, we can nevertheless begin to outline a portrait of Jesus and make a number of observations on the basis of the above experience of one Latino community's celebration of the triduum.

This Jesus is a concrete, historical, *flesh-and-blood* person, who, as such, is known in and through his *relationships*: he is the Son of God, son of Mary, our Lord, brother, friend, and *compañero*. As the first and foundational sacrament (*ursakrament*), Jesus reveals to us not only who God is (theology) but also who we are (anthropology)—inherently sacramental, relational creatures. This Jesus is the one who accompanies us in our suffering and whom we, in turn, accompany in his. This Jesus is, thus, the source of our community: we are one insofar as we all accompany Jesus together. This Jesus is, consequently, the source of those communal bonds which constitute us as persons and as a people, thereby giving us the strength to confront life's vicissitudes.

Jesus is, first of all, a flesh-and-blood human being who is with us today. Ours is a Jesus who bleeds . . . which is to say, a Jesus made of flesh-and-blood like us. The blood on his face, side, hands, and feet are the signs of his humanity; not the abstract "humanity" of the philosophers and theologians, but the flesh-and-blood humanity of those who dare to kiss his wounds.[48] There is, in our popular Catholicism, no separation between the concrete, particular "Jesus of history" and the spiritual, universal "Christ of faith." This Jesus, this Christ, is the same one we accompany today in his suffering, the one whose feet we kiss and whose face we caress. The body on the cross is no mere statue any more than the host on the altar is mere bread or the wine mere wine—or any more than an individual person is a mere voter, a mere consumer, a mere parishioner, or a mere "1." Similarly, our desire to touch and kiss the corpse is as much an act of faith in the concrete, historical reality of Jesus among us today as is our desire to eat the bread and drink the wine, or to love our neighbor, who is already a constitutive part of us. From the ever-present music, to the candlelight, to the aroma of the flowers, to the intermittent gasps heard from the crowd during the crucifixion, to the sound of the soldiers' pounding hammers, to the colorful sights of the market, plaza, and church,

---

47. Moreover, one must bear in mind that popular religion is, to a great extent, a religion of the home; to inquire about the Jesus of popular Catholicism, one would also have to examine the ways in which Jesus is present in the U.S. Hispanic home.

48. Why are modern Western Christians so suspicious of physical images (statues) but not of the abstract, mental images which inevitably fill the imaginational vacuum left when the physical images are removed? If we cannot see and feel Jesus with our bodies, we will inevitably "picture" him with our minds (or in our theology books). The danger of idolatry is at least as great in the latter case as in the former.

the physicality, sensuality, and particularity of Jesus Christ's presence among us is undeniable and unavoidable.

As the humanity of Jesus is not abstract, neither is his relationality. The relationships which define Jesus are themselves mediated and defined physically: as accompaniment, as "being with" or "walking with." These demand bodily presence: walking with Jesus to Gethsemane (*caminemos con Jesús*), kneeling in prayer with him in the garden, walking alongside him on the road to Calvary, kissing his feet on the cross, accompanying the corpse in the burial procession, touching the cold body, kneeling and praying with Mary at her son's tomb. It is this accompaniment that constitutes us as individual persons and as a community. More precisely, it is in our common accompaniment of Jesus on the cross that *he* constitutes *us* as individuals and a community. Again, this community is not an abstraction, or a merely "spiritual" reality; it is mediated by a mutual, bodily presence. Such a community of accompaniment is not possible in a disembodied way any more than it is possible for me to break "bread *with* another" (the literal meaning of *ad-cum-panis*) if I am not actually sitting at the same table with him or her. The *act* of accompaniment is what defines this community.

Undertaken actively and in mutual accompaniment, the community's confrontation with suffering can become a source not of despair but of strength. As constituted by his or her relationships with others, the individual person is intrinsically and by definition *never alone* in his or her struggles. Despite the suffering evoked and re-lived during Good Friday at San Fernando, there is no sense of despair or hopelessness in the face of that pain. On the contrary, the overwhelming sense is one of peace, strength, and life in the midst of pain. This is not the illusory and ephemeral strength of the "self-made man" but, on the contrary, the true and profound strength of the person who knows that he or she is not "self-made."

In this light, the U.S. Hispanic tendency to emphasize Jesus' crucifixion over his resurrection becomes more understandable: the resurrection already takes place when, as a community and as individual persons constituted by that community, we accompany Jesus and each other on Calvary. It is then that, in the person of the Crucified, we encounter the powerlessness of death in the face of our *common* life. Jesus is already resurrected when he dies accompanied by his mother and the other women—by the converted centurion whose words proclaim that Jesus' death is not the end—and by us, who walk with him from Gethsemane to the grave. Easter, then, is but a ratification of what has, in fact, already occurred on Calvary: the victory of life over death. The supremely human, crucified Jesus *is* the resurrected Jesus.

And this Jesus permeates Latino culture, from the bloodied images of the *Divino Rostro* found in so many Latino homes to the tortured and scarred Jesus hanging from crosses in Latino churches. Often these images are so life-like in the agony they express that, upon encountering them, we get goose bumps or, especially perhaps if we are "sophisticated moderns," we become embarrassed in their presence. This Jesus seems somehow gruesome, exaggerated, medieval, even psychologically unhealthy in his suffering. Yet there he is—and, in the Latino world, he is everywhere: "The crucified Jesus is painted or sculpted to appear in horrible pain. The crown of thorns, the nails, the blood, are all made to communicate real suffering, real torture, and real death."[49] This is not a Jesus we can ignore or avoid, either as casual visitors to a Latino community or, especially, as scholars and pastors seeking to understand and explain in theological language how God is present in that community.

Whatever our theology textbooks may tell us about the importance of Christmas and Easter, there is little doubt that, for Latinos and Latinas, religious faith is identified above all with the crucified Jesus. In our attempt to define and specify the socio-historical context of a Catholic U.S. Hispanic theology, we must understand that the Jesus who comes alive in popular Catholicism is not an abstraction or a "mere" symbol. Rather, he is a particular, concrete, historical person, with flesh and bones, a body, and a face which reveal the universal, spiritual Christ of faith—and he is made concrete in the performative, ritual act of "walking with." This is a popular religion which, as indistinguishable from life itself, is always embodied and enfleshed: like life itself. If this Jesus bleeds, it is not to sanctify suffering but to sanctify the flesh; and to sanctify the flesh is to see in it a sacrament, or symbol, of the God of Jesus Christ.

One cannot understand U.S. Hispanic popular Catholicism without understanding its essentially incarnational and, therefore, relational character: Jesus is not simply a spirit "out there" or even "in here"; he is a truly historical, flesh-and-blood man who *accompanies* us in our lives—as do our families and friends. The crucifixion of Jesus became present to the "Roman soldier" nailing him to the cross at San Fernando only because, in the physical action of hammering the nails, this poor Mexican man embodied, made concrete and particular, what had earlier been merely an abstract universal concept, "a Roman soldier." The Roman soldier was, for this man, no longer an abstraction. The Mexican parishioner was no longer just *playing* the part of the soldier; he now *was* the soldier. As the soldier, he was no longer merely pretending to crucify Jesus; he *was* crucifying Jesus. Thus, he could also now proclaim "Truly, this was God's son," no longer as the declaration of an unnamed Roman soldier but as *his own* profoundly felt belief. By physically putting himself in the place of the soldier, he recognized his own intrinsic relationship to the soldier, to the multitudes surrounding the cross, to Mary, and to Jesus Christ. His own identity was revealed in those relationships, which in turn presupposed the embodiment, or incarnation of the

---

49. Espín, "Tradition and Popular Religion," 70.

faceless, abstract "Roman soldier" of the biblical text in the concrete, particular, historical person of *this* Mexican man—and, thus, presupposed the incarnation of the faceless, spiritual "Christ of faith" in *that* other Mexican man who now *was* Jesus Christ.

For the U.S. Hispanic theologian, then, it will not be sufficient to read books about Jesus Christ, or even to study relevant dogmatic declarations or biblical texts—as important as these might be. We must instead look first—even if not only—to the concrete, historical presence of Jesus in our communities, for it is in our concrete, historical relationship to Jesus (e.g., by touching his wounds and kissing his feet) that we come to know him, as surely as it is in our concrete, historical relationship with our families and friends that we come to know these. We cannot relate to other persons except through the mediation of our bodies (e.g., intellect, touch, feelings, sight). The importance of this incarnational and relational quality cannot be overstated and, as we will see in our analysis of Marian popular Catholicism, is repeatedly reinforced in U.S. Hispanic popular Catholicism. These are a Jesus and Mary whom we can be with and come to know through this everyday *acompañamiento*.

The Anthropology of Mary

Like the Jesus described above, the Mary of U.S. Hispanic popular Catholicism is a very real, flesh-and-blood person, not a merely historical figure from the past, or a merely spiritual being in the present. She is one with her people, not in some abstract theological or spiritual way, but in the most concrete way possible, in the very color and features of her face, in her language, and in the physical make-up and position of her body and clothing.[50] That same face conveys her concern and compassion for her people in the reflected image of Juan Diego. Her language expresses her sense of intimacy with him, as his language expresses his intimacy with her. A similar intimacy is expressed in our own use of the diminutives *Madrecita* and *la Morenita* to address and refer to Mary. In the Guadalupe celebrations, the people's need for physical contact with Mary is as evident as is their need, in the Good Friday celebration, for physical contact with the crucified Jesus.

Mary too is defined by her relationships. These are not merely incidental to her identity; like Jesus, she does not have an identity *except in relationship*. Mary is never just Mary; she is also our mother, *comadre*, *compañera*, friend, and, above all, mother of Jesus. In the Good Friday celebration, Mary is always alongside her son, even after his burial. The last image we see on Good Friday is the image, in the celebration of the

---

50. Rodríguez, *Our Lady of Guadalupe*, pp. 22–30; Elizondo, *La Morenita*, pp. 83–86.

Pésames, of Mary kneeling at the tomb of her son, and the community kneeling beside her. In the Guadalupe story, Mary identifies herself as the mother of Juan Diego and the mother of God. As *la Soledad*, Mary experiences the most profound desolation and dehumanization, that of the abandoned, isolated individual. As the Crucified, Jesus experiences the same: "My God, my God, why have you abandoned me?"

Like Jesus, and like all persons, Mary is identified and known by her relationships; and, like Jesus', her relationships are never purely "spiritual" but are always mediated by physical embodiment, by physical presence, by *accompaniment*. When, in search of the beautiful singing he hears, Juan Diego discovers the radiant Lady on Tepeyac, her first words to him, her first request is that he come and accompany her: she asks him to walk up to her, to "come to her side."[51] She does not simply ask Juan Diego to pray to her in the privacy of his own heart and home, rather she asks that a temple be built on Tepeyac so that the people may be with her *there*; "spiritual" presence is not enough, she demands physical presence as well. Indeed, when one reads the narrative, one is struck by Juan Diego's constant trips from his house to Tepeyac, or from Tlatelolco to Tepeyac. Why would Mary make poor Juan Diego do so much walking, along such rough terrain, when she could simply whisper her messages to his heart, wherever he happened to be? For whatever reason, her relationship to him as mother to child depended on his presence with her on Tepeyac—and her presence with him. Likewise, the San Fernando community's Guadalupe is one whom the people visit, touch, kiss, and serenade, just as they kneel alongside the Sorrowful Mother on the night of her son's death. It is in these physical actions of accompaniment that her motherhood and compassion are revealed.

The acts of being with and accompanying Mary constitute and form us as a community in the same way as the acts of being with and accompanying the crucified Jesus do. Juan Diego's encounter with the Lady on Tepeyac was the birth of a new people from the ashes of conquest. A community that had been utterly destroyed is given new life, and continues to be born anew whenever people gather together at San Fernando—or hundreds of other churches—to visit with *la Morenita* and sing *las Mañanitas*.

It is this community which defines us and, by so doing, strengthens us to resist contemporary "*conquistadores*" bent on extinguishing our people. Guadalupe is no weak, passive mother; she is, instead, the mother whose physical identification with us—on Tepeyac, on the *tilma*'s image, in San Fernando Cathedral—as a people bound together by our common accompaniment of her and each other provides us with a common history, a common identity and, hence, a common source of strength. This Mary, then, is the bodily, flesh-and-blood rebirth of God's love at that

---

51. Siller, *Para comprender el mensaje de María de Guadalupe*, p. 64.

very moment in history when God's love had been extinguished, executed by the same people who claimed to be God's servants.[52] Wherever God's love continues to be threatened today, she remains its inextinguishable presence. Wherever poor "Juan Dieguitos" continue to be excluded, dismissed, and ignored, she continues to call them to her side, to Mt. Tepeyac, to San Fernando. There she affirms their identity and dignity as her children.

In its central, though implicit assertion of the absolute value of relationality and community, U.S. Hispanic popular Catholicism presupposes the foundational role of relationships in defining what it means to be a human being—and what it means to be a Christian. The human person is defined, above all, by his or her character as a relational being. Yet this relationality is not merely some static "essence" of the person, but an *active* relating in and through which the person defines him or herself, in interaction with others. Relationship is not something that "happens to" someone, something one "experiences" in a passive way, or something one "possesses"; it is something one *does*, the most basic form of human action since, through relationship, we discover and live out our identity as intrinsically relational beings.

In what we do we discover who we are. As suggested above, I do not experience myself as an individual person *until* I am confronted by another, in the face of whom I can now recognize my-self. Only when the newborn infant recognizes its mother as mother, i.e., as an-other, does the infant now recognize him or herself as other than the mother. Prior to that, mother and infant are one in the eyes of the infant. Analogously, only when we encounter an-other culture do we recognize the existence of our own culture as distinct; prior to that, we simply assume that our way of life and our interpretative horizon are universal. Not until I am exposed to another culture do I recognize myself as a cultural being, that is, as some-one who has a *particular* way of life; prior to that, I simply assume that my way of life is also everyone else's. By definition, such an encounter always entails an *inter*action.

In the story of Guadalupe, Juan Diego does not come to recognize his own identity as a human person, as some-one, until he encounters *la Morenita* on Tepeyac. Prior to that encounter, he had no sense of himself as a human being at all: "the people's dung."[53] By approaching and encountering Mary, he finds himself. In the process of relating to her he is able to discover his own identity and dignity as a person, an individual with his own particular experience and history, a self with intrinsic value, some-one whose identity cannot simply be subsumed within or

---

52. See Virgilio Elizondo, *The Future is Mestizo: Life Where Cultures Meet* (Bloomington, IN: Meyer-Stone Books, 1988), pp. 59ff.

53. Siller, *Para comprender el mensaje de María de Guadalupe*, p. 74; Elizondo, *La Morenita*, p. 77.

determined by Spanish history. Here, then, relationship and community are not *restrictions* on individual autonomy but are, on the contrary, *the condition of the possibility* of Juan Diego's autonomy as an individual person with a distinct identity irreducible to the identity imposed on him by the Spanish colonizers.

As an indigenous man, Juan Diego had come to view his life through the lenses of the conquering Spaniards, that is, he had come to see himself as a mere passive object of their actions, a mere instrument of their designs. He saw himself as, literally, a no-body who, therefore, could never truly "act" but could only be acted *upon* by others: he refers to himself as "a rope" and "a little ladder," two tools that are used by other persons and whose sole value comes from their usefulness.[54] The Spaniards were active agents who were making history; Juan Diego was merely raw material to be manipulated and molded by their hands. As a mere passive object, Juan Diego was incapable of entering into a human relationship with the Spaniards: a person cannot have a relationship with an object. Relationship presupposes *inter*action, i.e., action between subjects.

Juan Diego brings this self-understanding with him to Mt. Tepeyac. When Mary appears to him and asks him to act, to go to the bishop to insist that a temple be built on Tepeyac, he feels himself unable to do so: a no-body cannot act. In contrast to his own reluctance, *la Morenita* refuses to accept his deprecatory self-understanding and, instead, calls him "the dearest of my children," some-one capable of acting. Only at that point can Juan Diego, in fact, confront the bishop as one *person* to another.

The narrative expresses Juan Diego's newfound personhood in many different ways. Already at the very beginning of the story, we read that Juan Diego "dared to go where he was being called. His heart was not at all disturbed, nor did he have any fear. . . ."[55] He did not merely react instinctively, like one of Pavlov's dogs, rather he *dared* to approach the Lady who had called him. And his *heart* was confident. For the Nahuas, the heart was the "dynamic and active part of the person," whereas the face or countenance was the "static part of the person" associated with passivity.[56] Juan Diego would no longer be a passive object of history; he would now be an active agent of history.

Another indication of Juan Diego's dignity is that he begins to use the same language of affection and intimacy with the Lady that she uses with him: he refers to her as "my dearest Girl" and "the most forsaken [or smallest, dearest] of my Daughters." These appear strange as terms of address for the Lady, but they reflect the fact that Juan Diego now considers himself on equal footing with her.

---

54. Siller, *Para comprender a María de Guadalupe*, p. 74.
55. Ibid., p. 64.
56. Ibid.

Also, Juan Diego's trips to the bishop's palace were initially undertaken merely out of obedience to the Lady: the indigenous man resisted, considering himself unworthy. By the time of the third trip, however, Juan Diego "pleaded very much with her to send him immediately to see the Lord of the priests to take him her sign. . . ."[57] He was now an active, indeed eager, agent of his own action.

A further sign of Juan Diego's new-found personhood is his reaction to his uncle's illness. No mere instrument even of the Lady of Tepeyac, he chooses to delay his return trip to the bishop's palace, thereby disobeying her express command in order to help minister to his uncle. The "old" Juan Diego would never have dared disobey Mary in such a manner. Mary repeatedly urges Juan Diego to confront the bishop with her demands, thereby asking Juan Diego to risk doing the unthinkable, i.e., disobeying the bishop. Ironically, Juan Diego's willingness to disobey Mary is a sign that he is, indeed, a person, with needs and desires that cannot simply be subsumed within someone else's—not even those of Mary herself.

The reason for his disobedience is also significant: his desire to minister to the needs of his uncle. When conflicting with the human needs of his family members, his explicitly religious responsibilities would have to take a back seat.[58] As Siller points out, moreover, "in the Náhuatl world . . . the 'uncle' is the original center of the neighborhood, the roots of the people."[59] The uncle thus represents the community itself, which had been destroyed by the illnesses brought to Mexico by the Spaniards.[60] In the face of the community's physical needs, Mary's needs would have to wait. After Mary spies Juan Diego trying to sneak around her, he does not react with embarrassment or fear; instead, he nonchalantly asks Mary "How did you sleep? Are you feeling well?"[61] Then he asks her to be patient.

By giving him his personhood, Mary had also given him the freedom to act, e.g., to disobey her . . . and the freedom to interrelate as one person with another.[62] In the exchanges between Mary and Juan Diego, then, we see the conversion of Juan Diego from "the people's dung" to "the dearest of my children." He will no longer be merely a passive object of someone else's action, not even of Mary's action when her requests conflict with his uncle's needs. He is now a full-fledged human being, capable of relating to the bishop as one person to another, one subject to another . . . capable, therefore, of establishing a genuine *inter*relationship with another person. This new understanding of his ability to act becomes

---

57. Ibid., pp. 84–85; Elizondo, *La Morenita*, p. 78.
58. Siller, *Para comprender a María de Guadalupe*, pp. 82–85.
59. Ibid., p. 80.
60. Ibid.
61. Ibid., p. 82.
62. More precisely, perhaps, Mary helped Juan Diego experience and claim his personhood as an intrinsically relational being.

the basis for his relationship with the Lady. Only after the Lady assures Juan Diego that his uncle would recover his health does Juan Diego agree to go immediately to the bishop. Otherwise, Mary would just have to wait. Here we see that Juan Diego's identity as a unique person, as "*el otro*" (the other), presupposes a prior, more fundamental communality, "*nosotros*" (we others).[63]

What takes place at Tepeyac then is not an apparition but an *encounter*. The notion of apparition implies an active subject, which "appears," and a passive object, *to which* the subject appears. An encounter, on the other hand, implies an *inter*-action *between* two subjects—each of which "appears" to the other. The story of Guadalupe recounts a relationship which begins as the apparition of a subject (the Lady) to an object (Juan Diego) and ends as an encounter between two equal subjects, two full-fledged persons.

A community is defined by such intersubjective relationships.[64] A byproduct of authentic community is, thus, the birth and development of free and unique human persons. This belief is made explicit at the very end of the Guadalupe narrative when, accompanied by the many people who will help him build the temple, Juan Diego returns to see that his uncle has been cured. The uncle responds to Juan Diego's arrival with astonishment, not because his nephew had come to visit him, but because he had "come so well-accompanied and honored."[65] Before his encounter with the Lady, Juan Diego had been the most forsaken and abandoned of her children; now he is well-accompanied and honored. To be abandoned is to be nobody; to be accompanied is to be honored, a person. The people's accompaniment symbolizes his new, honored status as a full human being.

The fact that community does not extinguish but enhances individuality is a presupposition that defines all U.S. Hispanic theological reflection. Virgil Elizondo begins his book *The Future is Mestizo* with stories about his family, neighborhood, parish, and city; only after recounting these does he proceed to ask the question "Who am I?" The same is true of Justo González's book *Mañana* and Ada María Isasi-Díaz's book *En la Lucha*: each begins with an acknowledgment and discussion of its roots in the author's formative communities. Only as I have begun claiming my own history and communal identity have I become increasingly "free to choose," free to make my own personal decisions about how I will relate to that history and community, and how I will relate to my adoptive U.S. community.

---

63. The notion of "*nosotros*" as a collective subject is developed by the Argentine philosopher-theologian Juan Carlos Scannone in a series of articles appearing in the journal *Stromata*. See especially "Un nuevo punto," and "Filosofía primera e intersubjetividad."

64. See Scannone, "Filosofía primera e intersubjetividad."

65. Ibid., p. 93.

Authentic individuality and authentic community are not contradictory but mutually implicit. As the Lady of Tepeyac affirms Juan Diego's freedom, the true family does not suffocate the freedom and uniqueness of the individual members, rather it fosters that very freedom—without which there can be no real family, no real community of *others*, no genuine "nos*otros*."[66] Indeed, the true test of an authentic relationship or community is one whose participants are, like Juan Diego, free to disobey, to criticize, and to be different. Just as community is a prerequisite for individual freedom, so too is individual freedom a prerequisite for community. This, however, is not the ahistorical "freedom" of the autonomous, unsituated individual; it is, instead, a personal freedom which already presupposes the very relationality, situatedness, and community which is now freely accepted and appropriated, even if through conscious disobedience, criticism, or "rejection" (since, by definition, any rejection of a *constitutive* community can never be absolute). Authentic relationship presupposes unique, particular *otros*, or others; but these unique individuals themselves presuppose the relationships into which they were born and which, thus, helped form them as persons capable of acting freely (rather than merely being "acted upon" by others).

Wherever individual freedom and particularity are stifled, the organic understanding of the person has been supplanted by an individualism that views the uniqueness and freedom of the person (the particular) as threats to the community (the universal). In an organic anthropology, each person is not a mirror reflection but a *unique refraction* of the whole.[67] Like glass prisms that, each cut in a different form, refract the light into uniquely structured, magnificent rainbows of colors, thereby making visible a light that would otherwise be invisible to the eye, each person is the unique refraction of that common Light which becomes visible only in the radiance of each unique, particular rainbow. Without the prisms, without their individual uniqueness, the Light would remain invisible.

---

66. According to Juan Carlos Scannone, "the 'we' [*nosotros*] as such is revealed in the irreducibility of the 'he' and the 'you' to the 'I' . . . and that of the 'you' and the 'I' to the 'he.'" "Religión," 39. Every community is susceptible to the danger of denying that irreducibility (i.e., "otherness," or uniqueness): "just as the persecution of the particular and the different may indicate mere domination and repression, it is also possible that the desire to preserve certain customs will function in opposition to the individual who, in the midst of and enclosed within these customs, is denied access to more universal values." Camps, *Virtudes públicas*, 176.

67. As Scannone avers, the individual person "creatively appropriates" the wisdom of the formative communities ("Religión, lenguaje y sabiduría," 30).

[4]

Beauty or Justice?

The Aesthetic Character of Human Action

In the Guadalupe story, we see the connection between anthropology (Juan Diego attained a new understanding of himself as a *person* rather than as mere "dung") and human action (he arrived at this new understanding through his *interaction* with *la Morenita*). A relational anthropology, wherein the person is viewed as intrinsically social, is thus rooted in human action, or "praxis." Such an anthropology is not derived from metaphysical categories of "human nature" but, fundamentally, from human praxis itself, from our *interaction*, our *life* in community.

Yet this begs the question, What do we mean by human "action" or "praxis?" What do we mean, for instance, when we assert that the relationship between Juan Diego and the Lady of Tepeyac was an "encounter" that, as such, involved an "interaction" between two subjects? Only after we address this question will we be able to proceed to the further, methodological question, "What is the relationship between theology itself and praxis?" More specifically, what is the relationship between our knowledge of God, and the theological articulation of that knowledge, on the one hand, and our everyday lives, or "action," on the other? What is the relationship between what we *know* and how we *live*? What is the relationship between what we preach and what we practice?

Before explicitly considering the relationship of praxis to theology, therefore, we will 1) examine the significance of Latin American liberation theology for understanding the nature of praxis, or human action, 2) trace the historical development of the term "praxis" in order to locate liberation theology within that etymological history, and 3) demonstrate how a U.S. Hispanic theology, rooted in popular Catholicism, can deepen our understanding of praxis as the foundation of anthropology and theology.

Latin American Liberation Theology: The Primacy of Praxis

Perhaps the most significant contribution of Latin American liberation theologians to the church and theology has been their responses to these very questions. If U.S. Hispanic theologians, like most contemporary Christian theologians, have come to appreciate the significance of praxis for theological method, this is due, in no small measure, to the groundbreaking insights of liberation theologians.[1]

For liberation theologians, the person is defined more by what he or she *does* than by what he or she *thinks*. Thus, one's actions are the most accurate reflection of one's identity. If you want to know who I am, observe how I live my life, with whom I interrelate, to which activities I devote my time, energy, and resources. If you want to know what I believe, don't first ask me my thoughts; instead, look first at my actions. From these, one could find out more about my identity than from my answer to the questions, "Who are you?" and "What do you believe?"

In their critique of traditional Western theologies, liberation theologians have rejected those theologies which presupposed that Christian faith is, fundamentally, an intellectual assent to certain propositions or doctrines. They have likewise rejected any view of theology that understands the theological task as a purely scientific, rational exercise divorced from the everyday life and actions of the theologian himself or herself. Instead, argue liberation theologians, Christian faith must be understood as a *lived* commitment, and Christian theology as reflection upon that lived commitment in the light of the Scriptures. If the term "orthodoxy" refers to those "correct beliefs" which have traditionally functioned as the norm against which Christians' faith must be judged, liberation theologians remind us of the importance of orthopraxis, or "correct action," as the most basic norm of Christian faith. To know God is to do justice. To love God is to love one's neighbor. The validity of theological theories is always influenced by the type of human life, or "praxis," whence those theories issue. A Christian theology that issues from an un-Christian life will be no more credible to believers and non-believers than will the parental condemnation of lying be credible to our children if we ourselves are liars. Correct action ("orthopraxis") is never unrelated to our truth-claims ("orthodoxy"): the former calls into question the veracity of the latter.

Christian doctrine remains important as the Christian community's articulation of our lived commitment to Christ, and as the word of God which inspires and transforms our lives. But what most defines us as Christians is not our intellectual assent to those doctrines but our lived

---

1. See Allan Figueroa Deck, Introduction to *Frontiers of Hispanic Theology in the United States*, pp. xiv–xv.

commitment to Christ and our neighbor. Likewise, theology remains important as the community's reflection upon that commitment in the light of the Scriptures, but what makes that reflection credible and authentically Christian is, above all, its roots in the lived commitment to Christ and neighbor. Without those roots, theology remains inadequate, meaningless, irrelevant, and literally in-credible—or it may even directly legitimate injustice and oppression.[2]

It was precisely in the context of the Latin American experience of injustice and oppression at the hands of European conquistadores and missionaries that Latin Americans began to challenge European theologies that presupposed the primacy of theory, or beliefs, over praxis, or action. Already in the sixteenth century, Bartolomé de Las Casas had questioned the right of the Spaniards to call themselves "Christian" when their behavior with respect to the indigenous peoples of America was anything but Christian. Though the Spanish conquistadores and missionaries may have believed and preached correct Christian doctrine, their actions belied their words. They may have preached a Christian God of love, but their actions revealed that their real gods were the gods of Gold and Silver. Thus, their *true* beliefs were revealed more in what they did, their praxis, than in what they proclaimed, their doctrines and theologies. For Las Casas, the chief obstacle to the evangelization of the indigenous people was not their "idolatrous" native religions, but the idolatry of the Spanish "Christians," who preached love while committing murder, and professed belief in a transcendent God while worshipping Gold.[3]

Liberation theologians have retrieved the example of Las Casas, and the long Latin American history of exploitation, to insist that the most basic measure of one's faith is not theory, or one's intellectual beliefs, but praxis, or one's actions. Thus, liberation theologians have been instrumental in reminding us that the foundation and goal of Christian faith and theology must always be Christian life itself, a life of love and justice. Theology is never an end in itself, but is always rooted in and at the

---

2. On the relationship between orthodoxy and orthopraxis, see Gustavo Gutiérrez, *A Theology of Liberation*, Revised Edition with a New Introduction (Maryknoll, NY: Orbis, 1988), pp. xxxiii–xxxv, 8. On the role of praxis in theology, also see, especially, Juan Luis Segundo, *The Liberation of Theology* (Maryknoll, NY: Orbis, 1976); idem, *Faith and Ideologies* (Maryknoll, NY: Orbis, 1984); Clodovis Boff, *Theology and Praxis: Epistemological Foundations* (Maryknoll, NY: Orbis, 1987); Enrique Dussel, *Philosophy of Liberation* (Maryknoll, NY: Orbis, 1985); Rebecca Chopp, *The Praxis of Suffering: An Interpretation of Liberation and Political Theologies* (Maryknoll, NY: Orbis, 1986).

3. For a brilliant and moving analysis of the life and work of Las Casas, see Gustavo Gutiérrez, *Las Casas: In Search of the Poor of Jesus Christ* (Maryknoll, NY: Orbis, 1993).

service of the Christian community's ongoing, active commitment to Jesus Christ in society and history.

It is this understanding of faith and theology as rooted in the historical struggles of the marginalized Latin American community that has made liberation theology such an important inspiration to U.S. Hispanic theologians, including myself. When I entered theological studies, I knew that, for me, those studies could never be an end in themselves, but were one dimension of a larger, more fundamental vocation, the vocation of accompanying my own community in a common life of discipleship (though, as yet, I still identified that community with Latin America). The theological task, I was convinced, had to be more than merely the intellectual exercise of an autonomous scholar.

What Is Praxis?

As mentioned above, to say that praxis, or life, grounds the theological task is still to beg the questions: What do we actually mean by human "life" or "action?" What do liberation theologians mean when they speak of human life, human action, or "praxis?" What do *we* mean? These terms themselves presuppose an interpretative horizon against which they are defined: whenever we use these terms in everyday conversation, we presuppose those definitions and connotations prevalent in our own socio-historical context. The interpretative horizon which so influences our understanding of these terms is that of modern Western, post-Enlightenment society.[4]

The modern Western understanding of human action is greatly influenced by the individualistic anthropology outlined in the previous chapter, which understands human action as the action of an *autonomous* subject *upon* his or her external environment, itself construed as but a passive object of the subject's actions. Thus, other subjects, or persons, are themselves but passive, inert objects to be acted *upon*. Human action, or praxis, is thereby reduced to *technique*, or "practicality": the value of human action, or life, is predicated upon its practicality, or usefulness. This, in turn, implies the reduction of human action to mere *movement*: to act is to "go from here to there" in order to "make contact with" the object "upon which" one is acting. Thus, a person's interaction with another person is not substantially different from his or her "interaction" with a computer, a hammer, a pencil, or an automobile. Human action is thus reduced to the autonomous subject's physical, technical

---

4. While one might call ours a "postmodern" interpretative horizon, in the last three chapters I will take up the question of the relationship between modern and postmodern interpretative horizons, suggesting that the latter is essentially an extension of the former.

manipulation of the external world, which is perceived as merely the "instrument" of the autonomous subject's action.[5]

This notion of praxis as *instrumental action* (action-as-manipulation, defined by its usefulness and practicality) has functioned as the interpretative horizon for all modern Western interpretations of human action. Among the most influential of these, especially in Latin American liberation theology, has been that of Karl Marx. Marx's critique of liberal, capitalist individualism remained ambiguous precisely because, like a good modern thinker, he presupposed a similar understanding of human action, or praxis.[6]

For Marx, what distinguishes the human person from other animals is "conscious life-activity": "In creating an objective world by his practical activity, in working-up inorganic nature, man proves himself a conscious species being."[7] What defines, in turn, conscious life-activity is the act of production: "He begins to distinguish himself from the animal the moment he begins to *produce* his means of subsistence, a step required by his physical organization. By producing food, man indirectly produces his material life itself."[8] According to Marx, it is through the act of production, through the creative process of working upon our

---

5. On the modern notion of praxis, see Matthew Lamb, "Praxis," in *The New Dictionary of Theology*, ed. Joseph Komonchak, et al. (Wilmington, DE: Michael Glazier, 1987), 784–87; idem, *Solidarity with Victims* (New York: Crossroad, 1982); Jürgen Habermas, *The Theory of Communicative Action* (Boston: Beacon Press, 1984); idem, *Theory and Practice* (London: Heinemann, 1974); Hans-Georg Gadamer, "Hermeneutics and Social Science," *Cultural Hermeneutics* 2 (1975): 307–16; Richard Bernstein, *Beyond Objectivism and Relativism: Science, Hermeneutics, and Praxis* (Philadelphia: University of Pennsylvania Press, 1985); idem, *Praxis and Action: Contemporary Philosophies of Human Activity* (Philadelphia: University of Pennsylvania Press, 1971); Nicholas Lobkowicz, *Theory and Practice: History of a Concept from Aristotle to Marx* (Notre Dame, IN: University of Notre Dame Press, 1967); Joseph Dunne, *Back to the Rough Ground: 'Phronesis' and 'Techne' in Modern Philosophy and in Aristotle* (Notre Dame, IN: University of Notre Dame Press, 1993).

6. See Lamb, "Praxis"; Habermas, *Theory and Practice*, esp. pp. 168–69; Boff, *Theology and Praxis*, pp. 330–31; Dunne, *Back to the Rough Ground*, esp. pp. 168–226; Enrique Dussel, *Filosofía de la producción* (Bogotá: Editorial Nueva América, 1984), pp. 33–114; Victoria Camps, *Virtudes públicas* (Madrid: Espasa Calpe, 1990), pp. 104–22. On Marx's understanding of praxis, see Kostas Axelos, *Alienation, Praxis, and Technē in the Thought of Karl Marx* (Austin, TX: University of Texas Press, 1976).

7. "Economic and Philosophic Manuscripts of 1844," in *The Marx-Engels Reader*, ed. Robert C. Tucker (New York: W. W. Norton and Company, 1978), 76.

8. Karl Marx, *Writings of the Young Marx on Philosophy and Society*, ed. Loyd Easton and Kurt Guddat (Garden City, NY: Doubleday, 1967), p. 409.

physical environment, that we quite literally create ourselves as human persons: our products are the concrete, objectified expression of our very selves. Life-activity is thus defined as productive labor. To be a person is to work, to produce: "to be, man must make . . ."[9] For Marx, then, the human person is *homo faber*.[10] For Marx, writes Kostas Axelos, "productive labor, this creation of objects, is unquestionably the realization of the essential, substantial, and objective forces of man."[11]

When, therefore, the products of our hands are taken from us to be sold in the marketplace, what is, in fact, taken from us is our very selves, which we have put into those products. The individual's right to enjoy the fruit, or product, of his or her labor derives from this fundamental fact: the product of my labor *is* my very self, my own life, in concrete, objective form. For Marx, then, human alienation is defined quite literally, as the rupturing of the intimate, intrinsic relationship between the worker's life, as an act of production, and the worker's life, as the object which is produced. This alienation is, according to Marx, the very essence of capitalism. In capitalism, the workers' products are taken from them by the capitalist, to be sold for a profit in the marketplace; that profit is, at bottom, a part of the worker's very self extracted from the worker and expropriated by the capitalist. What is truly being sold is the worker himself or herself.[12]

Though this identification of human action, or praxis, with production is Marx's contribution to the history of the word "praxis," the term is itself a Greek word with roots in classical, pre-modern society. Aristotle's own anthropology, for example, is based on a particular understanding of praxis. He defines praxis as *all human activity whose end is internal rather than external to itself*, i.e., all human activity which is *an end in itself*. That human activity which is its own end, and is valuable *in itself*, is human intersubjective activity (interaction between human subjects),

---

9. Axelos, *Alienation, Praxis, and Technē*, p. 123.

10. Dussel, *Filosofía de la producción*, pp. 15–33. Hannah Arendt addresses the Marxist tendency toward a reductionist anthropology and understanding of human action by specifying *homo faber* as but one of the characteristics of human action, of which the highest is the *bios politikos*. She thus essays a critical retrieval of the Aristotelian distinction between praxis and poiesis (discussed below) in the light of a modern, transformative understanding of human action. See especially her *The Human Condition* (Chicago: University of Chicago Press, 1958).

11. Axelos, *Alienation, Praxis, and Technē*, p. 126.

12. On alienation, see Bertell Ollman, *Alienation: Marx's Conception of Man in Capitalist Society* (Cambridge: Cambridge University Press, 1971); Nathan Rotenstreich, *Alienation: The Concept and Its Reception* (Leiden: E. J. Brill, 1989); Axelos, *Alienation, Praxis, and Technē*, and Bernstein, *Praxis and Action*, pp. 48–50; Lobkowicz, *Theory and Practice*, pp. 293–372.

or human relationships.[13] These relationships have *intrinsic* value; they are ends in themselves, rather than merely means to some other, external end. Human action whose end is *external* to itself is what Aristotle calls "poiesis." The prototypical example of poiesis is the human activity of production. When we produce, or make something, the activity of producing or making has no intrinsic value or end. The end of production is not the action itself, but the object (product) which results from the action, *after* the action is already completed. Whereas praxis is its own reward, the reward of poiesis is in its results, what is left over *after* the activity of production is completed.[14]

The difference is analogous to that between "making a home" and "making a house." The value of the former resides in the activity itself. The end of home life is nothing other than the family's enjoyment of that life itself: "Productive techniques are needed to make a house. But a home is a doing, a performing, [not a "making"]. . . ."[15] The value of constructing a house, however, resides in the *product* of the activity. The end of the process of making a house is not the activity of construction itself, but the house that is left over *after* we have *finished* the activity: "An activity such as building a house would never be considered satisfactory if it did not stop, that is, resulted in a house built and finished."[16]

The difference between praxis and poiesis is also analogous to that between playing a musical instrument and *making* a musical instrument. When I play my guitar, I do so because I enjoy the music, the sound, the rhythm, etc. I enjoy the act of playing itself. The end is nothing other than my enjoyment of the activity itself. After I am through playing, the enjoyment is over. The "goal" of playing a musical instrument—i.e., the goal of performance—has been accomplished in the very act of performing itself: "playing the flute obviously has achieved its end a long time before it stops. In fact, once it has stopped, it is no longer of any

---

13. On the notion of intersubjectivity, see Bernard Lonergan, *Insight: A Study of Human Understanding* (San Francisco: Harper and Row, 1957), pp. 211–18, and Kathleen M. Haney, *Intersubjectivity Revisited: Phenomenology and the Other* (Athens, OH: Ohio University Press, 1994). For Aristotle, the prototypical examples of human intersubjective activity are political activity and moral conduct; these are the principal mediations of our relationships with each other, i.e., the principal ways in which we relate to each other as free subjects.

14. Aristotle, *Politics*, 1.4.1254; idem, *Nicomachean Ethics*, 6.4.1140. On the Aristotelian notion of praxis, see also the works cited in note 5 above, especially Lobkowicz, *Theory and Practice*, pp. 3–57. See also Enrique Dussel, *Filosofía de la producción*, pp. 33–41; Alasdair McIntyre, *Whose Justice? Which Rationality?*; and idem, *After Virtue: A Study in Moral Theory* (Notre Dame, IN: University of Notre Dame Press, 1981).

15. Lamb, "Praxis," 786.

16. Lobkowicz, *Theory and Practice*, p. 10.

value—precisely because it does not aim at a result beyond the mere 'doing' of it."[17] The end of the process of making a musical instrument, however, is not the enjoyment of the activity itself, but the final product, e.g., the flute, guitar, violin, or piano. Here, the value of the activity is derived primarily not from the activity itself—i.e., the physical labor involved in constructing a musical instrument—but from the *product* of the labor—i.e., the musical instrument which, having already finished my activity, I can now gaze upon and use with special pride. The value of productive activity derives from its effectiveness, or usefulness, in transforming the material environment (the wood or metal) in order to achieve a predetermined goal (the instrument itself, the final product).

By now, the difference between Marx's notion of praxis, or human life, and Aristotle's should be evident. For Aristotle, "life is action [praxis] and not production [poiesis]."[18] "If we assume that life may be described as some kind of an activity," writes Nicholas Lobkowicz, "it obviously is not an activity which reaches its completion by stopping and leaving behind something different from itself."[19] What makes human life *human* is precisely that it is an absolute value in itself—regardless of its productivity, usefulness, or practicality.

For Marx, on the other hand, what defines human action as human is precisely its productive capacity, the human ability to transform the environment.[20] Whether what one is transforming is raw wood, in order to make a house, or social structures, in order to make a "just society," or one's very "self," in order to make a "better person," what defines human life and action is its usefulness in achieving the desired result. Axelos notes the connection between "making" a product (praxis-as-labor) and "making" a just society (praxis-as-social transformation) implicit in the modern, Marxist notion of praxis, which reduces human action to mere technique, or instrumentality: "Naturalism, humanism, and socialism-communism are based on absolute productivity, practical activity, transformative praxis—in a word, on Technique. Technique is not reducible simply to machines and limited industrial production. It is the motor force of history. . . ."[21] To reduce human action to social transformation is to reduce it to productive activity, which is to reduce it to technique; and to reduce human action to technique is to reduce the human person to but a passive object, a mere instrument of production.

---

17. Ibid.

18. *Politics* 1.4.1254. Lobkowicz notes that "Aristotle uses this statement to show that a slave is an instrument of action, such as a dress or a bed which one uses without getting from it something beside and beyond the use" (*Theory and Practice*, p. 10).

19. *Theory and Practice*, p. 10.

20. See Dussel, *Filosofía de la producción*, p. 92.

21. Axelos, *Alienation, Praxis, and Technē*, p. 325.

In conceiving human action as fundamentally productive, Marx simply reflects the modern, post-Enlightenment emphasis on technique, or instrumental action, as the highest form of human activity: to be a human being is to produce, or to transform the environment. If the act of production is the prototypical human activity, then *all* human activity will tend to be judged by the criteria of production; whether in capitalism or socialism, the effectiveness of human action in transforming the environment will be the standard by which that action is evaluated. Human life will be viewed and valued as the means or instrument through which we produce a desirable product, whether that product is income and profit, food, or the classless society. Whether the desired result is economic profitability or the socialist "New Man", the value of human action will be determined by its usefulness in producing that result. For Aristotle, human life, or praxis, is essentially useless; life has no "use" other than the living itself. Yet, for Marx and modernity, the value of human life lies precisely in its usefulness.

It would, one should note, be an oversimplification to suggest that Marx at no time views human life as intrinsically valuable. On the contrary, the motivation for his entire scholarly project was precisely the liberation of human beings from social structures that treat their lives as mere instruments of production rather than as intrinsically valuable. Yet Marx was himself a product of a modern, post-Enlightenment, Western society that is less concerned with doing than with making, less with performance than with the results of the performance, less with enjoyment than with usefulness, less with living than with working. By making productive labor the defining characteristic of human life—i.e., that which distinguishes human life from animal life—Marx assumed the modern notion of human action, thereby introducing a contradiction and ambiguity into his own notion of human action: Is human praxis valuable in itself, or is it valuable only as "production"? Is praxis intrinsically valuable, or is it valuable only insofar as it is "useful"? Is human action a value in and of itself, or is it valuable only insofar as it contributes to or produces some valuable *result*? In his famous eleventh thesis on Feuerbach, Marx writes "The philosophers have only *interpreted* the world in various ways; the point is, to *change* it." What if it *doesn't* change? Were our actions, in that case, worthless? What about those philosophers? Do *their* lives have any value? In Marx, the distinction between action-as-an-end-in-itself and action-as-a-means-to-an-external-end thus becomes blurred and ambiguous.[22] The liberation theologian Clodovis Boff notes this ambiguity and its impact on our contemporary understanding of praxis:

---

22. For discussions of this ambiguity, see Clodovis Boff, *Theology and Praxis* (Maryknoll, NY: Orbis Books, 1987), pp. 330–31n.; Camps, *Virtúdes publicas*, pp. 109–110; Dussel, *Filosofía de la producción*, p. 71. One reason for the ambiguity is the overlapping meanings which Marx gave to his notions of work, activity, and creativity. See Ollman, *Alienation*, pp. 97–103, and Bernstein, *Praxis and Action*, pp. 11–83.

Aristotle sees a neat distinction between *praxis* and *poiesis*. Praxis is a form of activity characterized by its immanence: its development is its own end. . . . As for the second form of activity (*operatio-poiesis*) . . . we have a *transitive* activity: its finality is something other than itself. . . . In current usage, "praxis" means both types of activity discerned by Aristotle. . . . Primarily owing to the theological and historical pressure of Marxism, praxis is no longer understood as its own end, *Selbstzweck*, self-finalized activity, but on the contrary, as the production of an external result. Praxis is action resulting in an effect of transformation.[23]

Liberating Praxis

Latin American liberation theologians have been influenced by Marx's notion of human action as transformative. In the words of Gustavo Gutiérrez, "praxis that transforms history . . . is the very matrix of all authentic knowledge, and the decisive proof of that knowledge's value."[24] "Truth," asserts the Brazilian Rubem Alves, "is the name given by the historical community to those actions which were, are, and will be *effective for the liberation* of man" (my emphasis).[25] Yet along with this important insight of Marx, liberation theologians have inherited the ambiguity latent in Marx's notion of praxis. Marx's emphasis on human praxis as primarily productive, or useful, tends toward an instrumentalist view of human life and, thus, toward a depreciation of human life, or praxis, as an end in itself.

In liberation theology, the emphasis on *liberating* praxis, or liberating social action, reflects a similar ambiguity: Is liberation the *result* of praxis, that is, the "product" of our struggle to transform society? Or, is liberation a *concomitant*, or *by*product, of praxis—i.e., the change that takes place in us *as* we engage in that struggle? Do we become liberated only *after* and *as a result of* our social action, or do we become liberated *in the*

---

23. Boff, *Theology and Praxis*, pp. 330–31n. The shift in the understanding of praxis from Aristotle to Marx is also discussed by Dussel in *Filosofía de la producción*, pp. 33–114. The differences between the Aristotelian and modern notions of praxis are discussed by Victoria Camps in her *Virtudes públicas*, pp. 104–22.

24. Gutiérrez, "Liberation Praxis and Christian Faith," 19. On the influence of Marx's notion of praxis, see, e.g., Gutiérrez, *A Theology of Liberation*, p. 8; Boff, *Theology and Praxis*, pp. 330–31; Arthur McGovern, *Marxism: An American Christian Perspective* (Maryknoll, NY: Orbis, 1980), pp. 179–85; Chopp, *The Praxis of Suffering*, pp. 94–5.

25. Quoted in McGovern, *Marxism*, p. 180.

course of our action? Is praxis, or human action its own end and, thus, valuable in and of itself, or is praxis valuable only insofar as it leads to a liberated society?

This ambiguity is to some extent reflected in the numerous, diverse ways the term praxis is used in liberation theology. In its broadest sense, praxis is simply human historical action. Historical praxis is, in the words of Gustavo Gutiérrez, a person's "active presence in history";[26] and "theology will be critical reflection on historical praxis. . . . it is a process of reflection which starts out from historical praxis."[27] In this basic definition of human action as historical praxis, we can note a close similarity with Aristotle's identification of praxis with human life itself. In this sense, one might say that human liberation is not a goal but a concomitant of praxis; the poor become liberated *in the process of the struggle itself*, in the process of being actively present in history as human subjects. It is *in the very struggle* against oppression that the poor cease to be merely objects of someone else's action and, instead, become historical subjects in their own right.

Gutiérrez also gives praxis a second, more specific meaning: praxis refers to the specifically Christian form of active presence in history, namely, prayer and commitment to justice.[28] Thus, Gutiérrez defines theology as "a critical reflection on Christian praxis in the light of the Word."[29] Yet Christian praxis is specified even further. In a third, still more specific sense, Gutiérrez identifies this Christian praxis as liberating praxis: "The praxis on which liberation theology reflects is a praxis of solidarity with the interests of liberation and is inspired by the gospel. . . . Consequently, a praxis motivated by evangelical values embraces to some extent every effort to bring about authentic fellowship and authentic justice. . . . This liberating praxis endeavors to transform history in the light of the reign of God."[30] "Theology, then," he suggests, "will be reflection on faith as liberation praxis."[31] Thus, the praxis which grounds theological reflection is variously defined as historical praxis, Christian praxis, and liberating (or liberation) praxis.

---

26. Gutiérrez, *A Theology of Liberation*, p. 6. See also idem, "Liberation Praxis and Christian Faith," in *Frontiers of Theology in Latin America*, ed. Rosino Gibellini (Maryknoll, NY: Orbis, 1979), 22.

27. Gutiérrez, "Liberation Praxis and Christian Faith," 22.

28. See, e.g., Gutiérrez, *A Theology of Liberation*, pp. xxx–xxxiv, 5–12; idem, "Liberation Praxis and Christian Faith"; Chopp, *The Praxis of Suffering*, pp. 46–63.

29. *A Theology of Liberation*, p. 11. At the same time, however, he defines theology as "critical reflection on *historical* praxis" (my emphasis), p. 12.

30. Ibid., p. xxx. See also idem, "Liberation Praxis and Christian Faith," and Chopp, *The Praxis of Suffering*, pp. 46–63.

31. Gutiérrez, "Liberation Praxis and Christian Faith," 22.

This last meaning represents perhaps the most significant contribution of liberation theology to the church, reminding Christians that the lived commitment to social justice is not superfluous to but a precondition for authentic Christian faith. The struggle for justice is not an option for Christians, over and above their Christian belief and worship; the lived commitment to social justice is itself an essential, intrinsic dimension of any authentic Christian faith.

Yet this identification of human action with social transformation also leaves liberation theology susceptible to the modern tendency to define human action as production or technique, that is, as a means *to* some external end—in this case, the end of liberation. What, in other words, is the *relationship* between historical praxis, or praxis-as-an-end-in-itself, and liberating praxis? Is liberating praxis *foundational* insofar as it is "the praxis on which liberation theology reflects"? If so, the starting point, or *locus theologicus*, of theology will be the "endeavor to transform history." Yet such an understanding of praxis, as transformation, remains ambiguous. Is liberation theology fundamentally a reflection on human action as an end in itself (historical praxis), or on human action as an *instrument* of liberation (liberating praxis)? Is liberation but a *byproduct* of the struggle *within which* we become full human subjects? Or is liberation the end *product* of this struggle?[32]

As indicated in the first chapter, their insistence on the intrinsic connection between social transformation and the Christian faith has been, for me, one of the most inspiring insights of Latin American liberation theologians. My own experience in Latino communities, such as San Fernando, has also led me to question, however, any emphasis on the social transformative dimension of human action which would make this dimension itself foundational. In these communities, I have witnessed a type of empowerment and liberation taking place which, at least initially and explicitly, seems to have relatively little connection to any social or political struggles. Indeed, in many cases, empowerment and liberation are not explicit goals at all. Seemingly, the only explicit goals are day-to-day survival and, especially, the affirmation of relationships as essential to that survival. This affirmation is manifested in all those seemingly insignificant ways in which we love, care for, and embrace other persons. Central to the struggle for survival and relationships, moreover, is the community's life of faith, which also, at least on the surface, seems little related to social transformation.

---

32. On the ambiguity in liberation theologians' notion of praxis, see Chopp, *The Praxis of Suffering*, pp. 60–62; Hector Borrat, "Liberation Theology in Latin America," *Dialog* 13 (Summer, 1974): 172–76; and Robert Kress, "Theological Method: Praxis and Liberation," *Communio* 6 (Spring, 1979): 113–34.

Praxis as Aesthetics

If the notion of praxis as social transformation suffers from the ambiguity inherent in the modern conflation of praxis and poiesis, what other categories might we look to in order to address this ambiguity? A possible alternative category, I would suggest, is present within the Latin American intellectual tradition itself. As an alternative to the modern instrumental notion of praxis, Latin American philosophers of the early twentieth century began to emphasize *aesthetics*, or aesthetic experience, as the key category for interpreting human action.

The understanding of human action as essentially aesthetic is an important part of the intellectual heritage of U.S. Hispanics and Latin Americans. Before the emergence of theologies and philosophies of liberation in Latin America in the late 1950s and early 1960s, the most influential philosophical current in Latin America was that of the aesthetic philosophies. The preeminent public figure within this current was the Mexican statesman-philosopher José Vasconcelos (1882–1959). His systematic development of the concepts of *mestizaje* and *La Raza Cósmica* (The Cosmic Race) has made his ideas especially influential among Mexican Americans and, indeed, all U.S. Hispanics who have found in these concepts important sources of identity and empowerment.[33] Though Vasconcelos did not explicitly and systematically address the question of praxis, implicit in his many writings on aesthetics and mestizaje is a very definite understanding of the nature of human action. He proposes an aesthetic understanding of human action over against the instrumentalist understanding of European and Latin American positivists.

The guiding ideology of early twentieth-century Mexico was Comtean positivism: the assertion that human beings can know only that which is verifiable through empirical scientific analysis. The only acceptable criterion of rationality is that of empirical observation: all that we can know is what we can observe and verify empirically, with scientific certainty and objectivity. Through scientific observation of particular empirical data, we are able to establish logical correlations among them, which in turn allows us to formulate general hypotheses about the laws that govern the world. It is these logically-derived laws which, for positivism, are the only authentic form of human knowledge. This knowledge is then used to manipulate and arrange society in such a way that it will conform to these laws and, thus, function rationally and efficiently. Auguste Comte coined the word "sociology" to refer to the science of society, which operates according to its own political, economic, and ethical laws.

In positivism, then, reason is reduced to the process of establishing *logical* connections between particular observations in order to arrive

---

33. See, e.g., Guerrero, *A Chicano Theology*, pp. 19–20, 118–65.

at the underlying laws. Presupposed in these two axioms of positivism is a *separation* between subject (the scientific observer) and object (the data being observed), between the subject-as-observer and the external world. This separation is what makes possible the logical *manipulation* of the external world in order to organize it in accordance with the natural laws. When applied to politics, positivism then calls for the rational planification and reorganization of society. The result is the modern technocratic society, where every aspect of life is planned and organized according to scientific, technological criteria. Comtean positivism is thus one of the most important examples of the modern instrumentalist understanding of human praxis. In positivism, human action is valued and judged by its usefulness for bringing about the rational, planned society.[34]

The Mexican dictator Porfirio Díaz was a leading exponent of positivism. He attempted to structure Mexican society around his party of *Científicos*, learned "experts" schooled in the political and economic laws of society. To this positivism was added a Darwinian influence: among the laws of society are the laws of evolution and natural selection. These latter ensured, of course, that the privileged elite in Mexico would be favored by the government, since such favoritism would simply be a recognition of the law of natural selection.[35]

Positivism was the air that all Mexican intellectuals breathed at the turn of this century, but, by 1909, an anti-positivist movement was beginning to gain strength. In that year, a group of young politicians and intellectuals came together to found the *Ateneo de la Juventud*. Among its founding members were Antonio Caso, Diego Rivera, and José Vasconcelos. This group saw positivism as the ideological rationale perpetuating Díaz's dictatorship, the increasing Anglicization of Mexico, and the expansion of U.S. economic interests. The belief in the natural superiority of the white Anglo Saxon and European was justifying the destruction of the Mexican people and culture. During the revolution of 1910, the *Ateneo* began to draw up plans for the cultural rehabilitation of the country after the revolution.[36]

As a result of his political opposition to Díaz, Vasconcelos was exiled to the United States. After Díaz was finally overthrown, Vasconcelos

---

34. On positivism, see, e.g., Auguste Comte, *A Discourse on the Positive Spirit* (London: Reeves, 1903); idem, *Auguste Comte and Positivism: The Essential Writings* (Chicago: University of Chicago Press, 1983); and Anthony Giddens, *Positivism and Sociology* (London: Heinemann, 1974).

35. See Leopoldo Zea, *Apogeo y decadencia del positivismo en México* (México, DF: El Colegio de México, 1944); and Francisco Bulnes, *El Verdadero Díaz y la revolución* (México, DF: Editora Nacional, 1967).

36. John Haddox, *Vasconcelos of Mexico: Philosopher and Prophet* (Austin: University of Texas Press, 1967), p. 5.

returned to Mexico and, in 1920, was appointed Minister of Education. A leading proponent of public schools, he is considered the father of public education in Mexico. After leaving that office, he was unsuccessful in other campaigns for public office, including his campaign for the presidency of Mexico in 1929.[37]

The influence of positivism was not limited to Mexico, but extended throughout Latin America.[38] Likewise, the opposition was not limited to Mexico. Thoughout Latin America, politicians and intellectuals sought an alternative paradigm for understanding and organizing their societies. The new philosophies which emerged in Latin America as alternatives to positivism were the *aesthetic* philosophies. Among the leading exponents of the aesthetic philosophies were not only the members of the *Ateneo* in Mexico, but also scholars such as Alejandro Deústua in Peru and José Pereira da Graça Aranha in Brazil.[39]

In 1918, Vasconcelos published his *Monismo estético*, in which he hails the emergence of the aesthetic philosophies, "philosophies grounded no longer in pure reason, nor in practical reason, but in the mystery of aesthetic judgment. It is in the *special pathos of beauty* that I look for the unifying principle, capable of participating in the three forms of action, intellectual, moral, and aesthetic."[40] By the "special pathos of beauty," Vasconcelos means the "empathic fusion" between subject and object that takes place in the aesthetic experience (i.e., the experience of beauty, or a work of art), wherein the person, or subject, loses him or herself in the experience. When listening to a particularly beautiful piece of music, for instance, the person is caught up in the music, becoming one with it; the subject no longer experiences him or herself as separate from and "over against" the music but as "fused" with the beautiful sound itself. Rational, logical thinking separates and dissects in order to manipulate

---

37. Ibid., pp. 5–6.

38. See, e.g., Leopoldo Zea, *Dos etapas del pensamiento en Hispanoamérica: del romanticismo al positivismo* (México, DF: Colegio de México, 1949); R. L. Woodward, *Positivism in Latin America, 1850–1900* (Lexington, MA: Heath, 1971); Oscar Terán, *En busca de la ideología argentina* (Buenos Aires: Catálogos Editora, 1986); Mário Dias Ferreira dos Santos, *Filosofias da afirmação e da negação* (São Paulo: Logos, 1965).

39. See, e.g., Alejandro Deústua, *Estética general* (Lima: Imprenta E. Rávago, 1923; idem, *Estética aplicada: Lo bello en el arte: Escultura, pintura, música (apuntes y extractos)* (Lima: Imprenta Americana, 1935); idem, *Estética aplicada: Lo bello en el arte: la arquitectura (apuntes y extractos)* (Lima: Compañía de Impresiones y Publicidad, 1932); idem, *Estética aplicada: Lo bello en la naturaleza (apuntes)* (Lima: Rivas Berrio, 1929); José Pereira da Graça Aranha, *A esthetica da vida* (Rio de Janeiro, 1920).

40. José Vasconcelos, *Obras Completas*, 4 vols. (México, DF: Libreros Mexicanos Unidos, 1958–61), 4:16.

the external world; aesthetic judgment becomes one with the external world in order to enjoy and celebrate it.

For Vasconcelos, human interpersonal action is fundamentally aesthetic action. Only through an aesthetic, empathic fusion with another can I truly relate to the other as a person. In order to "relate" to another person, logical reason must reduce his or her life to a concept, a number, or a mere physical body moving through space. Logical reason can only deal in abstract generalities, so it is forced to turn human life into such an abstraction.

To relate to another as a person, I must "fuse" with him or her, that is, we must enter into each other not only as physical bodies—though, as we will see, this will also be essential—but as whole human beings. Thus, the only way we can "fuse" with each other is affectively, through empathy—in the same way as we "fuse" with a beautiful sunrise, or a beautiful piece of music. We can know objects through observation and logical analysis, but we can only know human persons through empathic love. "The law of aesthetics," suggests Vasconcelos, "is neither quantitative and causal, as in physics, nor utilitarian, as in simple ethics, nor logical, as in the rational process. The law of aesthetics is the law of love. . . . Not only is this compenetration through love not understandable rationally, it contradicts reason, whose mission is to develop an analysis, to create barriers with respect to every particularity."[41]

Thus, the inherently relational character of the person cannot, ultimately, rest on logical, rational, or even ethical grounds. Both reason and ethics are rooted in aesthetics, since the source of our desire to know and our desire to be good is the fundamental human desire for unity and identity.[42] Moreover, by their nature, neither logical rationality nor ethics can adequately mediate the experience of a living, feeling human person: "Rational understanding constantly follows the process of converting the personal into the impersonal, and this, properly speaking, is not to understand but to misunderstand."[43] In order to think about a person, I must turn him or her into a concept. In order to think about myself, I must turn my own life into a concept, called "Roberto Goizueta," which I can now analyze. What I am, in fact, analyzing is not my concrete, ongoing life itself, but my own *concept* of that life.[44] Logical reason cannot relate directly to life itself; it can only deal with concepts.

---

41. Ibid., 3:1304–5.

42. Ibid., 3:1284.

43. Ibid., 3:1210, 1214.

44. Vasconcelos' distinction here is analogous to the distinction which Bernard Lonergan draws between the subject-as-subject and the subject-as-object; see, e.g., Lonergan, *Method in Theology*, pp. 8–15. See also my *Liberation, Method and Dialogue: Enrique Dussel and North American Theological Discourse* (Atlanta: Scholars Press, 1988), pp. 108–111.

Likewise, ethics is not concerned with human action as an end in itself, but examines human action teleologically, with a view to its end: "All ethics implies the study of a norm imposed on that which in life is loose, ungovernable, chaotic, in order to transform it in accord with a redemptive end or aspiration."[45] In order to judge human action in light of its ends, ethics must, like logical reason, distort life: it must break down life, which is a dynamic, ongoing, fluid reality, into discrete "acts" which are then analyzed according to ethical criteria. Life itself—understood as a verb ("living") rather than as an object of analysis—is never ethical or unethical, rational or irrational: life simply *is*. Life itself is not a noun, but a verb: "beyond reason [*más allá de la razón*], not only beyond good and evil, in the fullness of a joy that neither reasons nor inquires but enjoys and, in the fullest sense of the word, *is*."[46]

While ethics and logical reason can help us to live a *better*, more *useful*, and more *reasonable* life, these can never be identified with life, or human action itself, since life is never reducible to either discrete acts or logical concepts:

> Just as the objects observed by the mind confirm our ideational representations and their relationships, the same objects, submitted to ethical judgment, provide intuitions of usefulness or uselessness. . . . Consistent with their experiential criteria, ethical values possess a more concrete reality, richer in substance, than that of ideas . . . yet ethical values are themselves surpassed by an aesthetic moment and a moment of conformation when these values become abstract. Thus, the ancient Platonic-Socratic trilogy, Goodness, Truth, and Beauty, as identical, corresponds to a gradation that proceeds as follows: Truth, Goodness, and Beauty, in ascending order.[47]

For Vasconcelos, then, logical reason is the most abstract human operation. The purest form of logical rationality is mathematics, which reduces human life to the highest form of abstraction, the number. Ethics is less abstract, since it concerns concrete human acts, rather than ideas or concepts. The least abstract, however, is aesthetics, which concerns not the separate acts, but the living itself. Thus, reason is superseded by ethics, but ethics is superseded by love, i.e., aesthetic, affective union. "In its highest form, ethics is aesthetics, that is, service out of love, not out of duty; service with joy and life, action as enjoyment, the final stage."[48] Both logical reason and ethics distort life by turning it into a "thing," whether a

---

45. Vasconcelos, *Obras Completas*, 3:766.
46. Ibid., 3:1458.
47. Ibid., 3:776.
48. Ibid., 3:1225.

concept or an "act." Only the aesthetic sense allows us to live life itself, as an end in itself rather than as some-thing to be understood or some set of acts with an ethical purpose. If life has no other purpose than to *be,* then the highest form of life—the only true and good life—is the life of enjoyment, the life of celebration and play: "Once action loses sight of a measurable, concrete, and finite end, it ceases to be work and is trans-formed into recreation."[49] Play, recreation, and celebration are the most authentic forms of life precisely because, when we are playing, recreating, or celebrating we are immersed in, or "fused" with the action itself, and those other persons with whom we are participating. Thus, we are in-volved in and enjoying the living itself. When we are playing, recreating, or celebrating, we are not concerned with whether these actions are true or good; we are only concerned with participating in the process. Were we to "step back" from the action to ask ourselves whether the game or celebration is rational or ethically justified, we would have already dis-tanced ourselves from the action, turning it into an *object* of analysis.

Insofar as, by living and enjoying life as an end in itself, we become one with life, we also become one with God. Celebration becomes liturgy. To Vasconcelos, the human desire for aesthetic union with others is nothing less than "the yearning for communion with the divine nature."[50] At this point, abstract ideas and practical ethical norms give way to the concrete life of love, which is best represented not by doctrinal concepts or ethical imperatives but by concrete human lives: "Religious moralists penetrate much deeper into the essence of the ethical when they give us as a norm the conduct of an exemplary life, the life of Christ or the Buddha, before giving us the Christian revelation."[51]

These lives are not only rational and ethical but also corporeal. Unlike logical reason and ethics, which require abstraction from corporeality, the aesthetic sense is rooted in our bodiliness itself, since life is always cor-poreal. Our aesthetic union with others and God is always mediated by our concrete, historical bodies. Love is always, therefore, erotic love. "The law of Eros . . . is the law of the heart. And the law of Eros is, in sum, the law of aesthetics."[52] Though the aesthetic sense is rooted in our interior life, the life of the heart, this interiority is never disembodied. Our bod-ily, lived existence is inaccessible to logical reason or ethics. Neither, how-ever, is our interiority accessible to reason and ethics, for reason can only conceive love as a concept and ethics can only judge love as a series of discrete, external acts separate from the act-or.

Finally, what distinguishes the aesthetic sense from the rational and ethical is the fact that, only through empathic love is there the possibility

49. Ibid., 3:1296.
50. Ibid., 3:1137.
51. Ibid., 3:1318.
52. Ibid., 4:768–69.

of a genuine communion which also preserves the particularity, or uniqueness of the individual persons. By reducing living existence to concepts, logical rationality reduces the particular to the general: the particular human life to "human existence," or the particular person to "humankind." Again, the most extreme—and therefore the most properly "rational"—case is that of mathematics: each person is simply the number "1." (In "one person, one vote," we have suggested, each "one" is indistinguishable from any other "one.") The only unity possible for logical reason is, thus, an arithmetic unity, the aggregate sum of all the particulars. The universal is, literally, the sum of the particulars (e.g., a community is merely the sum of its individual members). And, since these particulars are all abstract concepts—e.g., all "ones"—the very particularity and uniqueness of each "one" is destroyed:

> The abstraction equates those which, by their nature, cannot be equated. The principle of identity affirms that A is the same as A. This is a postulate applicable only to abstractions. In the real world, every A is A and is not identical to any other A, even less so to any B whatever. . . . One cannot add red plus yellow; to express the abstract and numerical link between the two heterogeneous realities, red and yellow, we say they are two colors, but the artist is not content with the obvious generic definition. One already knows that these are two colors; what concerns us is the quality which makes their combination fruitful. It is impossible to reduce one to the other, through a process of abstraction, without prescinding from the qualities of each: in fact, by combining them we discover that they engender the color orange, etc. The task proper to the artist is that of exposing and opposing colors in order to achieve harmonious effects. Far from reducing one element to another, the artist becomes attached to their differences; red should remain red and yellow yellow.[53]

Likewise, "the artist does not search for universals, the sculptor does not think of man in the abstract; on the contrary, . . . he will make efforts to enhance and make more precise the characteristics and peculiarities which mark out, from among all men, the man whose individual constitution is to be set forth, a man of war, a Mars or a Socrates. . . . We know the failure of those sculptures which represent war or wisdom in the abstract, and the poor dramas which in English are known as Everyman and Everywoman."[54] Since logical reason must reduce reality, in all its diversity, to concepts and numbers, true diversity can be encountered only in concrete life itself—thus, only through the aes-

---

53. Ibid., 4:874–75.
54. Ibid., 3:1321–22; see also Haddox, *Vasconcelos of Mexico*, p. 31.

thetic sense. Only in lived experience is yellow distinguishable from red.

If unity is conceived in arithmetic terms, every unique human life becomes merely one among many factors of an equation. Thus, "to say that the whole is the sum of the parts is to confuse book-keeping with philosophy, the accountant's total with the whole of creation."[55] In so doing, we "forget the difference between inanimate objects and living subjects."[56] The result is that, again, we reduce human life to an object indistinguishable from any other object. Since all "1's" are equal, "1" person is indistinguishable from "1" automobile. It is then but a short step to treating human persons like objects and, conversely, treating objects like human persons: e.g., we discard elderly human persons as if they were obsolete cars, or we "trade in" our old spouses for newer models while, on the other hand, we "fall in love" with our automobiles, cleaning them, polishing them, protecting them, and caring for them with the greatest affection.

According to Vasconcelos, only the aesthetic sense is capable of mediating, or expressing a unity between *persons*. "The distinction between the spiritual individual and the physical particle, and between the abstract, general proposition and the universal reality comprised of concrete beings is, then, the beginning of the distinction between logic and aesthetics. The ancient and typical error of logical rationality is rooted in this confusion of terms, as a result of which it [logical rationality] functions identically with respect to the relations between things and the relations between subjects."[57] Objects can only "relate" to each other externally, like billiard balls, while subjects relate to each other through empathic compenetration. I can know a billiard ball by looking at it, holding it, and analyzing it, etc. I cannot, however, know my wife through these means; I may know information *about* her, but I will not know *her*. I may know what she looks like, what color hair she has, and how tall she is, but unless I enter into a relationship *with* her—unless I love her—I cannot know her. Thus, to treat subjects like objects is to ignore the interior dimension of human life, i.e., the emotional, affective, and spiritual dimension.

Far from extinguishing either the dynamism or the particularity of each human life, an aesthetic unity intensifies that dynamism and particularity. Authentic love between persons results not in the dissolution of the particular lives, but in the full flowering of each life in its own particularity and uniqueness. The aesthetic unity is a unity of others, an empathic fusion of two unique persons. This, for Vasconcelos, is precisely the definition of Christian love, God's love: "And every particle, even

---

55. Vasconcelos, *Obras Completas*, 4:867–68.
56. Ibid., 3:1208–9.
57. Ibid.

the most humble, is incorporated into a whole which does not deper-
sonalize it, but increases and enlivens its essence. This is what we call
the aesthetic unity as opposed to the logical unity, the world of the spirit
as opposed to the world of pure intellect."[58] The aesthetic unity is mediated by each particular.

We discover the whole, or the universal, not by adding up the particulars, but by entering fully into their very particularity, *within which* we
will encounter their universal significance: "To know is to recognize the
specific phenomenal activity that, in each case, reveals to us the
Universe."[59] In the words of the poet William Blake, we can "see a world
in a grain of sand and a heaven in a wild flower."[60]

One example of this distinction is that of conjugal love, or marriage.
How would one know what the "universal experience of marriage" is all
about? What is marriage? According to the quantitative, arithmetic criteria of logical rationality, in order to know the meaning of marriage we
should marry as many persons as possible. Thus, the most knowledgeable person would be whoever has had the greatest number of particular
spouses and has experienced the greatest number of particular marriages
(perhaps a polygamist). According to the qualitative criteria of the aesthetic sense, however, in order to know about "marriage," an abstract
universal, one must enter fully into the depths of one particular marriage,
engage one's life completely in the life of one other particular person, and,
there—in that very *particularity*—uncover the *universal* meaning and significance of marriage. It is thus, out of one's own intensely-experienced,
particular marriage that one will be able to relate to and identify with the
particular marriages of other persons. Likewise, a man will understand
"women" better by living a profound relationship with his wife than by
having as many relationships as possible. It is through his particular relationship, or empathic fusion with this particular person that he is awakened to the inherently relational character of *all* human persons. It is by
enjoying and celebrating this particular relationship, his marriage, as an
end in itself that he is awakened to the value of all life, all human action,
as an end in itself. It is through his living interaction with this one other
person that he discovers who he is, and who all of us are.

For Vasconcelos, finally, the aesthetic sense is much more than a philosophical category; it is the source of the Latin American culture and people. The Latin American people are the progeny of the empathic fusion
which occurred historically between the Spanish culture and people, on
the one hand, and indigenous and African cultures and people on the
other. It was precisely through its openness to these "other" races and

---

58. Ibid., 3:1299.

59. Ibid., 4:888.

60. William Blake, *The Complete Poems*, ed. W. H. Stevenson (London:
Longman, 1989), p. 589.

cultures and its willingness to intermix and interrelate with them, that Spain gave birth to the Latin American mestizo people, *la raza cósmica.* This is the thesis Vasconcelos develops in his book *La Raza Cósmica,* published in 1925. Just as the aesthetic sense represents *"un salto de espíritu"* (a leap of the spirit) beyond the rational and ethical, so too does the Latin American mestizo community represent *"un salto de espíritu"* beyond homogeneous communities.[61]

Homogeneous communities impose unity by one of two means: exclusion or assimilation. Any other cultures will be either ostracized from the community, through exile, isolation, or outright extermination, or they will be forced to surrender their particularity in order to participate in the community. The homogeneous community thus always views itself as standing in opposition to and in competition with other communities. Vasconcelos saw the Anglo Saxon culture as the chief example of a homogeneous community. In North America, the Anglo Saxon people have created a "rational" society based on the extermination of Native Americans, the enslavement of blacks, and the isolation of these and other "minority" groups in reservations, ghettoes, and barrios throughout the United States.

The mestizo community, on the other hand, does not impose unity, but achieves it through empathic love. In so doing, the mestizo community affirms the identity of other persons as particular, unique, and different subjects (i.e., historical agents in their own right) who, as subjects, can be known only through love. The mestizo community is, by definition, open to mixing and interacting with other cultures and races without undermining the integrity of each particular culture and race: a mestizo is *both* Spanish and Aztec, or *both* Spanish and Nigerian. To deny either particular in either case would be to deny one's identity as a mestizo/a. For Vasconcelos, the chief historical example of the mestizo community is *la raza cósmica*:

> The central thesis of this book is that, increasingly, the different races of the world tend to mix, until they form a new human type. . . . Present circumstances favor . . . the development of interracial sexual relations, which lends unexpected support to the thesis that, for lack of a better term, I entitled: on the future Cosmic Race. It remains to be determined, however, if the unlimited and inevitable mixture is a fact advantageous to the development of culture or if, on the contrary, it will produce decadence, which now would no longer be merely national but global.[62]

---

61. Vasconcelos, *Obras Completas,* 2:908.
62. Ibid., 2:903–6.

As a mestizo race, the Latin American people have the responsibility of promoting a global mestizaje.

This implies, not a rejection of Latin American particularity, but a retrieval of its indigenous, African, and Iberian roots. The Anglo Saxons are incapable of carrying out such a historical mission since they "*committed the sin of destroying those races, while we assimilated them, and this gives us new rights and hopes of a mission without precedent in history* [italics in the original]." The historical reality of mestizaje is living proof that "precisely in the differences do we find the way; if we only imitate, we lose."[63] The mestizo/a is thus the bearer of humanity's future, for, by definition, the tradition of mestizaje "possesses a greater ability for sympathy with strangers," the very sympathy which is necessary for the formation of true community.[64]

Vasconcelos argues that this sympathy was at the heart of the Spanish conquest:

> This historical mandate begins to evidence itself in that abundance of love which enabled the Spaniards to create a new race with the Indian and the Black; dissipating [*prodigando*] the white stock through the soldier who gave birth to indigenous families, and Western culture through the missionaries who put the Indian in a condition to be able to enter the new age, the age of One World. The Spanish colonization created *mestizaje*; this indicates its character, specifies its responsibility, and defines its future. The English continued to mix only with whites and exterminated the indigenous peoples; they continue to exterminate them in the senseless economic battle, which is more efficient than armed conquest. This confirms their limitation and is the mark of their decline.[65]

The uniqueness of Latin American mestizaje resides in the fact that it issued from this "abundance of love"; it occurred not through "promiscuity" but through a "healthy aesthetic instinct," through the Spaniards' "officially sanctioned" openness to racial and cultural mixture.[66] Vasconcelos' interpretation of the Latin American experience of mestizaje in aesthetic categories thus led him to conclude that the conquest of the indigenous Indians by Spain was the model of empathic fusion.

If, in liberation theology, the identification of praxis with liberation contained latent ambiguities, Vasconcelos' interpretation of the Spanish conquest reveals the dangerous ambiguities inherent in his own project.

---

63. Ibid., 2:918.
64. Ibid.
65. Ibid., 2:918–19.
66. Grabriella de Beer, *José Vasconcelos and His World* (New York: Las Américas, 1966), pp. 305, 303.

In the following chapter, we will discuss these ambiguities in greater detail and suggest that, to address these lacunae, we should examine *the relationship between* the central insights of liberation theology, concerning the social transformative, or ethical-political character of praxis, and those of Vasconcelos, concerning the aesthetic character of praxis. As we flesh out the anthropological and theological implications of U.S. Hispanic experience, or praxis, we will draw upon these two key currents in our intellectual history. In so doing, we will also be entering into the centuries-old discussion about the nature of human action.

[5]

Beauty and Justice

Popular Catholicism as Human Action

In an attempt to address the ambiguity latent in the view of human action as liberating praxis, or social transformation, Latin American liberation theologians as a whole have been paying increased attention to the significance of popular religion for theological method. Indeed, whenever the social transformative character of human praxis is considered foundational for theology, popular religion will tend to be viewed with suspicion, as a form of praxis that, because often explicitly apolitical, cannot contribute to liberation and may, in fact, function as an obstacle to its realization. The increased attention to popular religion in Latin American liberation theology represents an important safeguard against this tendency and, to some extent, parallels the methodological attention paid to popular religion in U.S. Hispanic theology.[1]

The attention paid to popular religion has the effect, moreover, of underscoring the aesthetic dimension of praxis, so systematically developed and articulated by Vasconcelos (and thus represents a retrieval of

---

1. As I indicated in the discussion of popular religion in chapter 2, where I cited a number of works by Latin American liberation theologians, there has been, from the beginning, a certain current within liberation theology which has stressed the importance of popular religion as *locus theologicus*. Indeed, liberation theologians' views of popular religion have extended from a suspicion of its liberative potential, on one end of the spectrum, to an insistence on its centrality in the liberation process, on the other. Across the spectrum, however, the principal methodological category (i.e., the principal criterion for judging popular religion) remains that of "liberation." On the distinctions among the currents within liberation theology, see, especially, Scannone, "Enfoques teológico-pastorales," 262–71, and Candelaria, *Popular Religion and Liberation*. The point I make here is simply that, *as a whole*, Latin American liberation theologians are paying increased attention to popular religion (see Authur McGovern, *Liberation Theology and Its Critics* [Maryknoll, NY: Orbis Books, 1989], pp. 83–92).

an important aspect of the Latin American intellectual tradition, though in very different historical contexts and, consequently, in a critical manner). The symbols and rituals of popular religion are prime examples of the intrinsic value of beauty, and, hence, the intrinsic value of human life as beautiful, i.e., as an end in itself, for the goal of the community's participation in the stories, symbols, and rituals of popular religion is nothing other than that participation itself. The goal of the interaction among the participants, and the interaction between them and Jesus, Mary, and the saints, like that between Juan Diego and *la Morenita*, is nothing other than the interaction itself—which is to be enjoyed and celebrated. Popular Catholicism also represents the aesthetic character of human action in that popular Catholicism is perhaps the most important example of our U.S. Hispanic mestizaje. Popular Catholic symbols and rituals reflect an aesthetic, or "empathic fusion" of European, indigenous, and African elements. As we have already seen, for example, the narrative, symbols, and rituals surrounding Our Lady of Guadalupe combine both Catholic and Náhuatl elements; these are virtually inseparable.

For many U.S. Hispanic theologians popular religion has played a role similar to that played by liberation in Latin American liberation theology, namely, as *foundational praxis*, that paradigmatic human activity which grounds our theological reflection. In our attempt to do a theology grounded in the praxis of our U.S. Hispanic communities, we have often focused on popular religion as definitive of that praxis. If both Latin American liberation theologians and U.S. Hispanic theologians have tried to ground their theological reflection in the praxis of their respective communities, the former have emphasized the socio-political dimension of praxis (and hence the liberation struggle), while the latter have emphasized the racial-cultural dimension of praxis (and hence popular religion, the heart of U.S. Hispanic culture). This difference reflects, to some extent, the different socio-historical locations: the overwhelming *economic* poverty experienced by the people of Latin America, and the equally overwhelming sense of *cultural* alienation experienced by Latinos and Latinas in the United States.

If it is true that U.S. Hispanic theologians have tended to focus on the cultural dimensions of U.S. Hispanic experience, especially popular religion, what can the emphasis on popular religion—or, more specifically, popular Catholicism—contribute to our understanding of the nature of human praxis, or human action? Above, we saw how popular Catholicism reflects an underlying anthropology which views the person as 1) a sacrament 2) essentially and intrinsically related to others in community. These relationships 3) have intrinsic value as ends in themselves and, as such, 4) provide the person with his or her identity, or self, and an attendant sense of self-worth. This identity and self-worth, then, 5) empower the person to resist the dominant culture's attempts to destroy that identity through assimilation.

In what ways, then, can these aspects of popular Catholicism contribute to a more adequate understanding of human praxis, one which would avoid the dangers discussed above? We can begin to answer this question by observing that the five dimensions of the anthropology underlying popular Catholicism (listed above and discussed in chapter 3) reflect five corresponding dimensions of human praxis, or human action. As revealed in popular Catholicism, human action, or praxis is 1) sacramental; 2) essentially and intrinsically communal, or relational; 3) an end in itself; 4) empowering; and, therefore, 5) liberating.

Beauty as Revelatory: The Aesthetic Character of Human Action

In popular Catholicism, the people's action is mediated by physical symbols, such as the bread that is shared and the flowers placed on Jesus' corpse, by physical gestures, such as kissing the crucifix or kneeling alongside Mary, by physical movement and processions, by singing songs and playing musical instruments, and by the very physical effort exerted in preparing the church for the celebrations. Our relationship to God thus involves embodied *action* in the world; it is not merely a private sentiment or feeling. Neither is this embodiment merely a static, inert physical presence.

As always a concrete revelation of God (however beclouded and partial the revelation), human action can have no higher or more fundamental end: the fundamental end of human action—i.e., that which makes it "human"—is simply the action itself, the performance, the participation. For it is in the acting, in the performing, in the participation, in the living itself that God is revealed.

Therefore, the term sacrament refers not only to the revelation of God in creation, but also to the revelation of God in the person's embodied action in the world, in interaction and *participation*. This is typified by the San Fernando parishioner who played the role of a Roman soldier in the Good Friday procession. Reflecting afterward on his participation in the procession and crucifixion, he remarked: "Every year, the procession and crucifixion are basically the same. Every year I participate and, several times, I've played the part of one of the soldiers who crucify Jesus. I know the part almost by heart. And yet, each year when the time comes for me to pound the nails into Jesus' feet, I feel chills running down my spine and tears come to my eyes." God is revealed in the doing, in the active participation, in the hammering of the nails. It is in the act of walking alongside Jesus and all the others on the Via Dolorosa, and in the act of hammering the nails into Jesus' feet, that this man encounters God—in the most concrete, physical way possible. The only end, or goal, of the man's action is simply the action itself. What makes the man's participation sacred is not the end result, i.e., the completion of the drama, but his active involvement in the evolution of the drama. That is why, though he clearly knows how the story will end, he continues to find it revelatory—because the revelation occurs not at the end, but in the process itself, in the acting itself, in the performance itself. Consequently, his relationship with God is re-enacted whenever he participates in the ritual.

The same is true of all the other participants: the singers, the musicians, the clergy, the children who joyously run down the aisles tossing flower petals during the Easter Vigil, the women who scrupulously dress Mary and Mary Magdalen, the men who proudly prepare the Calvary scene early Friday morning, the mothers who lovingly raise their little infants' lips to the body of the Crucified, etc., etc. God is revealed less in the song than in the singing and playing, less in the sermon than in the preaching, less in the bread than in the breaking and sharing of the bread, less in the flowers than in the placing of the flowers on Jesus' tomb, less in the flower petals than in the children's running through the aisles while tossing the petals into the air, less in the figures of Mary and Mary Magdalen at the foot of the cross than in the act of dressing and preparing them, less in the Calvary scene than in setting up and preparing the Calvary scene, less in the crucifix than in approaching and kissing the crucifix . . . and, therefore, less in the resurrection, the end result, or "goal" of Jesus' life, than in the passion, the living of that life itself.

Turning once again to the Guadalupe story, we see that Juan Diego comes to appreciate the intrinsic, absolute value of his own life *in the course of his interaction* with the Lady of Tepeyac, his uncle, and the bishop. Juan Diego thus comes to value himself as a full-fledged historical subject, a person, only gradually and only *as* he interacts; not at the end of his interaction, as its "product." His sense of self-worth as a person emerges and develops *in* his actions, as their *by*product. Juan Diego becomes a person *as* he interacts with the Lady. He seeks nothing from his relationship with *la Morenita* except the relationship itself. In so doing, he comes to appreciate the intrinsic value of his own life—by appreciating the intrinsic value of his relationship with *la Morenita*. Juan Diego never sets out to achieve liberation (as an end result of his interaction with the Lady); at the outset, his sense of worthlessness precludes him from even conceiving the possibility that he might one day be able to speak to the bishop on an equal footing. He does not view liberation as a *goal* of his actions; given his initial deprecatory self-understanding, he *cannot* even conceive that, some day, he would be the invited guest of the bishop in the bishop's palace. He cannot conceive that, some day, he would dare to disobey the Lady of Tepeyac. At the outset, all that he knows is that *he wants to be with her*, and with his uncle. He wants to walk with them, to interact with them. *In the process*, he affirms and recognizes himself as a full human person, a historical subject, i.e., he is liberated.

U.S. Hispanic popular Catholicism reflects an understanding of human action as, above all, an aesthetic *performance*, an aesthetic praxis. All of the above actions are "useless," that is, they do not produce anything. More precisely, they are not undertaken primarily *in order to* achieve a result. Their value to the participant derives from the fact that these are not fundamentally the actions of one individual by him or herself, but actions *between* him or her and God, Jesus, Mary, the saints, and the other members of the community, both living and dead. Indeed, the very sacramentality of human action, as the active presence of God in the world, implies a relationality between God and world. Since a relationship is never a static reality, but a dynamic, developing interaction, God's sacramental relationship to us is embodied most fully, not in "the person" *per se*, but in the *acting* person. And because human action is always *inter*-action, it is always—even in our most private moments—relational. If community is an intrinsic aspect of my identity as an individual person, then anything I do has implications for those communities which have formed me and which I, in turn, help form; even in my most "private" moments, I am responsible to those communities and hence, ultimately, to the entire human and divine community, in which I necessarily participate.

The conscious choice to enter a relationship, however, may be made for a wide variety of reasons. One may have some emotional need that requires satisfaction through a relationship with another, or one may seek to use another to attain some desired goal. In such cases, human relationship can become a form of poiesis, or productive action, whose end is extrinsic; relationship here is merely a means to achieve some external end. While poiesis, or production, is a necessary aspect of human life, it does not *define* human action; a helpless, newborn infant suckling at his or her mother's breast and a mentally-ill homeless man wandering the streets alone are as much human beings as is the most successful entrepreneur. What *defines* human action as such is praxis, or *interpersonal* action, i.e., relationship. Even hermits are defined by the relationships which have formed them as persons and which they, thus, carry with them into the desert.[2] The most fundamental of these is, of course, the interpersonal relationship with God.

All the above examples, as well as many others that could be adduced, reflect the U.S. Hispanic understanding of religion as the living out of our relationships with each other and with God, Jesus, Mary, the saints, etc. Religion is, by definition, "*re-ligio*," or a *binding* back. By definition, then, religion *is* relationship, or relationality. The end of religion is nothing other than the living out of this relationality. This is nowhere more evident than in U.S. Hispanic popular Catholicism, wherein the community lives out and celebrates its relationships. Popular Catholicism is the liturgical celebration of life as an end in itself, life as *praxis*.

---

2. See Thomas Merton, *New Seeds of Contemplation* (New York: New Directions, 1961).

To suggest that popular Catholicism is the liturgical celebration of life, or embodied action, as an end in itself is to underscore the aesthetic character of human praxis. Precisely *as* embodied, human praxis is also beautiful. As a "yearning for communion with the divine nature," this beauty is the sacrament, or mediation of God's presence among us. If Tridentine Western theology stressed the fact that God is known in the form of the True (Doctrine), and liberation theology that God is known in the form of the Good (Justice), U.S. Hispanic theology stresses the fact that God is known in the form of the Beautiful.

A central theme of the Guadalupe story is the revelatory power of beauty. The story itself begins with music, the singing of the birds, and ends with flowers, the roses that Juan Diego takes to the bishop. The extended dialogues in which the Lady identifies herself as Mary are circumscribed by symbols of beauty which make that identification credible for Juan Diego. If Juan Diego believes what Mary tells him, it is not because her statements are self-validating or self-evidently true, but because they are preceded by beautiful, heavenly music and corroborated by beautiful, fragrant roses. The truth of Mary's statements is mediated by and revealed in the beauty of music and the flowers. Without the singing birds and the fragrant flowers, Juan Diego would not have encountered Mary and, even if he had, would not have believed her. It was in the music and the flowers that he knew her. Here, interpersonal action is defined and mediated by beauty. In the world of the Nahuas, beauty *is* truth. To know beauty is to know the truth; it is to know God.

If one defines human interpersonal action in aesthetic rather than instrumental categories, the understanding of praxis changes radically. As we have seen, in an instrumental relationship, there is always a subject, the "actor," and an object, that which is "acted upon" by the subject in order to achieve a desired result. When human action, i.e., the *interaction of subjects with* each other, is itself modeled after the instrumental, productive relationship of subject to object, one of the subjects is necessarily reduced to the status of an object controlled and manipulated by the subject to achieve some desired result. In this reduction of human praxis to poiesis, the ego, or subject, is the only active agent, with everyone else in his or her surroundings being reduced to mere instruments of the ego's designs. This, indeed, is the nature of the technological, or productive relationship. The subject must be in control of his or her environment in order to utilize it for the achievement of the desired end, whether that end be financial profitability or social transformation. Furthermore, this relationship of control presupposes a *distance* between the subject and object, which allows for such manipulation: I can only use a hammer if it is "out there," away from me, an object which I can grab with my hand and manipulate. Likewise, instrumental notions of social transformation tend implicitly to regard "the poor," "social structures," and "society" as abstract categories and objects which can be manipulated—by the social reformer, bureaucrat, or revolutionary—to achieve the desired result of "liberation."

However noble the ends of human action, if those ends are viewed as achieved *by means of* praxis, or human action, the value of human action will tend to be predicated upon that action's ability to bring about those ends. Human life then is no longer its own end; now it becomes but a means to another end, e.g., the achievement of a more just society. The ethical value of the ends themselves is ultimately irrelevant: the Spanish bishop was convinced that he had Juan Diego's best interests in mind. Even the most ethical ends, if understood as mere products of human action, will result in the instrumentalization and objectification of human persons. This is true also in the context of the individual person's life: whenever we view our personal lives as "projects" which we undertake (e.g., to "make" ourselves better persons, more successful persons, healthier persons, happier persons, etc.), we will tend to view our lives as *objects* which we work *upon* and mold (as we might mold a statue) in order to achieve the desired result. Our lives then become mere *products* of praxis, an end result for which we strive by means of our activity in history.

Social and personal improvement are certainly desirable goals. Paradoxically however, if we view human life as but a means to those noble goals, we will never attain them. If our goal is a just society, where all human persons are valued, affirmed, and loved as ends in themselves, as genuine "others," we cannot arrive at that goal through an instrumentalization of persons which contradicts the very goal itself. At its most basic level justice, like happiness, is not a product but a concomitant, or *by*product, of human life when that life is lived and valued as an end in itself. Like human happiness in general, social justice and personal growth or transformation are not directly-intended "products" of the "work" the individual person undertakes respectively "on" society, or "on" himself or herself. Rather, these are but *by*products of the person's interaction with *others*. In short, the only justice and the only true self-improvement or personal growth is that which is the unintended (directly, at least) consequence of the person's active *love* of others. This is simply another way of expressing the paradox of the cross.

Celebration becomes possible only when we cease making a project of our lives and our world. Workaholics, for example, are persons who believe they can achieve personal happiness by means of their action in the world. In the process, praxis, or life becomes little more than an instrument to be used to achieve that "happiness." The inevitable, ultimate result will be a life of *un*happiness—for the workaholic and all those around him or her. Likewise, any social movement whose goal is the creation of a more just society invariably undermines that goal if, in the process, persons come to be valued only or primarily in terms of their contribution to social transformation. This was a key failure of communist and state socialist societies, which assumed that the just society or the "New Man" are goals, or products, that can be "achieved" through human action in the world. Thus understood, human action is reduced to the act of technical manipulation in which human life (i.e., the person) is defined as an instrument of the revolutionary process. The value of human praxis is then judged on the basis of one single criterion: Does it promote the revolution? We very well know what happened to those human lives which were judged to be *counter*-revolutionary.

In sum, the achievement of freedom and justice, whether at the personal or social level, will be impossible if freedom and justice are viewed primarily as products of our efforts rather than as, fundamentally, implicit byproducts or concomitants of human lives affirmed and valued as ends in themselves. Only if and when our intersubjective relationships—as lived in our families, communities, and institutions—reflect such an affirmation will we have true freedom and justice.

Conversely, the clearest criterion for judging whether, in a particular society, human praxis has been instrumentalized is that society's treatment of its most "useless" and "impractical" persons, for example, the elderly, children, the handicapped, the poor, the unemployed, the terminally ill, the homeless. When life is valued, not as an end in itself, but as a means to the achievement of some other end, those persons unable or unwilling to contribute to that achievement will inevitably be marginalized, excluded, and destroyed. In a capitalist society, those unable or unwilling to contribute to economic growth and profitability will be marginalized; in a Marxist society, those unable or unwilling to contribute to the revolutionary transformation of society will be marginalized. When human life is not valued as an end in itself, human beings are objectified, turned into mere instruments for achieving some desired result.

As Vasconcelos maintains, the aesthetic relationship is of a very different kind. When we are in the presence of beauty, we *lose* our control and are swept up into the experience. Upon hearing the gorgeous singing of the birds, Juan Diego *was compelled* to follow the sound to its origins; he *was compelled* to interrupt his journey. He was no longer in control of his environment: the birds had as much control of the situation as he did. Indeed, he became one with the music, being swept along by the beautiful sounds. Here, the birds function as "subjects" not only acted upon by Juan Diego but, also, acting upon him: an *inter*relationship is established.

If praxis as poiesis implies control and distance, then, praxis as aesthetics implies a surrender of control and, in the words of Vasconcelos, an empathic fusion. If the former implies a subject-object relationship, the latter implies a subject-subject relationship. The aesthetic model first revealed in the Guadalupe story when Juan Diego hears the singing of the birds then becomes the model for Juan Diego's own relationship with *la Morenita*. As he follows the beautiful music, Juan Diego hears a soft voice calling to him and, again, is drawn instinctively to the beautiful voice. At its source, he finds a woman of radiant, glowing beauty. Again, he is captivated by beauty.

In the light of these different notions of praxis, one might go so far as to say that the remainder of the story becomes an account of Juan Diego's conversion from a technological, or instrumental understanding of human action to an aesthetic understanding. In the beginning, his surrender to her beauty and the beauty of the birds' music had become the basis for his empowerment as a person. The sign of this new person, some*one* who could confront the bishop as one person to another, would now be another symbol of beauty, the fragrant roses. The paradigm of human action would no longer be Juan Diego's initial, inauthentic "relationships" with the bishop and Mary, but would now be the later, transformed, and therefore genuine relationships with them. These relationships would themselves be mediated by the experience of beauty: the mellifluous singing of the birds, the radiant countenance of the Lady, and the sumptuous fragrance of the roses.

By interpreting the Guadalupe story as an account of one person's (and therefore one people's) conversion from an instrumental understanding of human praxis, where he was the "instrument," to an aesthetic understanding of praxis, we begin to see the important implications of this shift for our interpretation of the nature of human action. First, an understanding of praxis as aesthetic, or aesthetic praxis, makes possible a retrieval of the notion of praxis as self-finalized activity, or interpersonal activity as an end in itself. Therefore, secondly, the notion of aesthetic praxis precludes any objectification or instrumentalization of human life. Thirdly, whereas instrumental praxis implies a distance between subject and object, aesthetic praxis implies an affective union between two subjects. Fourth, that union is possible only insofar as we relinquish our absolute control of the relationship. Fifth, that relinquishment of control in order to enter into a genuine union with another becomes, paradoxically, the place where we discover our subjectivity, our freedom as unique persons capable of *inter*acting with other persons.

This freedom is at the same time a freedom *for* relationship and a freedom *from* the need to control the other. Only when we are freed from the anxiety created by the need to control others, or the need to be controlled by others, are we truly free. Thus, the highest form of aesthetic praxis becomes the act of celebration, wherein is affirmed the intrinsic value of human life as an end in itself. Whether in the eucharistic liturgy, the Good Friday procession, the Guadalupe celebration, "*el día de los muertos,*" the fiesta, or the *quinceañera*, the "useless," unproductive act of celebration is the aesthetic act *par excellence.*

When human action is instrumentalized, one's "life" becomes a problem to be solved, a plan to be carried out, or a project to be realized. My life becomes an instrument to be utilized to bring about the desired result or transformation. Consequently, I become enslaved to the desired result,

anxious to plan all aspects of my life so as to ensure its successful conclusion. Convinced that I am free because I am "in control" of my life, I
am actually enslaved by my very need to control—as is, of course, any
other person who happens to get in my way, thereby becoming but one
more object in my path, one more instrument for the realization of my
plans.[3] Needless to say, any genuine celebration of life is impossible for
either person in this situation. Celebration implies relinquishment of control; it implies a willingness to "let go." It thus implies an affirmation of
life as an end in itself: regardless of its products, its results, its outcomes,
or its conclusion, life is good.[4] For Latinos and Latinas, all human action
is, at bottom, a liturgical celebration.

Vasconcelos' use of aesthetics as a category for understanding human
action is also important in that it reminds us that, as embodied, human
action or praxis always has an affective dimension. It is through this
affective dimension that we can relate most intimately with others.
Furthermore, it is this affective dimension of praxis that precludes the
instrumentalization of human action. Without affect, human praxis is simply physical matter in motion and is, thus, no different from the "interaction" of billiard balls or bowling pins. Praxis is not embodied in just *any*
physical body; it is embodied in *human* flesh. The action and interaction
of physical objects is not praxis but mere physical movement, for praxis
presupposes human subjects. Consequently, any adequate understanding
of *human* praxis must affirm the affective character of praxis as "empathic
fusion" and not simply the movement of physical bodies.

Like our human relationships, the interaction with Jesus, Mary, and
the saints always involves not simply a "doing" but also a "feeling." Thus,
the liturgical actions may express anger, frustration, and impatience alongside trust, faith, love, and joy. Where one's relationship to Jesus is viewed
primarily as an instrument (poiesis) for bringing about some desired end,
one will likely avoid expressing the former "negative" feelings for fear
that they would threaten the attainment of the desired result. When, on
the other hand, one's fundamental goal is the *relationship* itself, or the
praxis itself, the expression of these emotions will come naturally—as a
natural and intrinsic dimension of the relationship. The sharing of any
feelings, however "negative," implies and affirms *inter*action, connection,
and relationship with the other person; the failure to do so implies and

---

3. The master's paradoxical dependence on the slave (i.e., the master's own
enslavement) was, of course, hypothesized by G. W. F. Hegel in his famous analysis of the master-slave dialectic, developed in his *Phenomenology of Mind*, trans.
J. B. Baille (London: George Allen and Unwin, 1964).

4. As Victor Villaseñor writes at the end of his autobiographical story *Rain of
Gold*, "It's a good life, no matter what!" *Rain of Gold* (New York: Dell, 1991),
p. 562. (It bears repeating that this is not an abstract or naive belief but one born
in the struggle against evil and death.)

affirms estrangement and alienation. One can risk angering the other person (e.g., Jesus, Mary) by acting angry, upset, disappointed, frustrated, impatient, etc., only when one *knows* that one's relationship with the other is unassailable.[5]

Only when intersubjective human action is lived out as an end in itself, as something to be affirmed and celebrated regardless of the "outcome," can relationships become sources of individual empowerment and human liberation. Otherwise, they will become sources of oppression wherein persons use and manipulate one another for the sole purpose of self-gratification. The affective dimension of human action is a key safeguard against this distortion. Insofar as human intersubjective action is affective, its only end is to be enjoyed and celebrated. In themselves, human feelings are neither good nor bad, neither right nor wrong; they simply *are*. *All* human feelings affirm and reinforce relationship and community. Only two things can destroy community: apathy (lack of feeling), or the destructive *expression* of human feelings (through, for instance, violence).

Domestic Life as Human Action

Instrumentalized praxis results in a depreciation of the affective character of all human action. Where affect is excluded from our understanding of human action, so too will our most intimate interpersonal relationships be excluded from our understanding of what constitutes and defines human praxis. Where the intrinsic ends of praxis—human life as an end in itself—are depreciated, domestic life will likewise be depreciated, for the life of the home is the paradigm of self-finalized praxis, i.e., relationships as ends in themselves. Otherwise, domestic life itself will be reduced to poiesis, that is, an activity of re-production which mirrors and supports the public activity of economic production.

A further consequence of the modern instrumentalization of human action is thus the exclusion of domestic life, as an end in itself, from the sphere of human action. When this occurs, the value of a person's life

---

5. The supreme importance of relationship as an end in itself is illustrated repeatedly in the book *Rain of Gold*. At one point, for example, the young Mexican boy Juan Villaseñor is giving God a tongue-lashing because Juan's beloved mother has been reduced to begging on street corners in order simply to survive. "'Oh God! . . . What's wrong with You? I thought we had a deal! . . . No one on earth has ever gone to church to see You more than my dear mother! . . . AND I'M MAD AT YOU, GOD! . . . I can't wait for You anymore! You've had Your chance to help us again and again and You've failed! Do You hear me, You failed!' . . . He wiped the sweat from his face and, strangely enough, instead of feeling abandoned by God, he felt closer to Him" (ibid., pp. 150–51). By engaging God—even if in anger—Juan reinforces his relationship with both God and his mother.

comes to be determined by his or her productivity in the public sphere, that is, in the marketplace or political arena: to be a human being is to participate in public life because that is the locus of production. Conversely, domestic life and its "private" relationships are not only depreciated but, indeed, excluded from the notion of human praxis altogether: since what makes one's life "human" is one's public accomplishments, one's family or "personal" life is ultimately irrelevant to the understanding of human action or the human person. Only in public does a person "make" history; what he or she does in the home is ultimately outside the realm of human history, and therefore insignificant, except insofar as the home life supports the person's public, productive achievements.[6]

In light of the U.S. Hispanic understanding of praxis as rooted in family and community, and in light of the domestic roots of popular religion, such a depreciation or outright exclusion of domestic life from the definition of human praxis would be unthinkable for Latinos and Latinas. The depreciation of domestic life and "private" relationships is especially painful since, for many U.S. Hispanics like myself, it is precisely in those relationships that we have found a "space" within which to preserve our culture, our traditions, and our language in the face of a "public life" in which these are denigrated. Thus, to define human action as what we "accomplish" outside the home is to dismiss, for example, my mother's struggles to pass our Cuban traditions and the Spanish language to her children.

Domestic life, moreover, is a principal locus of Latino popular Catholicism. In popular Catholicism, the divine family is found at the very heart of the human family; the home altar and devotions are at the center of the family's life. Before these relationships are explicitly political, they are *human* relationships—even those with Jesus and Mary are *human* relationships. As such, they imply a level of interpersonal intimacy.

Thus, for Latinos and Latinas, the understanding of human action, or praxis, must include our active participation in *all* our relationships, both private and public, both interpersonal and institutional, both natural and supernatural. Praxis is life as lived, i.e., "lived experience."[7] Thus, praxis involves not only social and political action but also our common, "private," day-to-day struggle for survival in an alien environment. As Ada María Isasi-Díaz writes, "the struggle is my life."[8] Praxis is the daily struggle, daily life as an end in itself. From the perspective of Latinas,

---

6. The most horrific forms of abuse committed by our public heroes (usually males) against their wives and children in "private" life are thus tolerated and, indeed, excused as mere unfortunate side-effects of those heroes' history-making public accomplishments.

7. See Ada María Isasi-Díaz's definition of "lived experience" in *En la Lucha*, p. 173, where she notes the connection between human subjectivity, or agency, and human experience. Lived experience is not passive but active.

8. Isasi-Díaz, "A Hispanic Garden in a Foreign Land," 99.

mujerista and Latin American feminist theologians have reminded us that human action can never be reduced to simply that activity undertaken in the public sphere, which is to say, the traditionally male sphere of activity. To define human praxis exclusively in public, political or economic terms is to ignore the daily lives of millions of poor women, who have traditionally and historically been excluded from the public sphere of human activity.

A proper understanding of human action must, thus, embrace both public and private spheres of activity, and the intrinsic relationship between them:

> Until very recently analysis has laid greater stress on the direct changes in the socio-economic-political structure than on the other, also structural, dimension of daily life. . . . The emergence of women has been largely responsible for the discovery of daily life issues as crucial to the struggle. Although it is often regarded as autonomous, daily life is in fact at the center of history, invading all aspects of life.[9]

In daily life we learn to value human relationships as ends in themselves and, therefore, as liberating and empowering.

However, in daily life we can also experience distorted relationships in which individual lives become valued not as praxis but as poiesis, as mere instruments of production, whether the "products" are babies (re-production), sex ("*making* love"), or a home life which, rather than an end in itself, functions as an emotional fueling station where we recharge our psychic batteries so that we can return to the Real World of the market-place the next day.[10]

When praxis is identified with public life, *all* human action—domestic and public—will be judged by the criteria of production and, thus, by its usefulness. When we come to value products (i.e., commodities) above everything else, we will relate to our own lives and those of everyone else as mere objects. Human action, in both the home and the marketplace, will thus become but a means by which we manipulate these "objects" in order to achieve the desired result, that is, in order to maximize our economic, political, or emotional profits. When they cease being useful, human relationships then become as expendable and interchangeable as last year's automobile model. Thus, the modern notion of praxis-as-poiesis leads both to an exclusion of domestic life, as an end in itself, from our understanding of human action (since, in this view, human action cannot have intrinsic value) and to the reduction of domestic life to poiesis.

---

9. María Pilar Aquino, *Our Cry for Life: Feminist Theology from Latin America* (Maryknoll, NY: Orbis, 1993), pp. 38–9.

10. Ibid., p. 39.

A further, apparently contradictory, consequence is the idealization, romanticization, and sentimentalization of domestic life and community life. The life of community, whose paradigm is the life of the home, comes to be viewed through rose-colored lenses, as private, emotion-laden, unstructured, and informal face-to-face relationships. Society, or public life, is in turn viewed as rational, objective, impersonal, formal institutions and structures. Community is idealized vis-à-vis "society," and domestic life vis-à-vis public life.

This dichotomy ignores the structured, institutional character of *all* human praxis: the family is also an institution. When domestic life is idealized in this manner, the exercise of political and economic power will be seen as a purely public endeavor with no connection to family life, now thought to be the exclusive locus of human affective, interpersonal relationships (the "haven from a heartless world"). The society comes to assume that Christian faith and values are fine in one's private relationships—in the home and, perhaps, in church—but, once one steps out into the Real World of the "rat race" they are irrelevant and out of place. In that Real World, interpersonal relationships (praxis) must be subordinated to the demands of economic production (poiesis). "Home is where the heart is"; in the marketplace, however, one must leave the heart behind and live as a "rat" in order to survive, produce, and succeed.

As feminists, *mujeristas*, and womanists have demonstrated, however, this separation between private and public realms merely masks the underlying reduction of domestic life itself to but a form of poiesis, or production; the instrumentalization of the worker in the markeplace is replicated in the instrumentalization of women in the home.[11] The man who, in his job, is treated as merely an instrument of production will, in his home life, treat his wife as merely an instrument of re-production. If women are treated as sex objects in marketing and advertising programs, they will be treated as sex objects in the bedroom. If scantily-clad fifteen-year-old fashion models (by law, mere children) are used as instruments for selling the latest *haute couture* designs, we should not be surprised to see those same children used as instruments of adult sexual gratification in the home: by divorcing domestic life from public life, we are able to glorify the first form of instrumentalization as successful "marketing," while condemning the second as "child abuse." The same action which, when undertaken in the public arena, is applauded and celebrated is, when undertaken in domestic life, deprecated and condemned. In the public realm, the sexual objectification and instrumentalization of children is to be expected—and is well recompensed. In the domestic realm, the sexual objectification and instrumentalization of children is deemed both

---

11. For an explanation of why idealization and instrumentalization (oppression) are not, in fact, contradictory but, rather, mutually implicit, see also chapter 6 below.

immoral and illegal: the perpetrator would be convicted of child abuse or statutory rape.

In reaction to the instrumentalization of public life, and the consequent relegation of human interpersonal praxis to the home, Marx and liberation theologians have stressed the socio-political dimension of praxis as social transformation. Yet, in varying degrees, this emphasis has also presupposed and, therefore, perpetuated the modern private-public dichotomy. For Marx, domestic life *does not exist* as an arena of human self-realization independent from economic production; it is but one aspect (the *re*productive aspect) of economic production.[12] Marx thus made the same error in analyzing the family in capitalism as he did in analyzing religion: he observed its historical abuses and concluded that they were intrinsic to the monogamous family (and religion) *as such*.[13]

According to Marx, the origins of the division of labor, the source of all injustice, lie in the monogamous family, "where wife and children are the slaves of the husband."[14] This (unjust) division of labor characterizes not only the *bourgeois* monogamous family—though it is most obvious here. As the original, "natural" division of labor is the act of re-production, the historical, monogamous family is, *as such*, a form of "latent slavery."[15] "The division of labor," writes Marx in *The German Ideology*, "was originally nothing but the division of labor in the sexual act."[16] Consequently, when, in the classless society, the division of labor disappears, so too will the monogamous family: Marx proclaimed the "withering away" of not only the state and religion, but also the withering away of the monogamous family.[17] Ultimately, family ties are an obstacle to the individual's identification of his or her own personal interest with the general interest of the society. The private is subsumed within the public. This is simply the logical consequence of the reduction of human praxis to social transformation.

---

12. See, e.g., Tucker, *The Marx-Engels Reader*, pp. 147–63; Axelos, *Alienation, Praxis, and Technē*, p. 117.

13. On the internal inconsistencies of Marx's critique of religion, see Juan Luis Segundo, *The Liberation of Theology* (Maryknoll, NY: Orbis, 1976), pp. 13–19.

14. Tucker, ed., *The Marx-Engels Reader*, p. 159; see also Axelos, *Alienation, Praxis, and Technë*, p. 120.

15. Ibid., Tucker, *The Marx-Engels Reader*, pp. 150, 159.

16. Ibid., p. 158.

17. In his more extensive writings on the family, Engels insisted that Marx did not foresee the dissolution of the monogamous family in the classless society, but only its realization (ibid., p. 745). Nevertheless, what Engels describes as the "realization" of the monogamous family would seem to imply the subsumption of domestic life within public life since, for Engels, the sexual freedom of both men and women (historically available only to men) is a prerequisite of true monogamy: "With the passage of the means of production into common property, the individual family ceases to be the economic unit of society. Private

Whenever praxis is identified with social transformation, the tendency will be to emphasize the overriding importance of public, social action. While liberation theologians have not explicitly subordinated the family to society, implicit in the emphasis on praxis as social transformation is a relative depreciation of praxis as domestic life.[18] This, indeed, has been a central critique made of liberation theologians by Latin American feminists. The irony is that it is precisely in this "private," domestic sphere that many poor persons live most of their lives—since they have been excluded from participating in public life. Thus, this depreciation of domestic life as praxis has resulted historically not only in the marginalization of women's experience but also in the marginalization of popular religion as a *locus theologicus*, since a principal realm of popular religion is precisely the home. The increased attention now being paid to both women's experience and popular religion as sources for theological reflection thus represents an important attempt to acknowledge and address this lacuna.

Relationships in the family always take place within and are, thus, conditioned by socio-economic structures and relationships; if women's lives are viewed as mere instruments of male self-gratification, this distortion will affect the boardroom as much as the bedroom, and women will be abused in both. Yet neither is domestic life merely an extension of social relationships. For women *do* continue to struggle against and resist this instrumentalization. In their everyday struggle, in the marketplace *and* in the home, women are able to experience their lives as praxis, as inherently

---

housekeeping is transformed into a social industry. The care and education of the children becomes a public matter. Society takes care of all children equally, irrespective of whether they are born in wedlock or not. Thus, the anxiety about the 'consequences,' which is today the most important social factor—both moral and economic—that hinders a girl from giving herself freely to the man she loves, disappears. Will this not be cause enough for a gradual rise of more unrestrained sexual intercourse, and along with it, a more lenient public opinion regarding virginal honour and feminine shame? And finally, have we not seen that monogamy and prostitution in the modern world, although opposites, are nevertheless inseparable opposites, poles of the same social conditions? Can prostitution disappear without dragging monogamy with it into the abyss?" (ibid., pp. 745–46). Thus, according to Engels (interpreting Marx) the oppression of women in the family will only be resolved with the rejection of the bourgeois moral arguments for monogamy, which have served only to mask its true, unjust foundations in the division of labor. And that will only happen when there is no bourgeoisie, in the classless society.

18. As I will note in the next chapter, though Gustavo Gutiérrez never reduces praxis to social transformation (and, indeed, criticizes those Latin Americans who have), it is in his most recent writings that he has more explicitly and systematically broadened his understanding of praxis, especially in the context of his discussions of the preferential option for the poor.

valuable, instead of as mere poiesis. The public and the private are distinct though intrinsically interrelated dimensions of human praxis.

In the context of the modern Western private-public dichotomy, the identification of women with private, domestic life and men with public life legitimates the oppression of women by excluding them from participation in the public sphere and in those public decisions which invariably impact domestic life. When we ignore the structural character of even domestic life, we will ignore the way those structures so often replicate the public, social structures which oppress women: "The macro-world enters in, is engendered, and is perpetuated from generation to generation through, among other factors, everyday life."[19] "The work of women in the private, domestic sphere," observes Isasi-Díaz, "is seen as complementary, as necessary but determined by what the work and the workmen in the public sphere need. When women do venture into the public sphere, their work there is not recompensed on a par with men's work, nor does it relieve women of responsibilities in the domestic sphere. The situation is similar among Hispanic women but not identical to what happens to Anglo women."[20]

Despite the abuse and oppression too often suffered by Latinas in the family, the family remains an essential element of Latina identity and, thus, an important locus for mujerista theology: in the words of Isasi-Díaz, "maintaining our families is an intrinsic part of our struggle."[21] Where private and public life are separated, family and community leave the injustices of public life untouched; where public and private life are interrelated, they can be a counter-cultural source of resistance *against* those injustices.

Popular religion is the principal bond that unites public life and private life in U.S. Hispanic culture. Popular religion has roots in the home, in family devotions and practices, in what Virgilio Elizondo has called "*la religión de las abuelitas.*" But it is also a public religion, a religion not only of the home but also of the church, the plaza, and the streets: "Popular religion embraces all this in a single whole."[22] Because it is both public and private, popular religion also functions as a bridge between the public life and private life. This has been especially true for Latinas. Since women play such an important role in popular religion, their experience in religious leadership often functions as an introduction into public leadership roles. Isasi-Díaz gives an example: "For María the church organizations provide a way of helping her community, of exercising her leadership in the community. There is little or no difference between the reason why she became involved in politics and the reason

---

19. Raúl Vidales quoted in Aquino, *Our Cry for Life*, p. 40.

20. Isasi-Díaz, *En la Lucha*, pp. 18–19.

21. Ibid., p. 19.

22. Aquino, *Our Cry for Life*, p. 179.

why she is involved in church groups."[23] The same could be said of our U.S. Hispanic children and youth, whose participation is also central to our popular religion.

The church itself stands at the crossroads, or the intersection of private life and public life. It is the central place where domestic life encounters the life of the public square. This fact is often symbolized, in Latin America, by the placement of the church within or across from the town's main plaza. Thus, the same physical area is home to worshippers kneeling in private prayer, priests presiding at eucharistic liturgies, prostitutes walking the streets, and gamecocks displaying their battle skills—and, often, all at the same time.

San Fernando Cathedral is itself in the main plaza of San Antonio. Many of the celebrations at San Fernando take place not only in the church proper but also in the streets and main plaza outside the church. The celebrations "spill over" into the city, and the city "spills over" into the church. Moreover, these celebrations are extensions of domestic religious life. No attempt is made to keep the three worlds apart—home, church, public square. There is constant interaction among the three. This interaction itself symbolizes the U.S. Hispanic understanding of human action. At San Fernando, the boundaries between the life of the public square, the life of common worship, and the life of domestic worship are fluid and porous. Participants in the Good Friday procession include political and business leaders, along with everyone else. Among the lectors in the celebration of *las Siete Palabras* are not only clergy and lay members of the parish, but also civic leaders and television personalities.

Like all human action, however, the praxis of popular Catholicism is susceptible to distortion. Like all forms of human action, popular Catholicism can become a kind of "poiesis," i.e., an instrument for the attainment of some particular result. In some cases, like the ritual of making "*promesas*," or promises to Mary, the action may appear to be an action undertaken with a view to some external result, i.e., the benefit which the participant hopes to receive in exchange for his or her promise. Yet underlying the superficial appearance is another, more fundamental reality: by definition, every promise presupposes and reaffirms an active participation in a relationship of interdependence. Discussing the case of a woman who makes *promesas* to the Virgin, Isasi-Díaz observes: "Often it has been said that people like her feel they can buy God's favor. Is it not instead a matter of the reciprocity of the relationship?"[24] When, in another example, the Mexican mother of a *pandillero* approaches the crucified Jesus at the rear of San Fernando Cathedral, kneels to pray for her son, and, before leaving, carefully attaches a photograph of her son to the

---

23. Ada María Isasi-Díaz and Yolanda Tarango, *Hispanic Women: Prophetic Voice in the Church* (Minneapolis: Fortress, 1992), p. 53.

24. Ibid., p. 49.

cross, her actions are, indeed, meant to bring about some external result, i.e., the protection and safety of her son. However, what underlies the surface motive is an implicit affirmation of the relationships among herself, Jesus, and her son, as symbolized by the placement of the photograph next to Jesus. That this is true is evidenced by the fact that—even if only to protest—she will keep returning to the crucified Jesus whether or not her prayers are "answered."

Popular Catholicism as Mestizaje: The Insufficiency of Aesthetics

Popular Catholicism is also an aesthetic praxis in that it embodies the Latino mestizo heritage and identity. As a key aspect of our popular religion, "mestizaje" has been retrieved by U.S. Hispanic theologians in our attempt to specify the particular social location of our theologies. The historical experience of mestizaje, or "empathic fusion," has been central to the Latin American self-understanding and, *a fortiori*, to the self-understanding of those Latin Americans who, living in the United States, now face what Virgilio Elizondo has called our "second mestizaje."[25] As an aesthetic category, it specifies the racial-cultural context of our theology, which draws upon the cultural, religious, and ethnic symbols and rituals of our communities. Consequently, we cannot address adequately the aesthetic character of human praxis if we do not, at the same time, retrieve the particular manifestation which aesthetic praxis takes in the history of the Latino community, where—as Vasconcelos saw—aesthetics manifests itself, specifically, as mestizaje. It is precisely this connection—between beauty and mestizaje—which can, for U.S. Hispanics, become liberating, for it is this connection which will be denied by the dominant culture.

The U.S. Hispanic refusal to accept easy dichotomies between nature and supernature, between body and spirit, between the historical Jesus and the Christ of faith, between individual and community, between community and institution, between public and private, or, as we will see, between affect and intellect is made historically concrete in our experience of mestizaje: we instinctively see the world as a fusion of "both/and" rather than as a separation of "either/or." Growing up in a bicultural, biracial, and bilingual environment, Latinos and Latinas are accustomed to living between two perspectives, two interpretative horizons—or, more accurately, three: the indigenous or African, the Spanish, and the North American. To be a U.S. Hispanic is thus to live in a world where differences—in cultures, perspectives, and interpretative horizons—are not dichotomized: what is "other" or "different" is not viewed as contradictory or wrong vis-à-vis what is "the same."

---

25. See his books, *Galilean Journey* and *The Future is Mestizo*.

Within a culture that extols racial and cultural purity, otherness and difference will always be seen as a threat to that purity: one cannot be *both* black and white; one is *either* black or white. Students of U.S. legal history know to what extremes this country has gone to specify exactly how much "black blood" a person will be allowed to have before he or she can no longer be considered "white."[26] The concepts of *mestizaje* and *mulataje* are alien to the U.S. understanding of race: a person is either white or black. Once again, one encounters the modern, post-Enlightenment tendency to view reality—and, therefore, human beings—through dichotomous lenses.

The history of mestizaje makes such easy dichotomies much more difficult to uphold, since they belie our own lived experience. This is not to say that U.S. Hispanics are not prone to the same racist attitudes as Anglos, but such racism is a betrayal of our own identity and history in a way that it is not for assimilated Anglos. When Latinos and Latinas turn against indigenous cultures, or against African culture, or against European culture, or against Anglo American culture, we are turning against ourselves, since these are all a part of our own history and identity, our own aesthetic praxis. On the other hand, North Americans have always *identified* themselves *over against* other cultures: over against the British, the Indians, the Africans, etc. The mestizo is someone whose very flesh and blood imply the possibility of being both Spanish and indigenous, both Spanish and African, both Latin American and North American . . . and, therefore, both body and spirit, individual and communal, etc. Our history of mestizaje provides us with a binocular vision. When one looks through a pair of binoculars, with each eye having a different angle of vision, one has a depth perception unavailable to the person who simply looks through one lens. Our experience of living in two worlds, or two interpretative horizons, at the same time makes U.S. Hispanics instinctively suspicious of anthropological or epistemological dichotomies.

The retrieval of Vasconcelos' notion of mestizaje as an aesthetic category is not, however, without ambiguity. This ambiguity is most evident in Vasconcelos' own interpretation of mestizaje.[27] On the one hand, he interprets the experience of mestizaje as that of an "empathic fusion" which, as such, preserves the particularity of the different cultures. On the other hand, he views Latin American mestizaje as an extension, or

---

26. See, e.g., F. James Davis, *Who is Black? One Nation's Definition* (University Park, PA: Pennsylvania State University Press, 1991); Thomas Byrne Edsall with Mary Edsall, *Chain Reaction: The Impact of Race, Rights, and Taxes on American Politics* (New York: Norton, 1991); Henry Louis Gates, Jr., ed., *"Race," Writing, and Difference* (Chicago: University of Chicago Press, 1985); and Michael Hanchard, "Identity, Meaning, and the African-American," *Social Text* 24 (1990).

27. The ambiguities inherent in Vasconcelos' thought are noted by Andrés Guerrero in *A Chicano Theology*, pp. 148–50.

evolution of white, Iberian culture and a result of the conquering armies' "abundance of love" for the indigenous women. Such an interpretation of the Spanish conquest and the history of Latin American mestizaje belies the fact that, with a few notable exceptions, the origins of mestizaje lie much more in the Spaniards' violent raping and pillaging of the indigenous people and their culture than in any "abundance of love." Indeed, this fact is immortalized in the powerful Mexican symbol of *la chingada*, (the violated one) or *la Malinche*.[28]

How could Vasconcelos, ostensibly concerned with affirming Latin American cultural identity, have so radically misinterpreted the Latin American experience of conquest and colonization? The answer lies, I would suggest, in his understanding of aesthetics as *"un salto de espíritu,"* or a "leap of the spirit" beyond ethics. This understanding contains an important ambiguity: In what sense is aesthetics "beyond" ethics? Is ethics left behind in the wake of this "spiritual leap?" If not, what exactly is the relationship between ethics and aesthetics? This ambiguity then informs his interpretation of mestizaje: as aesthetic action, "mestizaje" must be a "leap of the spirit" beyond merely ethical, or ethical-political action.

Implicit, moreover, in Vasconcelos' explanation of the relationship between aesthetics and ethics is a (too) close identification of aesthetics with affect, emotions, feelings, and love which effectively immunizes ethical-political action (and, *a fortiori*, rationality) from these same aspects of human action. More specifically, Vasconcelos identifies affect with feelings and feelings with love. Thus, ethical-political action becomes, by definition, unfeeling and unemotional action in the world. As the realm of affect, the world of art, music, and literature is viewed as a "leap of the spirit" beyond the realm of civil society.

Furthermore, Vasconcelos pays little attention to the economic, or poietic mediation of all human action. We have already seen how, in Latino popular Catholicism, human action is mediated by physical symbols. These, however, are not only religious symbols but also *products* of our labor: e.g., the beautiful dresses which the women of San Fernando so carefully placed on Our Lady and Mary Magdalen to prepare them for Good Friday, the pieces of bread distributed to the congregation at the end of the Holy Thursday liturgy, the eucharistic offering itself, the gifts we exchange with each other, the house which, through a family's interpersonal action (praxis), becomes a "home." Before these physical objects are religious symbols, they are economic products. Their religious meaning is mediated not only by their physicality in general, but by the specifically economic character of that physicality. The bread is not merely a

---

28. On the significance of *la chingada* and *la Malinche* in Mexican history and self-understanding, see the classic work by Octavio Paz, *El laberinto de la soledad* (México, DF: Fondo de Cultural Económica, 1973). See also Guerrero, *A Chicano Theology*, pp. 113–15.

physical object like any other; it is "fruit of the earth and *work* of human hands."

By way of another illustration, the inability to appreciate the complex ways in which family relationships are mediated by economic relationships is precisely the weakness of the contemporary sentimentalized, neo-conservative evocation of "family values." That is, neo-conservatives fail to recognize how the life of the "home" is not isolated from but embedded in ethical-political and economic relationships. It does little good to promote family values while, at the same time, supporting political and economic structures that, by promoting autonomous individualism and an instrumental understanding of human life, lead to the breakdown of the family.[29] When forced to make their way within such structures, family values have little chance of survival. We cannot promote family values unless we recognize that the "private," affective realm of love and relationship is mediated by the "public," material realm of economics and politics.

Since Vasconcelos fails to systematically integrate the material and social dimensions of human action into his aesthetics, his notion of mestizaje remains as idealistic and sentimentalized as the neo-conservative's notion of family values. Despite his opposition to modern positivists, then, Vasconcelos assumes their dichotomy between matter and spirit, between body and feelings, between one's exterior life and one's interior life. The only difference is that he opts for the opposite pole in the dichotomy. Mestizaje becomes an affective, emotional action which, as such, has superseded ethical-political action and, even more so, productive action.

The irony, of course, is that Vasconcelos is at pains to emphasize the bodily, erotic character of all aesthetic action, or empathic fusion. Yet, without ethical-political and economic specification, this bodiliness and eroticism themselves remain abstract concepts. After all, as bodies we *act* and *make* (products) as well as feel. Human action always has an ethical-political character since—given our relational or organic anthropology—human action implies a *relationship* between ourselves and our environment, especially other persons. This relationship always implicitly raises the ethical question: *How should* I relate to my environment?

---

29. Richard Rodriguez argues that "there is no such thing as family values in America, never has been. Our culture was formed in an act of defiance against a mad British king. To this day, we are disrespectful of authority. Pop. Dad. Father. The old man is a figure of mockery in American culture, Homer Simpson, Archie Bunker, mad King George. . . . Today's irony is that those same Americans who most loudly profess family values are the very ones most suspicious of recent immigrants from south of the border and Asia. In California a common complaint against Chinese immigrants is that they are too tribal, too family oriented. And those Mexicans. When are the Mexicans going to learn English and give up their family language?" ("When Did Americans Ever Embrace Family Values," p. 23).

That question, which arises with self-consciousness, is unique to human persons: an animal cannot be held morally responsible for its actions since it responds instinctively to its environment.

Human intersubjective action is, in turn, mediated by poiesis, i.e., the economic products of human labor. Art is always susceptible to political and economic manipulation. As Terry Eagleton has observed, aesthetic ambiguity is not necessarily humanizing and liberating: "It is unwise to assume that ambiguity, indeterminacy, undecidability are always subversive strikes against an arrogantly monological certitude; on the contrary, they are the stock-in-trade of many a juridical enquiry and official investigation."[30] Indeed, the most "revolutionary" abstract art is much more likely to be found in corporate offices and suburban mansions than in the houses and apartments of an inner-city barrio. Political propaganda and commercial advertising are clearer examples of instrumentalized art; these are forms of aesthetic praxis that, in the service of political and economic goals, have been reduced to forms of poiesis, or productive activity.

As Latin American liberation theologians and European political theologians have reminded us, religion is equally susceptible to the same manipulation and, thus, assimilation. What Johann Baptist Metz has called "bourgeois religion" (*"bürgerliche Religion"*) is simply the modern, post-Enlightenment degeneration of religion into an ideology that, by relegating religious faith and practice to the private, interior life of the autonomous individual, legitimates the values of modern Western culture.[31] Religion then ceases to be a celebration of life as an end in itself, becoming instead a silent accomplice in the perpetuation of an unjust status quo.

One of the most important historical examples of the intrinsic interrelationships among aesthetic action, ethical-political action, and poiesis is the conversion of Bartolomé de Las Casas. A loyal servant of the Spanish crown, Las Casas came to the Indies in 1502 as a priest and *encomendero* participating in the colonial "pacification of the island."[32] In 1514, however, his life was radically altered by an experience he had while celebrating the eucharistic liturgy. Gustavo Gutiérrez recounts the events:

> Preparing to celebrate Mass and preach to the Spaniards on Pentecost, and setting himself to studying the "sermons that he had preached to them that Easter [or: 'the previous Pentecost'] and others from around that same time, he began to consider within himself some of the declarations of Sacred Scripture; and, if I remember rightly, first and foremost Ecclesiasticus 34." Let us reproduce, as

---

30. Terry Eagleton, *The Ideology of the Aesthetic* (Oxford: Basil Blackwell, 1990), pp. 379–80.

31. Metz, *Faith in History and Society: Toward a Practical Fundamental Theology* (New York: Seabury/Crossroad, 1980), pp. 32–48.

32. Gutiérrez, *Las Casas*, p. 46.

Bartolomé de Las Casas himself does, the passage to which he refers, inasmuch as the exact terms it employs have great importance: "Tainted his gifts who offers in sacrifice ill-gotten goods!/Mock presents from the lawless win not God's favor./The Most High approves not the gifts of the godless./[Nor for their many sacrifices does he forgive their sins.]/Like the man who slays a son in his father's presence/is he who offers sacrifice from the possessions of the poor./The bread of charity is life itself for the needy,/he who withholds it is a person of blood./He slays his neighbor who deprives him of his living;/he sheds blood who denies the laborer his wages" (Sirach 34:18–22; in the Vulgate, 34:21–27). . . . after having seen the crimes denounced by Scripture actually committed in the Indies—indeed, having helped commit them, by way of insufficient protest—Bartolomé suffers pangs of conscience. He has now meditated upon the classic prophetic theme of the mutual exigencies of prayer or public worship, and the practice of justice. But this time he underscores the fact that the absence of the second entails the death of the poor. To deprive them of that is to kill them. Worse, we are dealing with a murder perpetrated by someone who dares to attempt to use the stolen thing to honor God. . . . it is like killing children before their parents' eyes. . . . Las Casas regards the offering of this kind of present to God (by offering it to the church) as blasphemous, as it makes God equivalent to a "violent and wicked tyrant". . . . the bread of the poor is their life.[33]

The key to Las Casas' conversion was in his sudden recognition, in the light of the Scriptures, that the eucharistic bread is "the bread of the poor," and that, in turn, "the bread of the poor is their life." In light of this recognition, he is forced to reconsider "his position in the nascent colonial system," and "forsakes his condition as a member of an oppressive system, whose contrariety to all justice and to God's will he has not until now perceived."[34] The conversion thus begins when Las Casas realizes that what had heretofore been, for him, a religious (aesthetic) symbol, the eucharistic bread, is *everyday bread* before it is ever "the eucharist." Everyday bread is the (economic) product (poiesis) of someone's labor; in this case, the labor of the Indians. The bread is, thus, the mediation, or objective representation of the very lives of the Indians. Having been extracted from them while they are allowed to go hungry, the bread is "ill-gotten." When this stolen bread is then offered to God as the sacramental, objective mediation of thanksgiving and praise (i.e., as the mediation of the aesthetic, intersubjective relationship between ourselves and God), what is really being offered is the blood of the Indians, of which the bread is the product. As a result, Las Casas is challenged to reassess his political role as a servant

---

33. Ibid., pp. 47–51.
34. Ibid., p. 47–48.

of the Spanish crown and his economic function as an *encomendero* who owns Indians. Las Casas thus implicitly recognizes that the only authentic act of worship (aesthetic praxis) is one whose material, or economic mediation (the bread) is itself the product (poiesis) of ethical-political and economic relationships in which human lives are valued as ends in themselves rather than as mere instruments of production.

Having realized that the bread was, instead, the product of the unjust, violent expansion of Spanish political might, and an economic system that promoted that expansion, Las Casas became an increasingly open critic of the Crown and "agreed to condemn openly the distributions or *encomiendas* as unjust and tyrannical, and then to release [his own] Indians."[35] The example of Las Casas's conversion is a powerful illustration of the fact that, unless we attend adequately to the ethical-political and economic mediations of aesthetic action (e.g., worship, or any intersubjective relationship as such) that action will be distorted, unjust, fraudulent, hypocritical, and, in the case of religious worship, blasphemous.

It is this fact that should be integrated into our understanding of aesthetics and mestizaje. By understanding aesthetics as a leap *beyond* ethics, and identifying aesthetics with the world of feelings, Vasconcelos is not sufficiently attentive to the *intrinsically* ethical-political and economic dimensions of aesthetic action. That is, empathic fusion is mediated, not only by feelings but also by action, and not only by our physical bodies, but also by the political, economic, and social structures in which we participate.[36]

If the ethical-political dimension of human action is subordinated to the aesthetic, as a prior, inferior stage in the latter's development, ethical-political struggles for justice and against exploitation will be subordinated to the desire for affective union—rather than seen as the necessary mediation of empathic fusion. If the highest form of human action is the ability to "feel with" another person, the ethical-political *responsibility* entailed in that empathy can too easily be evaded: true empathy is rooted and issues in ethical-political action, which must, in turn, be expressed through a transformation of unjust relationships of production. Empathy implies and is made manifest in ethical-political action.

Furthermore, when this fact is not given due attention, the ethical-political impediments to affective union will be underestimated. Thus, had Vasconcelos interpreted the encounter between Spain and Mexico as not only an aesthetic encounter between two cultures, but also as an ethical-

---

35. Las Casas quoted in ibid., p. 51.

36. See Guerrero, *A Chicano Theology*, p. 149. The insight, so central to liberation theology, remains inadequately addressed in European theological aesthetics, such as the otherwise masterful work of Hans Urs von Balthasar. See, especially, his *The Glory of the Lord: A Theological Aesthetics*, vols. 1–7 (San Francisco: Ignatius Press, 1982–1991), and *Theo-Drama: Theological Dramatic Theory*, vols. 1–5 (San Francisco: Ignatius Press, 1982–1992).

political encounter between a conquering army and an invaded people, which conquest was made possible through economic exploitation (i.e., slavery) he could not have mistaken rape and pillage for "an abundance of love." One culture can fuse empathically with another culture only if and when they are both already acknowledged as equal. One person can fuse empathically with another person only if and when they are both already acknowledged as historical subjects; it is, *de facto*, impossible for a conqueror and his victim to fuse empathically.

It is primarily through political and economic structures of oppression that that equality is denied. An openness to and a respect for other cultures is impossible where one culture has arrogated to itself such economic and political power that it is able to impose its own values and way of life on other peoples. It is not simply hatred, or a lack of love, that impedes the development of mestizaje, but the economic and political power to assert that hatred through one's ethical-political action in the world. If, for example, Latino art is excluded from major North American art galleries, it is not only because these are "prejudiced" against Latino culture but also because they have the economic and political ability to exercise that prejudice, and they do business in an economic and political environment that supports the prejudice. If, on the other hand, Latino art suddenly becomes *de rigueur* and begins appearing in art galleries—and Latino authors in bookstores, Latino actors in movies, etc.—one should not automatically assume that, therefore, the United States is now a mestizo society that has achieved empathic fusion with the U.S. Hispanic culture. U.S. Hispanics continue to be discriminated against and exploited. If, tomorrow, Latino art is again unpopular, i.e., unprofitable, it will again be withdrawn from the galleries. As Eagleton has pointed out, once art is removed from its ethical-political and socioeconomic context, it is "thereby conveniently sequestered from all other social practices, to become an isolated enclave within which the dominant social order can find an idealized refuge from its own actual values of competitiveness, exploitation and material possessiveness."[37]

Too often, the reduction of human life to its aesthetic and cultural dimensions merely masks an underlying despair or fatalism with respect to the political and economic dimensions of our lives. It is a defining characteristic of modern, post-Enlightenment men and women that we are forever in search of that single key which will unlock all the secrets of history and, when discovered, usher in a New Age of liberation. We are latter-day gnostics in search of that secret knowledge which will enable us to make sense of a history so often apparently senseless and, thus, to achieve a happiness so often apparently unattainable.[38] For those who,

---

37. Eagleton, *The Ideology of the Aesthetic*, p. 9.
38. See Eric Voegelin's notion of the "egophanic" character of modern ideologies; *The Ecumenic Age* (Order and History, vol. IV) (Baton Rouge, LA: Louisiana State University Press, 1974), pp. 261–2.

not long ago, were convinced that that key was the "war on poverty," income redistribution, or political revolution, the failures of the 1960s, socialism, and political revolutions throughout the globe could only be followed by disillusionment. The disillusionment, however, has not been with these specific economic and political programs but with economics and politics *per se* as "keys" to human liberation. (Recall that, in the dichotomous world of post-Enlightenment culture, everything is always all or nothing: either politics is all or it's nothing, either economics is all or it's nothing.)

What we have not given up on is the possibility of finding such a key. Culture is an attractive, alternative "key to history," especially since, if "cultural openness" is *the* key to human happiness and liberation, we can achieve these for ourselves and others without sacrificing our political and economic privileges, without having to leave our comfortable seats. If justice demands nothing more than an open mind, a room-full of pre-Columbian artifacts, and an "exposure" to other perspectives, then we can achieve justice without leaving the comfort of the suburban enclosure or the ivory tower. Is it mere coincidence that the current concern for multiculturalism gained momentum in the late 1980s and early 1990s, at the precise historical moment when the Berlin Wall was crumbling and the U.S. "war on poverty" was being declared a colossal failure? Or is it, rather, that cultural differences are, after all, "the last refuge of the defeated economist?"[39]

Cultural symbols and practices are *always* mediated by political and economic structures and relationships. The surest evidence that racial-cultural oppression exists in the United States is *political* and *economic*: despite individual success stories, African Americans and U.S. Hispanics continue to have much less access to economic resources and political structures than do white Anglos. Without that access, an authentic racial-cultural mestizaje is impossible. The true test of cultural openness is not the number of people who read the book *The House on Mango Street* or see the movie "Like Water for Chocolate" (as noteworthy and inspiring as these works might be), but the number of Latinos and Latinas who remain unemployed, underemployed, excluded from political participation, trapped in the urban cycle of violence, etc.

If, as Vasconcelos himself insists, authentic mestizaje can only take place between two subjects, or "others," the denial of otherness is an ethical-political act of coercion and violence that is carried out through both direct political action and economic exploitation. Like all other aspects of human existence, cultural symbols, expressions, rituals, beliefs, and values are mediated by ethical-political relationships and material products. To ignore this fact is to presuppose that "cultural understanding" and "cultural diversity" necessarily imply an authentic relationship of others,

---

39. "America's New Lifestyle is Just Hard Work," *The Economist*, reprinted in *The Chicago Tribune*, November 1, 1994, sec. 1, p. 23.

where particularity is affirmed and valued. It is to ignore the fact that the encounter between Spanish soldiers and indigenous women was not an example of cultural diversity, or inter-racial love, but of political and economic domination. The result may indeed have been a cultural and racial mestizaje, but one brought about by ethical-political and economic oppression, not by empathic fusion. By reducing culture and race to aesthetic categories, Vasconcelos undermined his own struggle against ethnocentrism and racism.[40]

While Vasconcelos' understanding of human praxis as fundamentally aesthetic represents an important corrective to modern, instrumentalist notions of human action, it misconstrues the relationship of aesthetic to ethical-political action. I would suggest that, rather than *superseding* the ethical-political, the aesthetic dimension of human action is *mediated by* the ethical-political; it is encountered and lived out *within* ethical-political action, as the deepest meaning and significance of the ethical-political. The aesthetic is not a final stage beyond the ethical, but the fullest sense *of* the ethical—and, for that reason, encountered only within the context of ethical-political action. Ethical-political action is, in turn, mediated by economic relationships and the products of those relationships.

In U.S. Hispanic popular Catholicism, we can note the intrinsic connection between the aesthetic, the ethical-political, and the economic. It is no coincidence that the extent to which a particular Latino community continues to participate in traditional, popular forms of religion is closely related to that community's level of economic and political integration into U.S. society: in Latin America as in the United States, the religion of the upper classes is often virtually indistinguishable from Iberian Catholicism. The religiosity of middle and upper class U.S. Hispanics often exhibits the characteristics of what Mark Francis called Euro-American devotionalism.[41] Thus, popular Catholicism is not only a cultural but also a class phenomenon. It is no coincidence that, as the Argentine theologian Juan Carlos Scannone writes, "In Latin America the poor and oppressed are the ones who more wisely have resisted cultural aggressions. It is they, as well, who preserve and condense the popular culture of Latin America."[42]

The aesthetic value of the symbols, stories, and rituals of popular Catholicism derives from their historical context in a people's everyday struggle for survival, a struggle against the political and economic exploitation which is the necessary instrument of racial and cultural marginalization. Only in the midst of that everyday resistance to dehumanization can the Good Friday procession and the Guadalupe celebrations

---

40. See Guerrero, *A Chicano Theology*, p. 149.
41. See Francis, "Building Bridges."
42. Quoted in Allan Figueroa Deck, *The New Wave: Hispanic Ministry and the Evangelization of Cultures* (New York: Paulist, 1989), p. 116.

be, in fact, aesthetic celebrations of life as an end in itself. Otherwise they serve merely to legitimate the dehumanization. The ethical-political and economic context in which popular religious expressions are carried out is crucial to understanding their significance. It matters that Juan Diego was a poor, indigenous man and that the bishop was a wealthy, powerful Spaniard. It matters that the San Fernando congregation is predominantly poor and Mexican—and that the cathedral is in a downtown area. It matters that women, children, and the elderly (i.e., the poorest of the poor) play such central roles in the celebrations. It matters that Jesus is the son of a carpenter. It matters that Mary is a young peasant girl.

An aesthetic affirmation of life as an end in itself, popular Catholicism takes root most firmly in those lives that are, in every way, most "useless" to our society, i.e., most economically and politically superfluous. The very emphasis on beauty, aesthetics, and celebration then—and only then—becomes, *de facto*, a subversive act in a society geared toward the accumulation of economic and political power.

When, on Good Friday, the people of San Fernando walk alongside Jesus through the streets of downtown San Antonio, traffic stops, workers peer out through store windows at the multitudes, shopkeepers close their stores to join the procession, and even television reporters turn off the cameras to walk with the people. What makes possible such an open, public disregard for the productive life of the city is that the people demonstrating such disregard by marching through the city streets are themselves deemed economically and politically unproductive and useless. The procession thus grows out of their everyday struggle to survive *as persons whose lives have intrinsic value* in a society that has systematically denied that intrinsic value. In this context, then, the Good Friday procession is the cultural-religious (i.e., aesthetic) expression of the everyday ethical-political and economic struggle for survival. The procession is not directly an ethical-political action, but its context and its consequences are: the context is the everyday struggle for survival, and the immediate consequences are the undermining—if only temporarily—of the city's economic efficiency and productivity.

In turn, the religious celebration represents the deepest significance of that struggle. Paradoxically, only when human action is not directly used (as poiesis) for ethical-political ends, but is instead affirmed as an end in itself, can praxis, in fact, be empowering and liberating. Only by valuing human action as an end in itself can any authentic liberation take place. After all, the goal of social transformation—whether capitalist, Marxist, or Christian—is the creation of a society in which human action will be valued as an end in itself: e.g., work will be fulfilling rather than dehumanizing, family life will foster personal identity rather than suffocate individual uniqueness. Paradoxically, only by remaining "apolitical," that is, only by remaining "useless," can aesthetic celebration have ethical-political and economic consequences. Only by remaining rooted *"en la lucha,"*[43] in the common, everyday struggle for survival as *itself* empowering and liberating (even if, as too often happens, that struggle is, in the end, "unsuccessful"—as Jesus' was), can the procession be, in fact, an aesthetic affirmation of life as beautiful, that is, as an end in itself.

This affirmation represents the deepest significance of all ethical-political action, which ultimately derives its value not from its results (its "product"), not from the achievement of an external end, but from the interpersonal relationships through which the struggle is carried on in one's family, community, and society. In this sense, the daily struggle to keep food on the table, to keep the children clothed, to educate them and provide for their safety, to help one's spouse deal with discrimination at work, to put up with that indignity in order to bring home a paycheck, to keep one's patience while one's ill brother or sister is shuttled from one hospital emergency room to another because he or she has no medical insurance—all of these common experiences, common forms of praxis, among the poor, are themselves forms of ethical-political praxis. It is here, in these everyday ("private") relationships, that, by continuing to struggle in the face of such dehumanizing conditions, the poor affirm daily the intrinsic value of their lives. It is *that* affirmation that is empowering, liberating, and, thus, the most fundamental form of ("public") resistance to oppression. The seedbed of all ethical-political action is the basic affirmation: I AM A PERSON . . . or, more accurately, WE ARE PERSONS . . . WE ARE A PEOPLE! The intrinsic connection between the aesthetic and ethical-political dimensions of human action thus reflects the intrinsic connection between its private and public dimensions.

Though the economic products of our labor are important as the objective mediations, or expressions, of our relationships, they must not, however, be identified with the relationships themselves. The food so lovingly prepared for the children, or the clothes so carefully stitched, or the hard-won paycheck are necessary mediations of the family's love, but they are not the love itself: love itself is not a product but the mutual affirmation and enjoyment of the other's life as as an end in itself (hence the distorted, instrumental understanding of love implicit in the phrase "making love"). Human relationships are not, at bottom, economic; human praxis is not poiesis. The aesthetic celebration of life reminds us that the ultimate goal of all human action is nothing other than the active participation in relationships and the enjoyment of those relationships, wherein the particularity of each person can be affirmed and allowed to flower. That, indeed, is the definition of the mestizo community, a community which, however, is not born from empathic love but from the ashes of violent conquest and a people's courageous resistance.

---

43. See Isasi-Díaz, *En La Lucha.*

Such an understanding of human action, or praxis, would retrieve the central insights of both Latin American aesthetic philosophies and Latin American liberation theologies. Human intersubjective action is "beautiful" and, as such, is its own end; the fundamental nature of human action is thus enjoyment, celebration, and worship; *and* human action implies ethical-political relationships mediated by economic relationships; the intrinsic beauty of life is experienced only *in* the struggle to make these more equitable. Worship and celebration are always aesthetic and ethical-political acts that are mediated by economic products and structures. Before the bread and wine are the body and blood of Christ they are the body and blood of the poor person; the bread was kneaded by some-*one* and the grapes were picked by some-*one*. "The apparent ugliness of the countenance of the oppressed," writes Enrique Dussel, "the withered face of the farmer, the hardened hand of the laborer, the rough skin of the impoverished woman (who cannot buy cosmetics), is the point of departure of the esthetics of liberation. It is entreaty that reveals the popular beauty, the nondominating beauty, the liberator of future beauty."[44] The only proper locus of aesthetics and worship is, thus, the ethical-political option for the poor. Yet the deepest significance of that option is not social transformation *per se*, but the celebration of everyday human life. This is why, paradoxically, it is among the poor, in parishes like San Fernando, that one will find the most vibrant and vital communities of celebration and worship.

---

44. Dussel, *Philosophy of Liberation*, pp. 124–25.

[6]

Rationality or Irrationality?

Modernity, Postmodernity, and the U.S. Hispanic Theologian

In the contemporary search for a *locus theologicus*, the subordination of the Good to the Beautiful, or the ethical-political to the aesthetic, is often accompanied—as it is in Vasconcelos's thought—by the subordination of the True to both the Good and the Beautiful. If, as Vasconcelos suggested, the affective, aesthetic sense is less "distanced" from our concrete, lived experience than are ethics or theoretical reason, which imply the ability to "step back" from our lives in order to analyze and render ethical judgment on them, then our most direct access to revelation is through the immediacy of aesthetic, or empathic fusion, through Beauty. Hence, for Vasconcelos, the highest form of aesthetics is worship, or mysticism, wherein we become one with Absolute Beauty itself. U.S. Hispanic popular Catholicism is, I have suggested, an example of this highest form of aesthetics. If Latino culture is defined by an aesthetic mestizaje, popular religion is the liturgical form of that mestizaje.

As Vasconcelos avers, modern, theoretical reason deals in concepts, and concepts always limit and circumscribe human experience: e.g., "love" is not "hate," and "joy" is not "sadness". The *concept* "love" can hardly encompass the full reality of the *experience* of love. Indeed, we often find ourselves speechless in the face of profound experiences of love or beauty. Modern rationalism, however, has tended to equate the concept with the reality. Implicit in this identification of the concept with lived reality, is the modern identification of the person with his or her *mind*: to be a human being is to *think*. This reduction of life to thought is best articulated in René Descartes' famous axiom: *cogito, ergo sum* (I think, therefore I am). This understanding of the person, or anthropology, presupposes a dichotomy between mind and body: according to Descartes, "this 'I'—that is, the soul by which I am what I am—is entirely distinct from the body, and would not fail to be whatever it is, even if the body did not exist."[1] Modern Cartesian rationalism thus reduces the living, embodied, concrete, historical person to a disembodied intellect, or "soul." What is concrete, i.e., life as lived, is reduced to a mere abstraction, i.e., life as analyzed.

That analysis is always necessarily *im*personal: "the validity and truth of 'rational' arguments is independent of *who* presents them, *to whom*, or *in what context*. . . ."[2] True knowledge is "certain, precise and objective."[3] To the modern rationalist, "*knowledge* cannot be obtained from subjective individual interpretation of empirical experience . . . to think it can is a dangerous (and possibly 'irrational') illusion."[4]

When taken to its logical conclusion, the modern reduction of lived experience to an impersonal, abstract concept results in the reduction of lived experience to that most impersonal and abstract of all concepts, the number: in the modern Western world, to be a person is to be a number. If only that is true which can be known with certainty and objectivity, then

> certain knowledge [can] only be had by removing oneself as far as possible from the world, as in the case of mathematics, or of analytical propositions which are true because they are tautological. . . . Mathematics is the paradigm of this view of knowledge. It treats the universe as an abstraction, and reduces it to numbers. Mathematics allows us to remove from our observations all that is

---

1. René Descartes, *Philosophical Essays of Descartes*, vol. 1, *Discourse on Method*, part 4 (New York: Bobbs-Merrill, 1960), p. 127.

2. Stephen Toulmin, *Cosmopolis: The Hidden Agenda of Modernity* (New York: The Free Press, 1990), p. 75. The Cartesian separation between body and mind is reflected in the modern identification of "word" with "concept." As concepts, words are disembodied, "objective," and independent of the persons who utter them. The biblical, semitic notion of "word" is, however, altogether different. Here, there is no separation between the word and the speaker: God's word is an expression of God's very being. (I am indebted to John Linskens for this insight.) This latter understanding is prevalent in Latino cultures. Hence, for example, the identification of personal honor with "one's word" and the personal disgrace and violation implied in any violation of one's word. Conversely, as word and person have grown increasingly separate in U.S. society, there has been a corresponding increase in the flippancy and carelessness with which we treat language: it is assumed that one can use the coarsest language, tell the occasional "white lie," use clever speech to manipulate others and further one's own ends, and break one's oaths with impunity, while nevertheless remaining a perfectly good person. There is no necessary connection, then, between who I am and what I say.

3. Thomas Spragens quoted in Crowley, *The Self, the Individual, and the Community*, p. 189.

4. Crowley, *The Self, the Individual, and the Community*, p. 186.

contingent and adventitious by rendering them in a language which is itself abstract and "value-free." . . . One of the great objectives of the European Enlightenment . . . was precisely to find a system which would afford men knowledge of themselves and of the principles of morality, but which would be analogous to mathematics in that it would provide utter certainty and not be dependent on experience.[5]

All reality, all truth, and all knowledge can be reduced to numbers and, thus, understood through mathematical formulas and computer programs. This conclusion is explicitly stated by Galileo: "Philosophy is written in this grand book, the universe, which stands continually open to our gaze. But the book cannot be understood unless one first learns to comprehend the language and read the letters in which it is composed. It is written in the language of mathematics. . . ."[6]

The reduction of truth and knowledge to that which can be known with certainty and objectivity had a further corollary: that alone is true, and counts as knowledge, which can be universalized, or generalized. What is particular is limited, partial, and thus "false": "*general principles were in, particular cases were out.*"[7] Here again we see the modern tendency to establish a dichotomy between the particular and the universal; in this case, between judgments based on particular, subjective experience (which cannot therefore count as knowledge but only as "mere opinion") and universal, generalized, and thus "objective" principles, the only true knowledge.[8] This dichotomy is the common legacy of modern liberal individualism (*ego* . . .) and rationalism (. . . *cogito*).

As Vasconcelos insisted, however, human experience is not as neat as the well-defined universal concept or the logically devised mathematical formula. Ambiguity, variety, diversity, and particularity are absent from the world of universal concepts and abstract numbers. A rational, logical statement is either true or false; it cannot be both. A mathematical equation is either true or false; it cannot be both. But our lived experience is not so neat and unambiguous. For instance, we often experience "mixed" feelings of both joy and sadness, or both love and hate, or both fascination and fear. In its search for logical certainty, theoretical or speculative reason distances itself from the ambiguities of human living while dividing and separating life, which is always fluid and amorphous, into discrete objects (e.g., "love," "hate," "joy," "sadness") to be analyzed, dissected, and manipulated to some rational end. In order to understand

---

5. Ibid., p. 187.

6. Quoted in Stillman Drake, *Discoveries and Opinions of Galileo* (New York: Doubleday Anchor Books, 1957), p. 73.

7. Toulmin, *Cosmopolis*, p. 32.

8. See Bernstein, *Beyond Objectivism and Relativism*, p. 126.

life, theoretical reason must turn it into an object of study, thereby limiting, circumscribing, and distorting its true character as fluid and amorphous. The particularity and uniqueness of each human life is sacrificed to the abstract, universal concept or number: each person is but "1" instance of the general concept "humankind". "All abstraction," avers Stephen Toulmin, "involves omission, turning a blind eye to elements in experience that do not lie within the scope of the given theory. . . ."[9]

Consequently, the judgments reached by theoretical reason have often been astonishingly unreasonable: the desire to create a completely rational world has resulted in a world torn apart by conflict, violence, distrust, fear, and anxiety.[10] The twentieth century has witnessed the often horrific human consequences of a disembodied, affectless reason. The modern dichotomies between subject and object, between the particular and the universal, and between mind and body, have legitimated the objectification of millions of persons and the consequent destruction of their bodies. After all, the basis of any totalitarian ideology or political system is precisely the reduction of particular, unique human persons to mere numbers, categories, or instances of some general, universal concept (e.g., "Jew," "black," "Hispanic"). A particular life becomes merely one instance in an infinitely repeatable set of identical instances: one "worker" among many, one "homemaker" among many, one "black" among many, one "Latino" among many, one "voter" among many, one "consumer" among many, etc. The person's life is thus objectified and, denied its particular and unique intrinsic value, can now be manipulated as an instrument to some external end: respectively, to increase production, to make a home, to pick the cotton, to pick the grapes, to get elected, to purchase the product, etc.

The archetype of the modern rationalist was Adolf Eichmann, who could so calmly and efficiently send thousands of persons to the gas chambers. Such an act was, for him, simply the logical solution to a logical problem, the "Jewish problem." To the modern rationalist, human society is a mathematical problem, and the goal of human action, or praxis, is to find and—literally—execute a solution to this problem. Technology then comes to the aid of this instrumental understanding of human action, providing the tools of efficiency. The modern, planned society is simply the political concomitant of modern rationalism. This was, indeed, the basis of Vasconcelos' opposition to the planned society of Porfirio Díaz, to positivism, and to rationalism.

Even by its own criteria, theoretical reason has too often yielded irrational results. Science and technology have brought not only improvements in health care and economic standards of living but also nuclear weapons, gas chambers, chemical carcinogens, agent orange,

---

9. Toulmin, *Cosmopolis*, p. 200.

10. On the difference between rationality and reasonableness, see ibid., pp. 75, 80, 198–201.

and ecological destruction. In early twentieth-century Chicago, the automobile "was being proposed as a [rational] solution to several ills. Their maneuverability would help relieve traffic jams involving fixed-route vehicles, they would eliminate the health hazards connected with manure and animal carcasses, and they would reduce the dense smoke from commuter trains because fewer trains would be needed."[11] The automobile's promise of mobility and freedom is called into question every day as millions of people sit immobilized in rush-hour traffic jams.[12]

Theoretical reason presupposes predictability (*if* we build cars, *then* we will reduce traffic jams and dense smoke), while human behavior (praxis) cannot always be so clearly foreseen: human beings are not mathematical equations that will always yield the same result (if x, then y). Consequently, the results of our "solutions" to "problems" are not always as positive as had been anticipated; every reductively rational solution has unintended, often disastrous consequences—precisely because it necessarily distorts and misconstrues the object of the presumed solution. Once again we are reminded of Walter Benjamin's dictum: "Every great work of civilization is at the same time a work of barbarism."[13]

In Catholicism itself, the post-Vatican II rationalization of the eucharistic liturgy has brought not only increased understanding of its meaning but also a loss of its aesthetic character (often expressed as a loss of the "sense of mystery" or a loss of the "symbolic power" of the liturgy). The intent of liturgical reforms may have been to increase lay participation in the liturgy, yet for many Catholics, an increased intellectual, rational participation has been accompanied by a decreased affective participation.

Theoretical reason seeks certainty and predictability, whereas life can never be fully predictable: Who could have predicted Auschwitz? At the time, many refused to believe that Jews were being exterminated—even in the face of overwhelming evidence. Indeed, even today there are people who stubbornly and irrationally refuse to believe that it happened. Theoretical reason so often results in the opposite of what it intends because theoretical reason necessarily distorts reality, turning it into an abstract concept or idea that can be controlled, analyzed, molded, and shaped so as to yield a predictable result, as does a mathematical formula: one plus one will always equal two. If we approach life as we approach a mathematical formula, we will expect life to be totally predictable; when it is not, we will expend every effort to *make* it so. In order to understand,

---

11. Alice Sinkevitch, ed., *AIA Guide to Chicago* (New York: Harcourt Brace and Company, 1993), p. 15.

12. I remember, several years ago, cracking an ironic smile when, caught in the middle of one such traffic jam, I heard a well-known oil company jingle played over the radio: "It's not just your car, it's your freedom."

13. Quoted in David Tracy, *Plurality and Ambiguity: Hermeneutics, Religion, Hope* (San Francisco: Harper and Row, 1987), p. 69.

conceptual thought divides reality into discrete objects, and separates the subject, the "observer," from his or her environment so that the subject will be able to control and manipulate the environment. Life is fluid; concepts are static. Life is relational; concepts are separate and distinct. Life is concrete; concepts are abstract. Life is ambiguous; concepts are certain.

It is against the *irrationality* of modern rationalism that Vasconcelos proposed his aesthetics. However, the emphasis on the aesthetic, or Beauty, as an antidote to the Cartesian, logical rationality of modernity, is not unique to Latin America; it is also present in much postmodern Western thought. Postmodernity is itself a vague concept that can mean many different things. Jean-François Lyotard defines postmodernity as "incredulity toward metanarratives": it rejects the possibility of a universal, generalizable language, experience, judgment, identity, or knowledge.[14] For the postmodernist, "truth" and "knowledge" are always radically particular, radically contextual, radically relative, radically ambiguous, and always in flux. Differences are fundamental; similarities and unity are illusory. Indeed, everything is difference, or otherness. This includes the self, or the subject, who is also radically heterogeneous, an artificial pastiche of radically disparate and ever fluctuating relations, identities, and experiences. The self as such (as some coherent and relatively stable entity which unifies all these differences) does not exist; what we call the "self" is simply "social location." The certainty and stability of the concept, as defining reality, give way to the ambiguity and fluidity of art and play: Descartes' *ego cogito*, and Marx's *homo faber*, give way to *homo ludens*.[15]

---

14. Jean-François Lyotard, *The Postmodern Condition: A Report on Knowledge* (Minneapolis: University of Minnesota Press, 1984), p. xxiv.

15. I am here limiting myself to "poststructuralist," or "deconstructionist" postmodernism. On poststructuralist postmodernism, see, for example, Honi Fern Haber, *Beyond Postmodern Politics: Lyotard, Rorty, Foucault* (New York: Routledge, 1994), esp. pp. 1–8, 113–16; Mark Kline Taylor, *Remembering Esperanza* (Maryknoll, NY: Orbis, 1990); Jonathan Arac, ed., *Postmodernism and Politics* (Minneapolis: University of Minnesota Press, 1986); Eagleton, *The Ideology of the Aesthetic*, esp. pp. 369–401; Jonathan Loesberg, *Aestheticism and Deconstruction: Pater, Derrida, and De Man* (Princeton, NJ: Princeton University Press, 1991); Jürgen Habermas, "Modernity Versus Post-Modernity," *New German Critique* 22 (Winter, 1981): 3–14; Hal Foster, "(Post)Modern Polemics," *New German Critique* 33 (Fall, 1984): 67–78; Seyla Benhabib, "Epistemologies of Postmodernism: A Rejoinder to Jean-François Lyotard," *New German Critique* 33 (Fall, 1984): 103–26; David Tracy, *Plurality and Ambiguity: Hermeneutics, Religion, Hope* (San Francisco: Harper and Row, 1987), esp. pp. 47–81; and Fredric Jameson, *Postmodernism, or, The Cultural Logic of Late Capitalism* (Durham, NC: Duke University Press, 1991); Andrew Ross, ed., *Universal Abandon? The Politics of Postmodernism* (Minneapolis: University of Minnesota Press, 1988); Andres Huyssen, *After the Great Divide: Modernism, Mass Culture, Postmodernism* (Bloomington, IN: Indiana University Press, 1986), esp. pp. 179–221.

In this, Western postmodernism has many similarities with the aesthetics of José Vasconcelos. Indeed, it is a testament to the marginalization of Latin American thought in Western intellectual discourse that Vasconcelos' thought is all but absent from postmodern discourse, despite the fact that what French philosophers were saying in the 1980s he had already been saying in the 1910s. Yet, since postmodern theories have become so influential in the North American academy and, even more importantly, since these theories reflect broader cultural currents in contemporary U.S. society, U.S. Hispanic theologians must themselves engage these currents, for they constitute an important dimension of the interpretative horizon of our theologies.

Like Vasconcelos, postmodernists propose an alternative to modern rationalism. An understandable response to the carnage wrought by the modern rational subject, for whom the intellect *is* the human person, has been to reject reason and the subject altogether, arguing that these are but artificial constructs with no foundation in reality. "Reason," argues the postmodernist, is nothing but the arbitrary connection between words in a text, as the self or "subject" is nothing but his or her "social location."[16] The logical and certain knowledge sought by modern reason is now thought to be impossible: because there is no universal history, there can be no "key" to history. The desire for logical certainty is then replaced with the ambiguity of aesthetics as the paradigm for human inquiry. Lived experience cannot be known through the logical, rational mind; it can only be "known" through the irrational, ambiguous feelings.

In postmodernism, the aesthetic is more adequate to concrete human experience, for the reasons Vasconcelos also gave: like our concrete lives, the aesthetic experience is affective, amorphous, ambiguous, inchoate, fluid, and intrinsically relational, so that the "subject" and the aesthetic "object" become fused as one. As in our concrete lives, the imposition of external, "universal" ethical or rational criteria on a work of art distorts the work of art by forcing its inherent ambiguity and "surplus of meaning" into the straightjacket of ethical and rational categories. The rational judgment is as artificial as the ethical judgment since both are imposed on lived experience from outside the experience itself. Likewise, ethical values themselves cannot be justified rationally, from "outside," but can only be "self-gounding, or founded in intuition."[17] Ultimately, a work of art is not right or wrong, nor is it good or bad; it simply *is*. To treat the work of art differently is to do violence to it.

The aesthetic sense, on the other hand, views reality as a network of fluid relationships, and fuses subject and object. By separating the subject from

---

16. See, e.g., Lyotard, *The Postmodern Condition*; idem, *Just Gaming* (Minneapolis: University of Minnesota Press, 1984); idem, *The Differend: Phrases in Dispute* (Minneapolis: University of Minnesota Press, 1988).

17. Eagleton, *The Ideology of the Aesthetic*, p. 382.

his or her environment, the "object of study," and by dividing reality into discrete objects of study, logical reason constructed the autonomous, isolated individual of modernity ("cogito, *ergo* sum"). By fusing subject and object, postmodern aesthetics "deconstructs" the subject as, in any sense, distinct or separate from his or her relationships, or social location. By defining the subject as the *thinking* subject, modernity canonized rationality; by deconstructing thought itself, postmodernity canonizes irrationality.

One contemporary alternative to the modern subordination of human praxis to theoretical reason is, thus, a return to praxis as aesthetic, i.e., *ir*rational, absurd, and indeterminate.[18] However, any identification of human action with irrationality implicitly accepts the narrow modern definition of rationality and, finding that this rationality lacks any foundation, opts for its opposite. By presupposing an identification of reason *as such* with *logical, speculative,* or *theoretical* reason (and thereby rejecting reason as such), these critics of modern rationalism simply assume the narrow modern definition of reason.

Vasconcelos, on the other hand, does not, at first glance, appear to opt for aesthetics *over against* reason, but to call for an *expansion* of our criteria of rationality beyond the logical, theoretical criteria of modern Western thought: "None of this is rational in the classic syllogistic or logical sense, but it is not at all irrational in the broad sense of the word, just as the work of the artist is not irrational."[19] Instead of invoking an irrationality that presupposes the modern definition of rationality, he challenges the validity of that definition itself. Yet here too his thought remains unclear. He does argue, for instance, that empathic fusion "contradicts reason."[20] In what sense, moreover, is beauty *"más allá de la razón"* (beyond reason)? In its "spiritual leap," does aesthetics leave reason behind? Or, instead, does aesthetics merely sublate reason, transforming it into something greater without thereby destroying it?

The latter, I suggest, would be the more appropriate understanding of aesthetics. If aesthetics is beyond logical reason, it does not thereby leave reason behind. If, for example, one defines reason not as "logical certainty" but as "understanding," then the logical rationality which led so many Jews to the gas chambers appears, not as "rational," but as an irrational *mis*understanding of human existence. It is impossible to understand another person simply by analyzing him or her rationally (through, for example, psychology or sociology); one must, above all, enter into a *relationship* with the other person in order to understand him or her. Likewise, one Diego Rivera mural may contribute as much to our understanding of the human condition—and, therefore, be as "rational"—as a hundred philosophical treatises.

18. Toulmin, *Cosmopolis*, p. 172.
19. Vasconcelos, *Obras Completas*, 4:891.
20. Ibid., 3:1304–5.

It is to this broader view of rationality that U.S. Hispanic theology must turn, for neither the modern nor the postmodern view is adequate. In fact, as I have indicated above, the postmodern and modern anthropologies, and, therefore, their correlative notions of human reason, are not fundamentally different.[21] Both views of human reason assume a disjunction between the intellect and the heart, between theoretical reason and "irrational" affect: modernity extols the former while deriding the latter, and postmodernity does the reverse.

Reason Beyond Modernity and Postmodernity

A theology grounded in popular Catholicism will, by definition, find this postmodern irrational definition of rationality inadequate and unacceptable. In popular Catholicism, theological truth is encountered not in clear and distinct ideas but in relationships; not in universal, abstract concepts but in particular, concrete sacraments, or symbols; not through observation but through participation, by kissing the statue, or walking with Jesus, or kneeling alongside Mary, or singing to Mary. In the Náhuatl world of Juan Diego, beauty *is* truth, and truth *is* beauty: "*flor y canto.*"

---

21. As the course of my argument suggests, I do not perceive in postmodernism so much a rejection or an alternative to modernity as the latest stage in modernity, or the full flowering of certain currents already present in modern thought (e.g., in 19th century German Romanticism, Nietzsche, Heidegger). The real complementarity of the modern and postmodern worldviews becomes most visible, however, not in esoteric academic treatises but in the dominant culture itself, where, as Terry Eagleton has suggested (see above), "postmodern" relativity, ambiguity, and chaos themselves become objects of "modern," capitalist consumption, thereby simply serving the (literally) egocentric aims of the modern, autonomous self. I thus concur with Jon Thompson's judgment that "what we are witnessing, among other things, is the working out of the logic of modernism in mass culture. In the near-global domain of mass culture, modernism is not superannuated but revivified. . . . The constant social challenge confronting modern art [and, I would add, philosophy, theology, and popular religion itself] is to avoid transforming its critical edge into just another easily consumed and easily forgotten commodity" (*Fiction, Crime, and Empire*, p. 39). For that reason, argues Thompson, "it would be more accurate to refer to postmodernity as '(post)modernity,' " though he, like I, "refrained from doing so because the constant repetition of the parentheses becomes tedious and overly insistent" (ibid., p. 179n.3). See also Hal Foster, "(Post)modern Polemics," *New German Critique* 33 (Fall, 1984): 67–78. By using the first person plural pronoun when referring to (post)modernity, I am indicating that, though a Latino, I—like, arguably, all North Americans—participate in and am influenced by the dominant (post)modern culture. This is especially true given the enormous influence of mass communication and media in the United States and, indeed, throughout the world.

It is in the singing of the birds, in the aroma of the roses, and, above all, in his encounter with the Lady of Tepeyac that Juan Diego comes to understand the truth of who he is, who she is, and who God is.

If lived human experience is inherently relational, embodied, and affective, then we cannot understand that lived experience through concepts alone. Interpersonal reality cannot be understood or known primarily through theoretical analysis, but through an aesthetic, affective, and active participation in ("fusion" with) the sacramental relationships, symbols, and rituals.[22] It is a reality which, like love, remains inaccessible and incomprehensible to the mere observer. Indeed, to the outside observer, popular Catholicism has often seemed superstitious, primitive, backward, and irrational.

Yet it is precisely as "irrational" that popular Catholicism and other forms of popular religion have found a degree of acceptance in postmodernism.[23] With its attraction to ambiguity, affect, indeterminacy, otherness, and difference, postmodernism can look to popular religion as an irruption of otherness and irrationality in society. This more positive view of popular religion is found, for instance, in much New Age thought, as well as in creation spirituality and some contemporary movements for

---

22. A "*reasonable* rationality" would thus be one which would respect the particularity and historical concreteness of the object of knowledge: knowledge of a mathematical equation, billiard ball, or a table, is different from knowledge of one's self, of another person, or of God. When that particularity is respected, we realize that the epistemological criteria and methods we use must themselves be different and appropriate to the particular object of knowledge. This, indeed, was a central insight of Aristotle, who distinguished three types of knowledge: *epistēmē* (theoretical knowledge), *technē* (technical, or productive knowledge), and *phronēsis* (practical knowledge, or wisdom). E.g., *Nicomachean Ethics*, 1139a27–28, 1178b20–21; *Topics*, 145a15–16; and *Metaphysics*, 1025b25. For explanations of Aristotle's threefold distinction, see Dunne, *Back to the Rough Ground*, esp. pp. 9–10, 227–74. It would thus be unreasonable to pretend that one can know God by using the very same methods and criteria one uses to know a billiard ball. Yet this distinction would not deny the possibility of knowing God, or knowing other persons; it would only insist that the methods and criteria appropriate to that knowledge are not exclusively those of, for example, the scientist. Likewise, the methods and criteria appropriate to our knowledge of the physical world are not exclusively those of the theologian.

23. See, e.g., the analyses of the postmodern fascination with popular culture, in Jameson, *Postmodernism*; and Anders Stephanson, "Interview with Cornel West," in *Universal Abandon?* ed. Andrew Ross. On the openness of postmodernism to non-rationalistic forms of religion and theology, see Thomas J. J. Altizer et al., eds., *Deconstruction and Theology* (New York: Crossroad, 1982); David Ray Griffin, *God and Religion in the Postmodern World* (Albany, NY: SUNY Press, 1989); James Alfred Martin, Jr., *Beauty and Holiness: The Dialogue Between Aesthetics and Religion* (Princeton, NJ: Princeton University Press, 1990), esp. pp. 164–96.

multiculturalism.[24] In addition, the postmodern emphasis on difference and otherness has made possible a certain openness to those persons who are "different from" and "other" to the dominant culture, race, gender, and class in society.

The greater openness of postmodern culture to popular religion is an improvement over the modern suspicion of popular religion.[25] Yet, for several reasons, this too must ultimately prove an inadequate and unacceptable interpretation of U.S. Hispanic popular Catholicism. The postmodern option for otherness and irrationality assumes the modern dichotomies between theory (theoretical reason) and praxis, between intellect and affect, between truth and meaning, between the particular and the universal, and between community and institution—all of which are alien to U.S. Hispanic popular Catholicism.

Popular Catholicism—and U.S. Hispanic culture in general—presupposes an integral, holistic, and organic anthropology. Consequently, a theology grounded in U.S. Hispanic popular Catholicism must, by definition, reject the theory-praxis dichotomy, including any option for praxis over against theory, or theoretical reason. We always act as *persons*, that is, as body (ethical-political praxis), spirit (aesthetic praxis), and intellect (reason). Ada María Isasi-Díaz observes that:

> *Mujerista* theology insists on the reflective moment of praxis, for it is precisely Latinas' ability to understand and think that is often questioned and debased. Praxis must not be equated with practice. Praxis is both intellectual enterprise as well as action; the dichotomy between intellectual activity and physical work is a fictitious one. . . . *Mujerista* theologians' insistence on the centrality of praxis, therefore, does not make our enterprise anti-intellectual, just as Latinas' self-construction as persons who struggle to survive does not mean that we surrender the intellectual enterprise to the dominant groups. Our insistence on praxis does not put reason and intellect aside. On what grounds can oppressors claim that Latinas' style of life, a style necessary to survive, is nonrational? On the contrary, those who struggle to survive are the very ones who can question the rationality of oppressors, who themselves are not capable of understanding this basic truth: that in the long run, only what benefits all

---

24. See, e.g., the work of Matthew Fox, especially in *The Coming of the Cosmic Christ* (San Francisco: Harper and Row, 1988); Fox's creation spirituality draws on Native American and Mother Goddess religious traditions, among others.

25. This is not to say that many postmodern scholars do not remain suspicious of religion but only that the postmodern worldview tends toward a greater cultural and religious openness and inclusivity than the homogeneous, rationalistic worldview of Western modernity. On postmodern critics' continuing suspicion of religion, see Tracy, *Plurality and Ambiguity*, pp. 82–114.

of humanity will really benefit them. Those whose daily bread is the struggle for survival are the ones who have grounds to question what is considered intelligent and reasonable by society at large.[26]

We can no more act only with our bodies than we can think only with our minds. Furthermore, the postmodern option for praxis (understood as "play") against reason—like Vasconcelos' option for aesthetics—often identifies praxis with affect and ambiguity, thereby assuming the modern dichotomy between intellect, or rational certainty, and affect, or ambiguity. While, again, this emphasis on affect may be attractive to U.S. Hispanics, any understanding of affect as irrational would be inadequate to U.S. Hispanic experience. Ada María Isasi-Díaz and other mujerista theologians, especially, have alerted us to the dangers of extolling affect at the expense of intellect, or reason.[27]

Any idealization of affect, otherness, irrationality, and ambiguity as alternatives to reason, theory, and logical coherence can only perpetuate the very dichotomy which has, for centuries, legitimated the marginalization of Latinos and Latinas. The idealization of affect (understood, in the modern sense, as the opposite of intellect and as, therefore, irrational) contributes to our continued marginalization and oppression in at least three ways: 1) by perpetuating dehumanizing stereotypes, 2) by forestalling the irruption of Latinas and Latinos as full theological subjects, and 3) by erecting a dichotomy between truth and meaning which misrepresents our lived experience.

One of the most insidious stereotypes of U.S. Hispanics—precisely because it is such an apparently attractive and innocent stereotype—is that of the emotionally warm, effusive, excitable, happy-go-lucky, fiesta-loving Hispanic. Another version of this is the passionate "Latin lover" . . . or, his "better half," the unconditionally loving, nurturing, and forgiving Latina. These stereotypes pervade our television programs, movies, and newspapers. The danger of such stereotypes is that they focus on particular positive aspects of U.S. Hispanic culture, the centrality of personal relationships and interpersonal affection, and identify these *aspects* with the *totality* of U.S. Hispanic culture—and, thus, the totality of U.S. Hispanic women and men.

When a part is mistaken for the whole, what results is a distortion of the concrete reality. When that part happens to be attractive and endearing, the idealized, or romanticized distortion is all the more appealing—even to those persons who are the object of the stereotype. The above stereotypes can be very seductive to U.S. Hispanics precisely because what is emphasized is an aspect of ourselves which we (appropriately) value very much.

---

26. Isasi-Díaz, *En la Lucha*, p. 170.
27. See, e.g., Isasi-Díaz, *En la Lucha*, pp. 166–85; Aquino, *Our Cry for Life*, pp. 71–77.

Yet, like all idealizations, this one has a dark underside. Where the only available anthropologies are the modern and postmodern, both of which view affect as irrational, to identify U.S. Hispanics with affect is implicitly to presume that U.S. Hispanics are irrational. Latinos and Latinas may then find acceptance as entertainers (e.g., musicians, movie actors) for Anglos: U.S. Hispanics then become the instruments through which the dominant culture, so alienated and estranged from the world of feelings, can *vicariously* experience that world—without, however, *itself* having to risk entering it. Latinos and Latinas then become accomplices in our own marginalization: the dominant culture can continue to be ruled by logical rationality because it has, as its complementary alter ego, Latino culture. The "rational" oppression of U.S. Hispanics is perpetuated and legitimated by the romanticization of our Latino culture as irrational: these are but two sides of the same coin. However, since the criteria for full participation in public life are still the criteria of dispassionate reason, U.S. Hispanics will continue to be excluded—unless we either assimilate or happen to be good entertainers, in which case, the more "Hispanic" we look and act, the more marketable we will be as entertainers.

The postmodern idealization of irrationality stems more from the inner logic and needs of modernity—with its isolation and, eventually, dissolution of the rational individual—than from any genuine affirmation of marginalized groups. Indeed, a Rousseauian romanticization of the irrational Noble Savage is no less dehumanizing, in the long run, than his or her relegation to an inner city barrio: he or she remains a savage, even if a "noble" one. To characterize the experience and values of U.S. Hispanics as irrational—even if in a complimentary tone—is thus to perpetuate our dehumanization: we remain but savages.

The Noble Savage is not the opposite of but the complement to the modern rational individual. U.S. Hispanic culture then develops a symbiotic relationship with the dominant culture similar to the relationship between this latter and so-called "high culture." Museums and concert halls can become places that Anglos frequent in order to experience feelings that they are unable and unwilling to experience in other areas of their lives (such as their own human relationships) and, more importantly, *so that* they will not have to experience them in other areas of their lives; when "love," "warmth," and "affective fusion" can be had in the secure comfort of a plush box seat, or in a museum of Latin American art, why should one risk the insecurity and vulnerability of actual human relationships?

Another analogy is one that feminists have often pointed out. The identification of U.S. Hispanics with affect closely parallels the almost universal identification of women with affect. Again, the result is an idealization of women-as-loving which absolves men of the responsibility to be loving. The family's "irrational" affective life, the "irrational" life of relationship (praxis), then becomes the exclusive domain and responsibility of "irrational" women, while "rational" men can be content to lead their productive (poiesis) lives in the "rational" Real World. The result is the classic symbiotic, or co-dependent relationship, in which neither person becomes a whole person. As we have seen, a further result is the oppression of the woman who, though (because?) she is idealized as emotional and loving, is simultaneously *derided* for this very same emotionality and *excluded* from the "non-loving," "non-emotional," "rational" Real World and, therefore, from participation in public life. Ironically, the idealization of domestic life as the domain of interpersonal relationships and "feelings," accompanied by the apparently contradictory identification of human life with rationality and productive activity (in the public sphere), imposes on women an unrealistic, overwhelming, and exclusive responsibility for family life, thereby excluding women from public life, and excluding family relationships from "rational," political and socioeconomic critique.[28] (Thus, as I suggested in the preceding chapter, the solution does not lie in a simple inversion of the dichotomy, which would depreciate family life by excluding interpersonal relationships and feelings from the definition of human action.)

Here again we see the intimate relationships among modern dichotomies: public/private, ethical political/aesthetic, intellect/affect, and, as we will see, truth/meaning. Like U.S. Hispanics as a group, women as a group (as well as African Americans and other marginalized peoples) have historically been identified with the second element in each of these dichotomies—and white Anglo men have been identified with the first. All forms of idealization or romanticization presuppose a distorting, dichotomous epistemology, thereby masking, and thus legitimating underlying forms of oppression.

The other side of idealization is always oppression. The same Spanish language which is romanticized as "mysterious" and "exotic" by movie and record producers is rejected as intellectually unsophisticated by French, German, and English speakers. The same woman who is idealized for being loving is simultaneously demeaned for being irrational. The same woman who is idealized for being nurturing is treated as a beast of burden. After all, the same body that is used for nurturing can be used for cleaning and scraping. The same Latina or Latino who is idealized for the free-spirited fiesta is abused as a "wetback." The same African American who is idealized for her or his "soul" is abused as a "nigger." The same adolescent who is idealized for her or his physical youthfulness and vigor is abandoned to the violence of the streets, the

---

28. As Honi Fern Haber warns, "if the realm of the private is equated with the 'merely aesthetic,' . . . it is made impervious to political critique, resistant to change on a social level" (*Beyond Postmodern Politics*, p. 75).

drug trade, and deteriorating schools. In the end, all are savages—noble or otherwise.

Anyone attempting to bridge this disjunction by living in the worlds of affect and intellect at once is sure to encounter tremendous difficulties and, indeed, resentment. This will certainly be true of U.S. Hispanics who attempt to enter the rational Real World (e.g., politics, business, the academy, the church). To do so effectively, one will likely have to sacrifice one's identity and learn the ways of the rational Real World. The dichotomous dominant culture cannot comprehend the Latino tendency to bridge dichotomies. In the Anglo world, for instance, the Latino tendency to mention God (*Si Dios quiere.* If God wills it.) or Jesus, Mary, and Joseph in the course of everyday conversation will be deemed an unwarranted intrusion of the private, irrational, religious world into the public, rational Real World. Even among explicitly religious persons, such as priests, ministers, and, above all, theologians, the mention of Jesus Christ in everyday conversation—especially in any way which might imply actual religious belief—would be an embarrassment.[29] In that world, no touching will be allowed, since the act of touching constitutes an equally unwarranted intrusion of the impure, irrational body into the world of pure, rational intellect, or an unwarranted breaching of the individual's autonomous existence. In that world, no one will display any emotions in public lest they be dismissed for being "out of control."[30] As U.S. Hispanics living in between cultures, neither of these cultural attitudes is alien to us; what is alien to us is the unbreachable border that separates, divides, and excludes. To the dominant culture, on the other hand, the border is essential.

Consequently, postmodernists can afford to be irrational and to write gibberish in the name of ambiguity and indeterminacy; as well-educated and well-published scions of the Western intellectual tradition, their

---

29. On the embarrassment occasioned, in U.S. society, by public displays of religious belief, see Stephen L. Carter, *The Culture of Disbelief: How American Law and Politics Trivialize Religious Devotion* (New York: Basic Books, 1993).

30. I remember, as a young boy, being involved in one of our regular family discussions. (In typical Cuban fashion, it was really several overlapping discussions going on at once—with each of us keeping track of and participating in all the conversations simultaneously.) As usual, this one became quite passionate and heated—which is to say that it was a typical, everyday discussion. At the end, one of my relatives looked at me with some concern and warned me, "This type of discussion is fine here, since this is normal for us. But, when you are having a discussion with '*americanos*,' be sure not to show *any* emotions. If they see you displaying any emotion at all, they will stop listening; they will assume you have become irrational and lost control." That comment made such an impact on me that I have remembered it until today. For "*americanos*," to be rational is to have no emotions and, conversely, to have emotions is to be irrational.

rationality will not be questioned. The white, male, Euro-American theologian's postmodern avowal of the irrationality of his discourse may be considered chic and sophisticated. After all, he is rational *by definition* (especially if he is German or French), so his circumlocutious mumblings are viewed as signs of a creative and insightful intellect at work.

Only those persons whom the dominant culture already considers "rational" have the luxury of "opting" for irrationality. Only those who continue to benefit from the rationality which modernity has already presumptively ascribed to them by virtue of their gender, class, race, or culture can afford to extol the virtues of irrationality. The rest of us will simply be considered irrational ipso facto. The irrationality and ambiguity of Anglo-American, French, or German scholars will be taken for profundity of thought; the irrationality and ambiguity of Third World scholars will be taken for mere ambiguity and irrationality. Third World peoples are already presumed to be irrational and mindless—by modernity and postmodernity alike. The difference is that, while modernity disparaged the irrationality of the savage, postmodernity celebrates it.

African American, feminist, and U.S. Hispanic theologians do not have the luxury of proclaiming our "irrationality" as a sign of a superior intellect. Since we have never been considered to have rational intellects in the first place, to comply in the postmodern characterization of our experience as irrational would be to comply in the perpetuation of the very Noble Savage stereotype that has denied us our intellects and, therefore, our ability for rational thought. Should an Anglo male philosopher speak unintelligibly, he will be considered brilliant; should a Latina speak unintelligibly, she will be considered ignorant. Indeed, should any Latina or Latino speak at all—especially in Spanish—she or he will be deemed ignorant, since Spanish is considered *per se* an "irrational" language, a language of the emotions. The message conveyed to me in the course of my own education, and still communicated in many subtle and not-so-subtle ways is this: only in French, German, and English is it possible to think and speak rationally, with intellectual sophistication.

Is it mere coincidence that, just when U.S. Hispanics, African Americans, and Native Americans—so long excluded from the world of rational discourse—are engaging in a rational, *critical* way the dominant culture and its intellectual elites, those same elites throw up their hands and declare all intellectual arguments to be irrational? The deconstruction of the subject is similarly suspect. For centuries, the modern Western, rational subject has been the axis of history, in relation to whom Third World peoples were simply heathens, barbarians, and non-persons. Now that we heathens, barbarians, and non-persons have finally begun to enter the historical stage as rational subjects in our own right, we are informed that the stage has been disassembled, or deconstructed; that "history" and the rational subjects are, after all, merely artificial constructs, a modern illusion.[31] At the very historical juncture when Latinos and Latinas are asserting our historical subjectivity and the value of our own experience as *locus theologicus*, we are now advised that the historical subject does not exist and that value is an arbitrary, artificial construct. At the very historical juncture when we are articulating and developing a theological language that will allow us to enter into "rational discourse" with the church and academy, we are advised that reason does not exist, only intuition, ambiguity, and irrationality.

None of the notions of reason and rationality available in Western post-modernity is thus adequate for U.S. Hispanic theologians. Each remains beholden to a destructive dichotomy that denies the intellectual capacity, and rationality, of Latinas and Latinos. To identify a whole people with but one aspect of their lives is, literally, to dehumanize them. The task for U.S. Hispanic theologians will thus be to articulate an understanding of the theological enterprise which will avoid these distorted anthropologies and epistemologies.

The liberation of the poor has not only an aesthetic dimension, not only an ethical-political dimension, not only a socioeconomic dimension, but also a rational dimension. The liberation of the poor implies the emergence of historically marginalized persons as full-fledged *rational* historical subjects. Juan Diego was not only a better person than the Spanish bishop; he was also a more intelligent, more rational, more reasonable, more knowledgeable person—even if much less educated in the ways of logical rationality: "The wisdom [of the people], though it is ethical and practical, has logical, speculative value. . . . without lacking a speculative *lógos*, it is an ethical, practical, and affective, or rather human-global

---

31. In his critique of Jean-François Lyotard, Jon Thompson notes the ethnocentric and, therefore, dangerous character of the postmodern deconstruction of history: "From the perspective of many writers, especially those from developing nations or marginalized situations within the developed world, Lyotard's notion that history is 'unpresentable' is a luxury they can ill afford, for the denial of history amounts to a denial of identity and particular historical experiences [ironic, given the postmodern option for particularity against universality]. There is a sense, then, in which the denial of reality (and ultimately of history) found so often in the work of intellectuals from the developed world is a position that is facilitated by not being one of history's victims, for whom 'the nightmare of history' is inescapable. For these intellectuals, a privileged place in an international, predominantly capitalist social and economic order enables the occlusion of even the negation of 'the real.' This point is dramatized in the contrast between Franz Fanon's work, which engages history, and the later work of Jean-François Lyotard, which elides it. This is not to suggest that an intellectual's position vis-à-vis the developed world wholly determines his/her response to the question of reality, but rather that this subject position is one of a number of crucial (and determining) factors" (*Fiction, Crime, and Empire*, p. 180n.9).

knowledge, in which freedom, rationality, and the creative imagination participate simultaneously."[32]

The modern glorification of theoretical reason has had a further destructive consequence. With the Enlightenment, theoretical reason became the exclusive mediator of "truth." That alone is considered "true" which can be determined with scientific certainty; all else is superstition or illusion. Thus, the intellectual pursuit of truth became divorced from the *meaning* of that truth for human life: while rational truth is impersonal, objective, and certain, meaning is personal, subjective, and ambiguous. A corollary of the dichotomy between theory and praxis was thus the dichotomy between truth, as reductively theoretical, and meaning, as reductively experiential.

This split has become reflected in our universities, where the "hard sciences," the paradigmatic arbiters of truth thus conceived, are separated from the humanities, the arbiters of meaning. The sciences deal with "objective" truth, whereas the humanities deal with "subjective" meaning: e.g., the value of scientific knowledge depends exclusively on whether it is "true" (for everyone) while the value of a novel, a work of art, or a religious belief depends exclusively on whether it is "meaningful" (for me, or for us). The social sciences are caught somewhere in between; indeed, this split is often replicated within each social science as the conflict between (objective) quantitative and (subjective) qualitative methods: e.g., between quantitative political science and qualitative political philosophy.[33]

---

32. Scannone, "Religión, lenguaje y sabiduría," 35. Juan Diego's knowledge was not primarily scientific, or theoretical, but practical. As opposed to theoretical knowledge, which abstracts from particular, concrete experience in order to make general, universal judgments, practical knowledge is rooted in particular, concrete experience and relationships. Thus, ethical concerns are always at the core of practical knowledge. This practical knowledge of the poor may be better rendered as "practical wisdom" to indicate its holistic, concrete character. This is the knowledge born in the struggle for survival, which demands extraordinary intellectual resources (see ibid., and the interviews with Latinas in Isasi-Díaz, *En la Lucha*, and Isasi-Díaz and Tarango, *Hispanic Women*). This, furthermore, was the distinction that Aristotle drew between *theoria* and *phronesis*, or practical knowledge (*Nicomachean Ethics*, 6.8; 1142a14–15; see note 21 above). "For him," writes Stephen Toulmin, "every ethical position was that of a given kind of person in given circumstances, and in special relations with other specific people: the concrete particularity of a case was 'of the essence.' Ethics was a field not for theoretical analysis, but for practical wisdom, and it was a mistake to treat it as a universal or abstract science" (*Cosmopolis*, pp. 75–6). What makes rationalism so *un*reasonable is that it severs the intrinsic, intimate relationship between reason and ethics, abstracting prematurely from human intersubjective action, or praxis.

33. See Lamb, "Praxis."

In theology, the separation of truth from meaning has resulted in the separation of the "rational" theological enterprise from the "irrational" faith life of the theologian and his or her community. The task of academic theology is then limited to the theoretical analysis of theological and religious claims and practices; the question of the meaning of those claims and practices is left to the wishy-washy, ambiguous world of the pastoral minister or, perhaps, the pastoral theologian. This is reflected institutionally in the separation between university theology departments (the world of "scientific" theology), on the one hand, and seminaries, pastoral studies institutes, and campus ministries (the world of "irrational" faith) on the other. Theology belongs to the public world of theoretical reason, the realm of truth, while faith belongs to the private world of affect, the realm of meaning.[34]

The postmodern reaction to this dichotomy has been, predictably, to assume the dichotomy while opting for its opposite pole. Thus, once-"objective" modern reason is dethroned, we are left only with "subjective" meaning. If objective, scientific methods cannot lead us to truth, then truth *per se* must not exist. All that we can hope for is "meaningful" experiences which, as "meaningful," are *inaccessible* to rational analysis and judgment; the statement, "this particular experience or theory is meaningful for me," is *ipso facto* incontrovertible and must be accepted at face value, since to judge it according to rational criteria would be to impose on it external, alien, and artificial categories. Truth, then, is reduced to meaning: whatever is meaningful for me is, *ipso facto*, "true"—and *only* for me. Rational certainty is replaced by sheer indeterminancy and ambiguity, since the story which is true to my experience is not necessarily true to yours, and the work of art which is meaningful for me is not necessarily meaningful to you. Indeed, the very notion "that there are nonlinguistic things called 'meanings' which it is the task of language to express" must ultimately be rejected, since such a notion "perpetuate[s] the idea of language as a medium. . . ." that the human "subject" uses to create him or herself rather than that by which the "subject" is created.[35]

Furthermore, since any adjudication between your truth and mine, between your social location and mine, between your experience and mine, would require the artificial imposition of external categories on our experiences in order to mediate between them, such adjudication is impossible. All experience is self-validating, or self-justifying. Indeed, the very term "validation" would be deemed inadequate since it presupposes a norm, or standard, against which an experience or position may be judged, or validated. Every human experience, claim, or position—like every human feeling—is neither true nor false; it simply *is*. All propositional statements are reduced to their "social location," or social context, and

---

34. Ibid.
35. Haber, *Beyond Postmodern Politics*, p. 45.

are thus incapable of being either verified or contradicted by those not likewise situated. Mutual understanding and rational dialogue are also impossible between persons with different experiences, since only those persons who share one's own social location (e.g., one's own gender, race, class, culture) have any access to the ideas that emerge from that particular context. Since, ultimately, the experience of each person is unique, no mutual understanding can be possible. To presume that we can thus understand each other would be to presume the possibility of transcending our particular experience by stepping outside of our own social location. The only contact possible between particular groups and persons is, consequently, affective contact: feeling with another . . . but "feeling" understood as irrational, for the possibility of rational communication is excluded. Postmodernism thus reacts to the modern, rationalist assimilation of all particulars within the ahistorical, abstract, general concept by absolutizing the "irrationality" of the particulars.

The Truth of U.S. Hispanic Popular Catholicism

The postmodern absolutization of particularity places U.S. Hispanics, and other historically marginalized groups, in an ambiguous situation. This situation is outlined very clearly by Justo González:

> . . . oddly enough, the emerging theology is posing anew the old medieval question of the nature of universals. . . . The new theology, being done by those who are aware of their traditional voicelessness, is acutely aware of the manner in which the dominant is confused with the universal. North Atlantic male theology is taken to be basic, normative, universal theology . . . every valid theology must acknowledge its particularity and its connection with the struggles and the vested interests in which it is involved. . . . This, however, leaves us in a difficult position, similar to that of the extreme nominalists of the Middle Ages. Their difficulty was that if universals have no reality beyond the mind, thought has no correspondence to reality, and all statements are so particular as to be meaningless. Our present-day problem is that if theology is always concrete and expresses particular struggles and vested interests, all communication between various segments of the church becomes impossible. This is clearly not the case. The taped conversations on the Bible of a group of fisherfolk on Lake Managua, translated and published in English, became a best seller in the United States and in other parts of the world . . . A sermon by a black preacher in South Africa is received with a loud "Amen" by Asian-American women in California. The insights of an Afro-American theologian are translated into a variety of languages spoken in the poorer nations of the world. Clearly, there is a universality to these very concrete and par-

ticular theological expressions. Yet this is not the universality of abstraction but rather a very different sort of universality that is achieved, paradoxically enough, by being very concrete.[36]

González goes on to argue that, in fact, the revelation of the universal in the particular appears as paradoxical and contradictory only for logical, theoretical reason. If this is so—as I believe it is—then the postmodern rejection of logical reason is itself based on that which it claims to reject, namely, logical reason; again, postmodernism reveals its thoroughly modern character.

For the Christian, however, the understanding of the relationship between the universal and the particular is rooted in the incarnation itself, in the "scandal of particularity": the universal God is revealed *in the particular* person of a first-century Jewish carpenter's son from Nazareth.[37] Universals do have a "reality beyond the mind" and thought does have a "correspondence to reality." Theoretical reason is not alien to human praxis; what is alien to the lived experience of Latinas and Latinos (and all human beings, *qua* human) is the *dichotomy*, or disjunction between theory and praxis and, its corollary, the dichotomy between universal, normative truth and particular, subjective meaning. If human praxis is, indeed, intrinsically relational, or intersubjective, then it is also intrinsically open to self-transcendence, or universality. Unless the human person is no more than a billiard ball, that openness to universality presupposes an intellectual, as well as an affective and ethical-political openness beyond one's particular lived experience.[38] If community is the

---

36. González, *Mañana*, pp. 51–2. See also his "Metamodern Aliens in Postmodern Jerusalem," in *Aliens in the Promised Land,* ed. Isasi-Díaz and Segovia.

37. González, *Mañana*, p. 52–3.

38. The self-transcendence that takes place in intersubjective praxis, or "empathic fusion," thus has an intellectual dimension, which Hugo Meynell calls "cognitive self-transcendence": "What do I mean by 'cognitive self-transcendence'? I mean by it the capacity of conscious subjects to know things and states of affairs that exist apart from and beyond themselves and their societies. If I know that the majority of the earth is covered by water, I am evidently exercising cognitive self-transcendence in doing so since, though I am certainly dependent upon my society in knowing it (since I never collected all the relevant evidence for myself), the majority of the earth's surface might still have been covered by water even if no human beings or other rational creatures had ever evolved to know about it. . . . To deny cognitive self-transcendence is to be driven to the remarkable conclusion either that there are no states of affairs that obtain prior to and independently of human beings and their societies, or that we can never get to know that such states of affairs obtain. . . . But it might be objected that it is one thing to exercise one's mind in such a way as to come by well-founded judgments and so to approximate to true judgments, but it is another to obtain knowledge of a real world supposed to exist prior to and independently of anyone's mind or its exercise.

source of individuality, then the possibility of transcending one's individual experience and one's own "truth" is *presupposed* in human praxis. Only if the individual, or the "social location," is autonomous and self-sufficient can the possibility of incommensurable human experiences and incommensurable "truths" or "meanings" even arise.

The possibility of mutual understanding—not simply mutual empathy—is thus itself intrinsic to an organic, relational anthropology.[39] The possibility of mutual, shared understanding implies, in turn, the possibility of shared norms—mediated, always, by the particular perspectives through which they are revealed.[40] More specifically, shared norms are mediated by praxis, that is, by the *active relationship* between particular others. Truth is not fundamentally a thing but an event. As a *human* event, it demands intelligibility—again, unless what are interacting are not human persons of spirit, mind, and body, but mere billiard balls. "One 'knows' the truth," contends Juan Carlos Scannone, "in an ethical relationship (with others, with God) which is intrinsic to the '*nosotros*'; though, nevertheless, the '*lógos*' and knowledge are not reduced to '*éthos*.' "[41] It is in intersubjective praxis that we transcend our particular experiences, not only physically and affectively but also intellectually.[42]

Where the lived experience of each person or group is seen as *absolutely* unique and incommensurable with the experience of other persons or groups, the possibility of a self-transcending truth that is rational and

---

However, after all, it can be shown that these are not two things, but one. . . . when we loosely contrast 'our world' or 'the world for us' with the world of other social groups, do we not really presuppose that the belief-systems of other societies are themselves parts of the real world that we may discover by use of the same capacities? After all, we make discoveries about other people's systems of belief just as we make discoveries about barium, white dwarfs, and hyraxes . . ." "Philosophy After Philosophy," in *Communication and Lonergan: Common Ground for Forging the New Age*, ed. Thomas J. Farrell and Paul A. Soukup (Kansas City: Sheed and Ward, 1993), 140–43.

39. See Scannone, "Filosofía primera e intersubjetividad," esp. 370–73.

40. Again, in the words of Meynell, "the considerations that lead to the view that cognitive self-transcendence is possible also vindicate the possibility of moral self-transcendence, which is the making of true judgments that are not merely a matter of personal preference or social *fiat* about what is good or bad, better or worse . . . *Horribile dictu*, we are driven by the considerations that I have brought forward to believe not only in Truth with a capital T, but in Goodness with a capital G." Ibid., pp. 144–45.

41. Scannone, "Un nuevo punto de partida," 32.

42. See Jürgen Habermas, *Legitimation Crisis* (Boston: Beacon, 1975), esp. pp. 109ff.; Bernstein, *Beyond Objectivism and Relativism*, esp. pp. 171–231; Sandel, *Liberalism and the Limits of Justice*, pp. 172–73; Helmut Peukert, *Science, Action, and Fundamental Theology: Toward a Theology of Communicative Action* (Cambridge, MA: MIT Press, 1984), esp. pp. 163–245; and Lonergan, *Method in Theology*, esp. pp. 57–99.

normative must be denied.[43] The pursuit of truth, undertaken as a common, intersubjective praxis (and, therefore, as *meaningful* for that praxis), is then replaced by the quest for meaning, undertaken by each individual within the confines of his or her own experience. The beatific vision is replaced by the "meaningful experience." Meaning is, in turn, conceived as radically particular: what is "true for me" is not "true for you," and vice versa.

Postmodern culture reacts to the modern sacralization of universal, *theoretical* truth by rejecting the possibility of truth altogether. Once one accepts the modern, conceptualist identification of normative truth with theory, one also implicitly accepts the modern separation of universal truth, valid for all, from particular meaning, valid only for the particular person or group. It then becomes impossible to conceive of meaning as in any way normative, or universally true since the ideas and concepts of theoretical reason can never fully comprehend and express the meaning of human praxis. Consequently, when universal reason is deconstructed so too is any possibility of universal norms, or truth. What remains is meaning—radically particular, ambiguous, indeterminate, and irrational. In this context, the question of the truth of a work of art or a religious practice is never asked; all that matters is, instead, whether the work of art or the religious practice is "meaningful." Then for instance, U.S. Hispanic popular Catholicism becomes but one among many equally valid, because equally meaningful expressions of religious experience—and valid *only* for U.S. Hispanics.

---

43. As Meynell notes, the denial of normative truth is self-contradictory, since it presupposes what it claims to deny. "It is self-destructive to deny that I can ever make a true statement, since if that denial is true, it constitutes a falsifying exception to itself. . . . Also, it is self-destructive to deny that I can ever have rational grounds for making a statement. Either that statement itself is made by me on rational grounds, in which case it constitutes a falsifying exception to itself; or it is not, in which case it is not to be taken seriously. . . ." Meynell, "On Truth, Method, and Gadamer," 218. And again: "the claim that cognitive self-transcendence is impossible . . . is actually self-destructive. One may consider the statement, 'Cognitive self-transcendence is impossible.' Is this supposed to state a truth that is the case independently of the attitudes and convictions of the person who utters it? If it is, that very utterance exemplifies cognitive self-transcendence. If it is not, it follows that there is another subjective viewpoint no less intrinsically worthy of respect, from which the contradictory claim is true—that cognitive self-transcendence is possible." Meynell, "Philosophy After Philosophy," 141. Moreover, the claim that my social location and experience are different from yours already presupposes that I have some (self-transcending) knowledge of your social location and experience—which knowledge I am using to distinguish yours from mine. Again, I cannot claim that my cultural perspective is particular and unique to me unless and until I have some knowledge of other cultural perspectives—which knowledge would already imply the possibility of self-transcendence. See ibid., pp. 146–47.

Yet our lived experience is very different: the meaning of the cross or Guadalupe is experienced not only as meaningful, or "true for us," but as normative and true, period—precisely *because* it is true for us, and we are intrinsically related to others. If all human praxis is intrinsically relational, its meaning is never entirely private, or *absolutely* different, which is to say that the meaning of praxis is never *absolutely* ambiguous and particular. In light of its anthropology and praxis, U.S. Hispanic popular Catholicism cannot be viewed as radically ambiguous, meaningful only to U.S. Hispanics, and, therefore, unable to make any normative truth claims.

All such interpretations presuppose a very different horizon of interpretation, anthropology, and notion of human praxis. Popular Catholic narratives, symbols, and rituals can be perceived as radically ambiguous only when viewed from outside, by observers under the sway of modern and postmodern presuppositions. From the inside, the narratives, symbols, and rituals are experienced as not only meaningful but also as theologically *true*. Symbols are both the end *and* the source of rational understanding; in the words of Paul Ricoeur, "the symbol gives rise to thought, but thought always returns to and is informed by the symbol."[44] Aesthetic experience not only transcends theory; it also gives birth to theoretical reflection. Those forms of aesthetic experience, those narratives, symbols, and rituals "which are assumed to disclose permanent possibilities of meaning and truth," become what David Tracy has called the "classics" of the community's tradition.[45] The narratives, symbols, and rituals of Latino popular Catholicism are such classics because they disclose *"permanent* possibilities of meaning *and* truth." The scandal of U.S. Hispanic popular Catholicism to both the modern and the postmodern scholar is precisely that, for us, these practices reveal universal, indeed cosmological truth—that, therefore, is normative for everyone. Guadalupe is meaningful for us because it is true for everyone—and it is true for everyone because it is meaningful for us. If the story of Guadalupe is not meaningful for many Anglos, it is not, for that reason, any less true—for *everyone*. Particular meaning mediates universal truth.

"Yet we are not dealing here with a mystery [or truth] *behind* the phenomenon," asserts Scannone, "but in and beyond it (not a spatial but an ethical 'beyond' . . .)."[46] To say that U.S. Hispanic popular Catholicism makes normative claims is not to say, then, that those claims to truth can be imposed on others. This is not an ahistorical, conceptual "truth" which denies the particularity of human praxis, or which is unconcerned with

---

44. Quoted in David Tracy, *The Analogical Imagination: Christian Theology and the Culture of Pluralism* (New York: Crossroad, 1981), p. 13.

45. Ibid., p. 68.

46. Scannone, "Filosofía primera e intersubjetividad," 384.

the question of the *meaning* of truth for particular human persons and communities; it is not an "abstract universal which would manifest itself univocally in each culture, changing only its accidental forms, nor a Hegelian-style concrete universal, which in dialectical form would subsume into itself absolutely all the particulars. . . ."[47] On the contrary, this universal truth is always mediated by the particular meaning of U.S. Hispanic praxis, or Latino popular Catholicism: it is, thus, a "*situated universal.*"[48] As such, this normative truth can be and is mediated also by the praxis of other particular persons and communities—otherwise, it could never be communicated to others.[49] As a truth grounded in human praxis, it is a truth grounded in and emerging from the *relationship* between "*others*" and thus, by definition, cannot be imposed on others from outside without thereby surrendering its claim to normativity—that is, without becoming "false" by undermining the very intersubjectivity that defines human praxis.

If truth is grounded in praxis, in the interrelationship of others, any attempt to impose that truth on those others, thereby denying their very

---

47. Scannone, "Religión, lenguaje y sabiduría," 31.

48. Ibid. In order to distinguish a particularity, or situatedness, that denies the possibility of universal truth from a particularity which mediates universal truth and is, thus, open to transcendence and communication beyond its own situation or perspective, Scannone refers to the distinction, in Spanish, between the two verbs "*ser*" and "*estar*," a distinction not present in the English language, which would translate both of these verbs as "to be": " 'Estar' comes from 'stare,' to be standing, in a firm but not fixed manner (and, in that sense, not definitively permanent); it implies a determination, but not an essential one. 'Ser,' on the other hand, comes from 'sedere,' to be sitting, and implies that which is definitive or at least habitual, it points to that which is essential in a way already previously and ontologically determined and, therefore, well assured. The mere juxtaposition of the Spanish forms: 'I am sick' [*estoy enfermo*] (contingently, not constitutively) and 'I am sick' [*soy enfermo*] (by nature or, at least, by constitution, as if by a kind of second nature), or of the forms 'I am well' [*estoy bien*] . . . and 'I am good' [*soy bueno*] . . . illustrates it sufficiently. We say 'I am at the beginning' [*estoy en el principio*] (of some task, of some process . . .), but we translate the prologue of the Gospel of St. John saying: 'in the beginning was [*era*; the past tense of *ser*] the Word,' and we continue thus: 'and the Word was [*estaba*; the past tense of *estar*] in God, and the Word was [*era*] God.' Consequently, '*estar*' has a more situated or circumstantial sense, to be firmly (standing) but disposed to walking, and it does not express the essence of things in themselves, as does the verb '*ser*.' " Scannone, "Un nuevo punto de partida," p. 38.

49. As Meynell observes, "few judgments are better grounded than that there are other beings besides myself who also make judgments and furthermore are acquainted with sensations, feelings, joys, griefs, and other conscious events and episodes in the same way that I am myself." "On Truth, Method, and Gadamer," in *Communication and Lonergan*, eds. Farrell and Soukup, 219.

otherness and difference from us, implies the degeneration of praxis into a poiesis that treats other persons and groups as mere objects of our action. An imposed truth is not a truth grounded in praxis but a "truth" grounded in poiesis, in a rejection of the particularity and fundamental (though not absolute or irrational) ambiguity of human praxis; it is a judgment arising not from interaction, empathic fusion, and mutual understanding but from instrumentalization, coercion, and violence. It is, therefore, no truth at all, but the most fundamental of all falsehoods.

Thus, one cannot claim that one's intersubjective praxis is normative, and understand that to mean that it can be imposed on (or *made* meaningful *for*) the lives of other persons and communities, without thereby entering into a self-contradiction. To attempt to impose devotion to Guadalupe, for instance, would be, *de facto*, to deny the truth of Guadalupe. To impose the Christian faith, as Bartolomé de Las Casas so clearly saw, is to deny the very truth we claim to profess.[50] Only if one first defines praxis not as inherently relational but as autonomous can the possibility of an "imposed truth" arise. Only where the particular and the universal are perceived as contradictory is the notion of an imposed truth *not* contradictory. That, indeed, is the history of modernity, from Columbus, to Descartes, to Kant, to Rousseau, to Eichmann, to proponents of English-only laws.

The normative claims of U.S. Hispanic popular Catholicism are of a different order. Popular Catholicism derives its transformative power among U.S. Hispanics precisely from its ability to embody and express universal, theological truth across generations, but to do so *through the particular* meaning that the narratives, symbols, and rituals have in the lives of U.S. Hispanics. The possibility of communicating with and understanding another person beyond the self presupposes an affirmation of the other's own particularity: "dialogue presupposes ethical otherness."[51]

Paradoxically, only by affirming the uniqueness of *this* or *that particular* truth can one affirm that truth as normative beyond the particular: only if one recognizes and affirms the *uniqueness* of the Guadalupe story vis-à-vis other Marian apparitions will one be able to perceive the universal truths revealed in that story. Only if I affirm your own concrete particularity and uniqueness will I be able to understand how your own life and history reveal a universal truth that is also true for me. If, as we saw in chapter 3, the affirmation of the particular *as* particular is what reveals its relationship to other particulars, then the affirmation of particular meaning as particular is what reveals its implicit normative claims, that is, its claims to universal truth: "genuine objectivity is the fruit of

---

50. Gutiérrez, *Las Casas*, p. 99–191.
51. Scannone, "Un nuevo punto de partida," 34.

authentic subjectivity."[52] "Mutuality," writes Ada María Isasi-Díaz, "asks us to give serious consideration to what the other is saying, not only to respect it but to be willing to accept it *as good for all*" (my emphasis).[53] Elsewhere, she explains that, "instead of attempting to present a universal voice, our attempt has been to point to the universal by being as specific as possible. . . . radical immanence is a different way of understanding what up to now has been called transcendence. . . ."[54]

As mentioned earlier, not until the infant first recognizes the mother as "mother," that is, as other than him or herself, can the infant know his or her own identity as "child." Consequently, only at that moment can the infant know the *truth* of the statements "my mother loves me" and "I love my mother." Prior to that recognition of the mother's particularity, the truth is itself unrecognizable because, since there is no "other," and therefore no "I," neither can there be any mutual love. However, when the other finally appears as "mother," the one at whose breast the infant is suckled, what is revealed and recognized is a truth (the reality of a mutual love) that, as *inter*subjective, is not limited to either the particular experience of the mother or that of the child. It is a truth that emerges *from the interaction between* two particular persons and that, therefore, transcends each of them. As Juan Diego's knowledge of the truth of who he is and who the Lady is emerges from the interaction between them. Our knowledge of who we are, as U.S. Hispanics, and who Jesus is emerges from our interaction with him in the Holy Thursday and Good Friday processions.

Yet postmodern culture is decidedly uncomfortable with any truth claims, since it presupposes the modern notion of truth as an ahistorical, conceptual, impersonal universality in the absence of which all is sheer indeterminacy and ambiguity. Since the subject does not exist neither can intersubjective truth. Thus, postmodern Western theology must interpret the narratives, symbols, and rituals of U.S. Hispanic popular

---

52. Lonergan, *Method in Theology*, p. 292. The human impossibility of achieving an ahistorical "objectivity" need not lead to a rejection of objective truth altogether. Indeed, as noted above, there is no more objective truth than that each of us is a unique subject: "To be 'objective' in one sense is to pursue one's inquiries as though nothing so 'subjective,' and therefore presumably non-objective, as human feelings, desires, sensations, acts of coming to understand or misunderstand, judgments for adequate or inadequate reason, and so on, existed. . . ." Meynell, "On Truth, Method, and Gadamer," 218. See Lonergan's notion of objectivity and the "virtually unconditioned," in *Insight*, pp. 279–316, 375–84, 549–52; and *Method in Theology*, pp. 37–8, 75–6, 238–39, 262–65, 338.

53. Ada María Isasi-Díaz, "A Hispanic Garden in a Foreign Land," in *Inheriting our Mothers' Gardens: Feminist Theology in Third World Perspective*, ed. Letty M. Russell, Kwok Pui-lan, Ada María Isasi-Díaz, and Katie Geneva Cannon (Louisville: Westminster Press, 1988), 97.

54. Isasi-Díaz, *En la Lucha*, p. 63.

Catholicism as particular, meaningful, irrational, and ambiguous *over against* the universal, true, rational certainty of, for instance, "official" Catholicism. Otherwise, the "irrationality" of Eastern religions and Mother Goddess religions will be *pitted against* the "rationality" of Christian confessionalism.

Were popular Catholicism—indeed, were Christian faith—simply a meaningful, ambiguous experience incapable of making any transcendent, normative claims, it would not have moved, transformed, and empowered so many people, so many of our own mothers, fathers, and ancestors, to make courageous, self-transcending commitments and sacrifices. "So obvious a truth of our cultural lives," observes David Tracy, "seems to be widely ignored; at least any claim to truth in the classic is quietly but effectively disowned. . . . Any normative claim to knowledge, any suggestion of truth for the classic is often shunned as that higher form of both category confusion and bad taste dear to the elitist."[55] It is thought, at best, a quaint curiosity that millions of people actually believe that the story of Guadalupe is true—not just for Mexicans but for everyone—rather than merely a meaningful legend with no normative status. In a contemporary Western society where the highest compliment that can be paid any religious belief or practice is, not that it is true, but that it is meaningful, or "interesting," Guadalupe is, at least, meaningful (for some) and interesting.[56] If popular Catholicism can make no normative truth claims beyond the U.S. Hispanic community, then it will remain as but one more interesting social phenomenon, meaningful and true for a marginal minority but irrelevant for the larger U.S. society.

The practical results of postmodern culture's allergic reaction to any truth claims are, again, disastrous. Claims to universal truth and knowledge become the exclusive purview of science and technology, while the arts and religion become merely matters of private, personal taste.[57] The separation of public life from private life now manifests itself as a separation of the public, normative truth claims of the sciences from the private, ambiguous meaning of the arts and religion:

> Whenever the technoeconomic realm controls the list of candidates for the meaning of what will count as shareable, as public, as knowledge, as truth, then the entire realm of culture—and all the candidates for classic status—must either be levelled to the conventional masked as the ordinary, or retreat into the privacy of some overcrowded reservation of the spirit. We already know

---

55. Tracy, *The Analogical Imagination*, p. 109.

56. See ibid., p. 111.

57. Recall the Kantian disjunction between "objective knowledge" and "merely subjective, private feelings"; see Bernstein, *Beyond Objectivism and Relativism*, p. 126.

what alone will count as truth in the public realm: the methodi-
cally controlled results of the technical realm in all its forms. The
rest is taste, or emotion, or "art." And art, finally, becomes a matter of the private vision of the artist: The spontaneous genius of
the great Romantics has become the artistic "celebrity" of
today. . . . Meanwhile, the relative but real autonomy of the work
of art . . . is destroyed by private ideologies employing psychological, sociological or theological forms of reductionism. In that
kind of unhappy situation it is perhaps not so strange that aesthetic theories can sometimes join ordinary language understandings of the reality of art as mere personal preferences, private tastes.
The discussion ends where it might begin: with one of the few Latin
phrases still common parlance in all Western languages: *de
gustibus non est disputandum.*[58]

When the intrinsic connection between particular meaning and universal
truth is severed—that is, when the meaning of particular experiences is
not recognized as mediating universal truth—art, literature, and religion
lose their ability to subvert the dominant culture because, by becoming
privatized, they lose their ability to engage that culture at all. Some individual Anglos may, indeed, find meaning and truth in Latino religious
narratives, symbols, and rituals, but the dominant culture as such *cannot*
do so as long as its "openness" to U.S. Hispanics is governed by postmodern anthropological and epistemological presuppositions.

The individual exceptions, together with our own experience as U.S.
Hispanics, indicate the artificiality of the truth-meaning dichotomy. In
concrete, particular human praxis, we do not experience meaning as radically ambiguous or indeterminate, as incapable of being communicated,
or mediated publicly—even if never completely—through the public objectivity of words and ideas. We experience art and religion as not only
meaningful, but as also true, as having a relatively autonomous and objective reality beyond our own particular social location. Without that
relative objectivity, which is mediated by intersubjective praxis, art and
religion (like the family, as we saw above) are doomed to remain merely
private affairs that, as purely "private," are immune to rational critique
and ethical-political judgment:

Yet do either those aesthetic theories grounded in "taste," or ordi-
nary-language understandings of the nondisputability of "taste,"
really fit our actual experience of the work of art? . . . the authentic experience of art is quite the opposite: We find ourselves "caught
up" in its world, we are shocked, surprised, challenged by its star-
tling beauty *and* its recognizable truth. . . . When we ignore the

---

58. Tracy, *The Analogical Imagination*, pp. 109–110.

actual experience of art by imposing alien aesthetic theories of taste upon it, we are tempted to misinterpret the experience as a purely, indeed, merely "aesthetic" one. In a manner analogous to our attempted alienation of ourselves and our own effective history into the realm of historicist privacy masked as autonomy, we may deny that the work of art [or religious practice] has anything to do with what we name knowledge, truth, reality. . . . For publicness and truth, the autonomous subject will look elsewhere: to those forms of thinking guaranteed as scientific and technical. . . . The work of art . . . is always interesting, sometimes even fascinating. . . . But art does not provide an encounter with anything we can call truth about ourselves or reality.[59]

Works of art, and religious narratives, symbols, and rituals, are not experienced either as objective realities "outside" and over against ourselves *or* as merely private, emotional, irrational experiences. Instead, if authentic aesthetic and religious experience "captures us" and we find ourselves "caught up" in it, then that experience is in some sense objective, since it is not merely internal to the self.[60] When one travels, for instance, through the Rocky Mountains, one is caught up into their majesty and splendor. The extraordinary vistas raise the hairs on the back of one's head and send a chill down the spine. Such a reaction is not merely arbitrary and subjective, but an appropriate, subjective response to an external, objective reality: the overwhelming natural beauty of the mountains. Not only a "meaningful experience," aesthetic, or empathic fusion is also a revelation of self-transcending truth.

Moreover, when we give ourselves over to beauty, whether natural beauty, works of art, or religious practices, these transform our lives. They are not merely private "aesthetic" experiences, emotional "highs" independent of the rest of our lives. Rather, they impact the way we *live* our lives (praxis) *and* our understanding, or knowledge (theory) of our lives and our world:

In entering into an experience of a genuine work of art we risk entering a "game" where truth is at stake. . . . When I enter a game, if I insist upon my self-consciousness to control every move, I am not in fact playing the game. . . . Pure subjectivity can account for an inability to play, a refusal to act, an impossibility of ever entering any game other than one's own self-designated role, the narcissist game where one is sole actor and sole spectator. But pure subjectivity cannot account for the actual experience of playing any game. . . . Whenever we actually experience even one classic work

59. Ibid., pp. 110–111.
60. Ibid., pp. 111–15.

of art we are liberated from privateness into the genuine publicness of a disclosure of truth.[61]

Absolute ambiguity leads to absolute paralysis. If we are not playing a common game, but each of us is playing his or her own game (or each social group is playing its own game), what can I possibly learn about my game from yours? Thus, the dominant culture may tolerate the U.S. Hispanics' "game," but will not view it as having any *necessary* connection to or implications for its own game. Thus, our irrelevance and marginalization will continue.

Theological Pluralism in a Postmodern World

In theology, the emphasis on social situation and particular meaning has manifested itself in the proliferation of theologies self-consciously grounded in particular perspectives: black theology, feminist theology, womanist theology, mujerista theology, liberation theology, U.S. Hispanic theology, etc. These are all reactions against the Western, male, white theologians' traditional failure to recognize the particularity of their own theologies, instead imposing these as objectively true and universally meaningful; only Western, male, white theology has been considered Theology, pure and simple, with a capital "T" and without the need for any adjective. "What is said in Manila," writes Justo González, "is very relevant for the Philippines. What is said in Tubingen, Oxford, or Yale is relevant for the entire church."[62]

The truth, however, ought to be precisely the reverse. What is said in Manila ought to be considered relevant for the entire church—because what is said in Manila is what alone presupposes the uniqueness of all particular peoples, since it is being proclaimed by a particular people whose own uniqueness has historically been denied. Because it presupposes the value of particularity, what is said in Manila implies the possibility that what is said in Yale may be true; but, because it presupposes a denial of particularity, what is said in Yale denies the possibility that what is said in Manila may be true. If, as Scannone avers, "dialogue presupposes ethical *otherness*," those groups whose own otherness, or particularity, is denied are the ones in the best position to judge when and where a truly universal knowledge—i.e., one arrived at in dialogue between others—has been achieved.

Yet, in the contemporary socio-historical context, a contrary emphasis on the particularity of every *locus theologicus*, e.g., U.S. Hispanic experience, over against the ahistorical, universal context of Western

---

61. Ibid., pp. 113–14.
62. González, *Mañana*, p. 52.

theologies will itself tend to be read through the *equally Western* prism of postmodernity, with its absolutization of particularity, otherness, ambiguity, and indeterminacy. The resulting fragmentation and mutual marginalization of theological discourse has at least two important consequences, both of which undermine the liberative intent of these theologies.

First, modern Western theologians are effectively immunized from any critique. If I am correct in my suggestion that postmodernity is but a stepchild of modernity, rebelling against its parent while unaware that this rebellion is itself a fundamental form of dependence, then the interpretative horizon of both is essentially the same: postmodernity assumes the dualistic, dichotomous anthropology and epistemology of modernity. If this is true, then what appears as an openness to other perspectives or other cultures is, in fact, an "openness" still controlled by and understood within one particular perspective, that of the dominant Western postmodern (*née* modern) culture. After all, contemporary advocates of otherness and multiculturalism were not always *post*modern; before their "conversion," they too were modern rationalists; theological discourse continues to be determined and regulated by Western, white males.

This creates a problem for postmodern culture: how to admit other perspectives into the dialogue (so as to ensure "multiculturalism") without, however, surrendering the right to frame the dialogue within the interpretative horizon of postmodernity. A solution to this problem is provided by the postmodern absolutization of the particular: Western, white male theologians can now invite these other perspectives into the dialogue with the implicit understanding that, as particular and other, these perspectives are "true to the experience" of only those persons who share the particular perspective or social location. Thus, U.S. Hispanic theology may indeed be considered true, but only for U.S. Hispanics, since it is a reflection of "their" particular experience. Anglo theologians *may* learn something from U.S. Hispanics but *need not* do so; their pedigree as theologians will be in no danger should they turn a deaf ear to Latinas and Latinos, nor will they be excluded from the academy or the church. What is demanded is simply tolerance and, perhaps, an affective openness that does not require—indeed precludes—an intellectual openness: e.g., U.S. Hispanics may represent a *practical* challenge to Christian *pastoral* workers, but certainly not an *intellectual* challenge to Christian *theologians*. Yet, conversely, U.S. Hispanic theologians *must* learn Anglo theologies to be credible theologians and be invited into the theological dialogue—even if the dialogue assumes that our theologies will be relevant only to other Latinos and Latinas.

In the context of postmodern pluralism, then, U.S. Hispanic theology will often be accepted as one of the many particular theologies which, as particular, are meaningful and, therefore, "true" for their particular constituencies—in this case, U.S. Hispanics. Such acceptance will appear, on the surface, as a welcome alternative to the exclusion of U.S. Hispanic experience from the totalizing, universalizing, and ahistorical embrace of modern, rationalist theologies. Beneath the surface, however, little really changes. "What is said in Manila" will still be relevant only for the Philippines. If modernity marginalized the voices of the poor, postmodernity may listen, but only as one who curiously listens in on someone else's conversation, since, as the voices "of the poor," these can ultimately be understood *only* by the poor themselves. It is *their* conversation and, as such, does not necessarily implicate the (equally particular and unique) conversation being carried on among the wealthy, powerful, and privileged. By absolutizing particular perspectives and, thus, making any genuine communication or understanding between them impossible, each particular perspective is effectively isolated from the rest. The beneficiaries are the same privileged, dominant groups of that modern society which "post" modernity had supposedly left behind.

The non-existence of Latinos and Latinas in our contemporary context is not achieved only by forms of outright exclusion but also by an ostensible inclusion in a postmodern cultural pluralism whose internal structure and presuppositions foreordain our invisibility. Once it is assumed that the experience of a person or group is 1) self-validating and, therefore, "valid" and "reasonable" only for that person or group, and 2) inaccessible and incomprehensible to other persons or groups, the possibility of both dialogue *and* critique is denied. Where mutual understanding is impossible, so too is critique. What is denied is the ability to make a difference in *another* person's life, since, we are told, it literally "doesn't make any difference" what our experience and values are as long as they are *ours*. If all experiences and values are equally valid, equally irrational, then our experiences and values as U.S. Hispanics are valid for us and, as such, ought to be respected and listened to—but they can make no claims on non-Hispanics, e.g., the dominant groups. Moreover, if all experiences and values are arbitrary and irrational, then there is, literally, no reason why the dominant groups should see themselves implicated in what we have to say. Those groups become effectively immune to criticism; after all, they have as much right to their positions as we to ours. For the poor, relativism implies marginalization and exclusion; for the privileged, whether modern or postmodern, relativism implies protection from those who are marginalized and excluded.[63]

---

63. Honi Fern Haber notes the ambiguous nature of the postmodern celebration of difference, openness, incoherence, and otherness with respect to marginalized groups: "In making us aware of the artificiality of closure, the law of difference makes politics radically plural, and this can make us more sensitive to, and tolerant of, difference. . . . The problem with the law of difference . . . is that taken to the extreme (treated as a universal principle), as it is in some present formulations of a politics of difference, it has the unintended consequence of excluding the possibility of oppositional politics. The politics of difference must

Concrete examples of this form of marginalization abound. Because of this fragmentation and marginalization, for instance, it is unlikely that any university would consider hiring U.S. Hispanic theologians if it did not have a sizeable Latino student body. The underlying assumption is that U.S. Hispanic theology is meaningful and important only for Latinos and Latinas; if these are not available to take classes in U.S. Hispanic theology, there is no need to offer the classes at all. Indeed, even when the classes are offered, they will be offered as electives, since, for the modernist, (particular) U.S. Hispanic theology is not (universal) Theology and, for the postmodernist, U.S. Hispanic theology is not feminist theology, or black theology, or Native American theology, etc. (all of which will also be electives). U.S. Hispanic theology might be taught, but as a compartmentalized, isolated, and thus marginalized perspective with no intrinsic, or essential relation to either (white European male) Theology or to other "perspectival theologies."

A second major consequence of this fragmentation of theology into particular theologies is the increased conflict and competition among particular theologies, especially Third World and feminist theologies. This, in fact, is the surest sign that an authentic pluralism or multiculturalism does not exist: the access to those material resources necessary

---

be reconceptualized to accommodate the fact that if any and all closures are terroristic, then the Other will never be given a chance to form itself as a political force. It will remain unpresented and unpresentable. And since, in fact, political systems (power regimes) which exclude or marginalize otherness do exist [see, in chapter 5 above, the discussion of the ethical-political and socioeconomic mediations of aesthetic praxis], then insofar as the law of difference can be used to keep the Other from articulating itself as a coherent, even if contingent identity, the law of difference serves the dominant and dominating order. It becomes a tool of colonization and keeps the Other defenseless. . . . the postmodern repudiation of all grand narratives, where this is equivalent to disallowing all closure, is unacceptable from the position of those involved in oppositional struggles. Postmodern politics is *not* a viable option on this description for it repudiates the formation of community and of coherent subjects, both of which are necessary to the identity formation of otherness. . . . any notion of a politics of difference which accepts the postmodern/poststructuralist disjunction: either difference or similarity leaves no locus for politics: no community, no self, no viable political theory. . . . My suggestion is that . . . the subject of oppositional struggle is subjects-in-community and not the subject in isolation; nor is it no subject at all" (*Beyond Postmodern Politics*, pp. 130–34). The threat posed by postmodern, anti-rational pluralism to marginalized groups is also adverted to by Jon Thompson: "What is sacrificed [in French postmodernist theory] is the analytical equipment by which contemporaneous experience can be placed in a historical context, analyzed, and then, at least partly, understood. The death-of-history strain of postmodernism has to a very large extent internalized the totalizing, imperial ideologies of late-twentieth-century monopoly capital, which subliminally, and sometimes overtly, suggest that resistance and opposition are impossible" (*Fiction, Crime, and Empire*, p. 166).

for making one's voice heard (e.g., access to the media, educational institutions, religious institutions, political decision-making) remains controlled by the same dominant groups—again, human relationships are always mediated by poiesis, or economic relationships. This access is increased, but only in a limited way, ensuring that all the various particular perspectives ("special interest groups") will have to fight with each other for this limited access. Thus, a limited number of scholarships may be made available to "minority candidates," leaving it up to the African American, U.S. Hispanic, Native American, and Asian candidates to fight over the funds. The result is that these groups, marginalized by modern rationalism, which absolutized the universal, continue to be marginalized by postmodern multiculturalism, which absolutizes the particular—while ensuring that one particular perspective continues to control access to the dialogue by providing the interpretative horizon, and the economic and political structures, within which the dialogue will be carried out.

By fostering this fragmentation and marginalization, moreover, postmodern multiculturalism begins to look a lot like modern liberal individualism. If the latter presupposed that society was composed of isolated, autonomous individuals, the former presupposes that society is composed of isolated, autonomous "social locations" or groups. The "deconstruction" of the individual ego, or subject, leads not to community but to increased isolation. The individual's claims to rights and freedoms are now deemed to be merely arbitrary claims based on an individual's particular experience, and thus not rooted in any pre-existent, commonly accepted order or tradition, such as "natural law" or "history"—since all such orders and traditions are themselves arbitrary constructs. Unable to either affirm or deny the truth-claims or value-claims of another, the individual or group is left with two options: extinguish the other, or defend the other's right to assert his or her claims as self-justifying and, therefore, unquestionable. The only acceptable option for the postmodern culture is, of course, the latter. Either we defend the *equal* value of all experiences and positions, thereby promoting freedom, or, if we continue to insist that certain experiences or positions are more valid than others, we inevitably do violence to these others by excluding them from our discourse, thereby promoting tyranny. *Any* closure would imply *total* closure and, hence, violence.[64]

---

64. As Haber points out, the problem is not the affirmation of otherness and difference, which is always a fundamental prerequisite for human community, but the *universalization* of otherness and difference, i.e., the assumption that *all that exists* is sheer otherness and difference, and that, therefore, *any* limitation of otherness and difference is necessarily, *ipso facto* totalitarian. She argues that difference is not universal but temporary (*Beyond Postmodern Politics*, pp. 113–34). This is similar to Scannone's distinction, above, between "*estar*" (suggesting a temporary and changing identity) and "*ser*" (suggesting an essential and unchanging identity).

If the above analysis is correct, the reduction of the individual ego to his or her social situation, and the consequent dissolution of the subject, do not represent a supersession of modern, Enlightenment individualism and rationalism; on the contrary, they represent the final stage in the historical development of liberal individualism and rationalism. To paraphrase Karl Marx, the inevitable end of individualism is the end of the individual; the exaltation of the individual, autonomous subject leads ineluctably to the self-destruction of that same subject; and the inevitable end of rationalism is the end of reason.

In modern liberal individualism, the self is but an empty void, a *tabula rasa*, which is given shape and content through the individual's free, autonomous, rational choices in the course of his or her life. Once postmodernism unmasks the arbitrary and capricious character of these choices—and, hence, of individual identity—all that remains is the *tabula rasa*, the empty void, the "selfless self." The "socially unsituated self" must eventually self-destruct, becoming *nothing but* "social situation."

Likewise, the deconstruction of modern reason and the exaltation of affect as feelings and emotions do not lead to a broader, more adequate understanding of rationality, but to the dissolution of all rational discourse. When rational discourse is no longer possible, since each particular social location is incommensurable with any other, only irrational relationships are possible: either a mindless, affective affirmation of "otherness" or an equally mindless conflict among the disparate, particular perspectives.

As in modern liberal individualism, when, in postmodern culture, it is no longer possible to make qualitative judgments about the validity of particular positions, the only available instruments for adjudicating among those positions will be quantitative. The pursuit of truth is then reduced to the pursuit of sheer numbers. Dialogue is reduced to lobbying and interest-group pressure. With the advent of postmodernity, the goal of modernity will thus have been achieved: the person will have been reduced to a number, whether the number on a vote tally, the number on a survey, or the number on a bank account. In the end, that will be deemed "true" which has the greatest numbers on its side. That will be deemed "rational" which is believed by the greatest number of people. Thus, like modern rationalism, postmodern irrationalism ultimately reduces the person to a mere number.

Is Theological Pluralism Possible?

Contemporary discussions concerning the rights of marginalized groups, or the desirability of multicultural programs and intercultural understanding take place in a modern-postmodern social context which reflects the above presuppositions, or interpretive horizon. These will be the same presuppositions which will underlie any discourse between U.S. Hispanic theologians and our interlocutors in the U.S. church, the academy, and society; the interpretative rules and presuppositions governing a dialogue between a dominant culture or group (e.g., the North American academy) and a marginalized culture or group now seeking entrance into the dialogue (e.g., U.S. Hispanics) will be those rules and presuppositions already governing the dialogue, namely, the rules and presuppositions of the dominant culture or group.

What, then, would be the implications for U.S. Hispanic theologians of the interpretative presuppositions underlying contemporary calls for theological and cultural pluralism? As Latino and Latina theologians seek to develop a theological scholarship rooted in the experience of our U.S. Hispanic communities, how might those presuppositions influence both our *articulation* of that experience and the dominant groups' *reception* of our scholarship? As *U.S.* Hispanic theologians, we will necessarily share at least some of these presuppositions: How might they affect our self-understanding and our understanding of the theological task?

Like most Latin American liberation theologians, U.S. Hispanic theologians are products of European and North American theological departments and schools. We are thus products of the Enlightenment. Indeed, the very notions of human rights and liberation at the heart of Third World theologies are notions inherent in the Enlightenment tradition itself—even if not always practiced. That tradition informs our interpretation of the world, the Scriptures, and our experience. If we critique U.S. society, it is precisely to insist that our adopted country live up to its noble ideals. If we proclaim the inherent dignity of the Latino and Latina, our rights to "life, liberty, and the pursuit of happiness," it is to remind the dominant culture of its own foundational values, which reflect an Enlightenment reading of the Judeo-Christian Scriptures.

Those values are asserted as incontrovertible and unassailable, safeguarding the equal dignity of all persons as children of God. To deny the value—and, *a fortiori*, the theological value—of anyone's experience by excluding him or her from public dialogue and participation is thus to contravene both human and divine law. It is precisely on this basis that the North American tradition of pluralism rests, and against which demands for pluralism and multiculturalism are made. Yet this tradition of pluralism, based as it is on the inherent value of the person, is understood and interpreted within the context of a modern liberal individualism whose logic leads, ultimately, to the deconstruction of the individual subject, the rejection of the very notion of "inherent" value, or normative truth, and, hence, the betrayal of Enlightenment ideals. Originally viewed as a necessary *corollary* of certain fundamental truths, e.g., that "all persons are created equal and endowed by their Creator with certain inalienable rights," pluralism is now viewed as a necessary consequence of the *absence* of *any* fundamental truth. The internally contradictory logic of modern liberal individualism has thus undermined its original intent.

The implications for U.S. Hispanic theologians seeking entrance into a multicultural, pluralistic theological dialogue are significant. If our contemporary interpretative context is, indeed, located on some continuum between modern individualism and rationalism on one end and postmodern deconstruction on the other, our theological reflection will likewise be developed within this continuum—at least if we desire to communicate with a North American audience, whether Latino or non-Latino. Whether we like it or not, our theologies will be interpreted within that continuum and its underlying presuppositions.

Within that continuum, moreover, an authentic pluralism is not possible. Given the options provided by modern liberal individualism and postmodern deconstruction, an affirmation of U.S. Hispanics as rational historical subjects and a consequent affirmation of the right of U.S. Hispanic theologians to equal participation in ecclesial and academic deliberations, is not an achievable goal—precisely because what such an affirmation would entail would be, not integration into a pluralism whose contours are already set, but the right to help shape those very contours. U.S. Hispanic theologians do not seek so much to be one more voice in the theological dialogue as to help construct the parameters of that dialogue; we seek to help shape not only the content of theological discourse but also the very foundations and presuppositions which underlie and guide the discourse.

The principal reason that, in our contemporary context, pluralism is not possible is that the postmodern assumptions governing North American interpretations of pluralism, multiculturalism, cultural diversity, etc. are internally contradictory. The *affirmation* of human dignity and freedom as values inherent in the human person is predicated upon the *denial* of those—and all—values as inherently artificial, subjective, and arbitrary. The liberation of marginalized persons as rational historical subjects in our own right is, in turn, predicated upon the denial of our—and all—subjectivity as an artifice with no concrete, historical reality. The desire for rational dialogue with other peoples and cultures is predicated upon the denial of any common epistemological or experiential ground for that dialogue and the rejection of any criteria of rationality. The affirmation of the human dignity of marginalized peoples is predicated upon a denial of our humanity by denying us our capacity for rational thought.

The contemporary North American interpretative context thus moves from: 1) the presupposition that the isolated, or socially unsituated individual is the essential foundation of society, to 2) the presupposition that a dichotomy exists between the individual and society, to 3) the presupposition that pluralism precludes, therefore, the possibility of self-transcending, normative truth claims, to 4) the postmodern reduction of the individual subject to his or her "social location," to 5) the disintegration of the individual subject, to, finally, 6) the presupposition that "society" is an artificial collection not, now, of isolated individuals but of equally isolated and incommensurable "social locations." The unsituated self begets its mirror image, the unsituated social location.

This evolutionary and dynamic process, in turn, obscures: 1) the continuing limitations imposed by this dominant interpretative context on any discussions of pluralism or multiculturalism, 2) the strict dichotomy between the particular (whether the individual ego or a particular social location) and the universal (humanity, society, community) that undergirds both modernity and postmodernity, and, therefore, 3) the inability to conceive of pluralism or multiculturalism as anything but a collection of equally valid, disparate, and incommensurable experiences, meanings, and social locations—since the only alternative would be a preferential option for one particular individual or social location (take your pick) over another. Such an option would, of course, be untenable as it would *de facto* undermine the freedom and equality of other particular individuals or social locations, which have as strong a claim to "truth" as any other individual or social location:

> Pluralism and liberalism are the same thing, identical in what they oppose—the sectarian, the merely political, the exclusionary, the normative—and in what they valorize—the free marketplace of ideas, the suspension of judgment, the imaginative and sympathetic consideration of points of view other than one's own. . . . It is because he speaks (or thinks he speaks) from so secure and admirable a position (the position, paradoxically, of having no position) that the pluralist is so often complacent and even self-righteous. He believes himself to be a person of exemplary generosity, distinguished from other men and women by a capacity to entertain any number of perspectives and to refrain from insisting too strongly on his own. Whatever else a pluralist is telling you, he is also telling you that his heart is in the right place . . . the right place is every place and therefore nowhere at all.[65]

For U.S. Hispanic theologians to enter into and promote pluralism, as thus construed by the dominant groups, would necessarily reinforce our

---

65. Stanley Fish quoted in Jim Merod, *The Political Responsibility of the Critic* (Ithaca: Cornell University Press, 1987), p. 110. As Merod points out, however, "the irony is that his [Fish's] apparent dissent underwrites the very pluralism he scorns" (ibid.). As do, I would add, my own and everyone else's critiques of U.S. individualism and pluralism. Consequently, any supposedly absolute rejection of the dominant culture—in order to choose, for example, Mexican or Cuban culture—would not only represent a denial of our U.S. Hispanic mestizaje ("both/and"), but would also be literally impossible since it would deny our concrete historicity.

continued marginalization by isolating us as but one "social location" among many others of equal validity. Such a conception of pluralism is intrinsically antithetical to the very foundation of U.S. Hispanic theology and other Third World theologies; that foundation is the *preferential* option for one particular group, one particular social location, one particular set of experiences and values over other groups, social locations, experiences and values—on the basis of which all these others can and must be judged. To be a U.S. Hispanic theologian is, above all, to listen to and read the word of God from within the privileged interpretative horizon of *the poor*. A preferential option for the poor,[66] by definition, accords priority to one group and social location over others—and thus makes the interpretative horizon of that particular group and social location the privileged norm for judging others.

In North American pluralism, however, such an option can only be but one among other equally valid options. That is precisely how U.S. Hispanic theology will be treated: as one among many equally valid and "enriching" options. A pluralistic, multicultural society is one that multiplies the number of available options (whether political, economic, religious, or cultural) without according explicit preference to any—"I'm OK, you're OK." Implicit preference continues to be accorded, however, to the dominant culture's interpretative horizon. This horizon is assumed as a given, historical fact and, as such, not open to question: the single universal, normative truth is that there is no universal, normative truth.

Whatever its multicultural intent, such a pluralism ironically perpetuates the violence inflicted on marginalized groups and, indeed, compounds that violence by forcing these groups to turn against each other, thereby deflecting criticism and opposition. When communication between groups is assumed to be impossible—since, for instance, an African American male's experience is totally different from and incommensurable with a Latina's experience—the only remaining criteria for making political, religious, economic, and cultural judgments and decisions are quantitative criteria. At this point, multiculturalism degenerates into a

---

66. This term itself emerges especially in the Latin American post-Vatican II church. Called for initially by the Latin American bishops at their conferences in Medellín and, especially, at Puebla, the preferential option for the poor has been most systematically developed and analyzed by Latin American liberation theologians. Prominent among these, as we will see in the following chapter, has been the Peruvian theologian Gustavo Gutiérrez. For early uses of this term in Latin American episcopal documents, see CELAM, *Medellín conclusiones: La Iglesia en la actual transformación de América Latina a la luz del Concilio*, sec. 14.III.9–11. (Though the term itself is not explicitly used at Medellín, the bishops call for the church to give an "effective preference to the poorest and most needy sectors"; ibid.) The term becomes explicitly used at Puebla; see CELAM, *Puebla: La Evangelización en el Presente y en el Futuro de América Latina*, esp. secs. 733–735.

competition among different groups for the sources of quantitative validity (e.g., votes, scholarship monies, or sheer demographic numbers). Modern individualism's unrestrained competition among autonomous individuals for the quantitative sources of value (e.g., votes, money, demographic numbers) is now replicated by postmodern multiculturalism's unrestrained competition among autonomous "social locations" for those same quantitative sources of value. The point here is not that quantitative criteria should be insignificant in making social decisions, but that, in contemporary U.S. society, these are the *only* criteria available. When the possibility of moral suasion and rational argumentation no longer exists—since the criteria of morality and reason vary from social location to social location—power, influence, coercion, and, in the final analysis, violence become the only available avenues for asserting the validity of one's own experience and values. In the end, absolute ambiguity will generate the very violence which its purveyors so abhor.

To U.S. Hispanics, the violence intrinsic to postmodern pluralism and multiculturalism is not of merely ethical or theoretical import. This incipient violence is also a profoundly practical concern, since it undermines precisely the ability of marginalized groups to assert the *rational validity* of our experience and values. If, in the United States, "truth" and "rationality" are determined by such quantitative criteria as financial resources, who will be the arbiters of truth and reason? Whose rationality and which truth will be reflected in social decisions and imposed, coercively if necessary, on other groups? For U.S. Hispanics, therefore, the issues of pluralism and multiculturalism within contemporary U.S. society cannot be resolved unless and until we answer the prior, more fundamental question: *Whose* pluralism? *Whose* multiculturalism? *Whose* rationality? *Whose* truth? The very definition of theological pluralism and multiculturalism is governed by the demands of human historicity, a historicity which not only limits but also makes possible normative truth claims. For U.S. Hispanic theologians, then, the task is to articulate an understanding of theological pluralism that is rooted in and attends to the *particular* experience of U.S. Hispanics as aesthetic, ethical-political, rational—and *preferred*.

[7]

Hacia Una Teología de Acompañamiento

The Preferential Option for the Poor and the Proper Place of Theology

Before there can be authentic pluralism there must be authentic justice: this ethical-political principle is implicit in a relational, organic anthropology. Genuine pluralism presupposes a praxis that is genuinely intersubjective, between particular, unique others. Consequently, the preferential option for the poor is a necessary precondition for authentic pluralism. If mutual respect and understanding presuppose a relationship of others, oppression, injustice, marginalization, and exclusion are the names we give to the denial of the particularity and otherness of certain persons, namely, the poor. Thus, as long as there are poor persons there can be no pluralism.

The connection between an organic anthropology and the option for the poor suggests that the Latin American origin of this term is not accidental. As an epistemological category, the preferential option for the poor could only have emerged within a culture which had an organic worldview; it could not have emerged within a worldview that pits the universal (the good of the whole) against the particular (the good of a part, e.g., the poor). Within an individualistic worldview, the scriptural command to do justice—as a *necessary* implication of our very humanity and creatureliness—is literally inconceivable; instead, that command will be interpreted as a mere *suggestion* that one autonomous individual help other autonomous individuals. Where there is no necessary connection between persons there can be no necessary ethical-political imperative to love others.

Thus, when read in the context of contemporary U.S. society, the preferential option for the poor—as developed most systematically by Latin American liberation theologians—is susceptible to misinterpretation. When interpreted within the dominant culture's interpretative horizon, the option for the poor is understood in a very different manner. If the individual is opposed to community, then the option for the poor will be interpreted as an option for some individuals, the poor, *against* other individuals, the privileged—and as, therefore, an option against the common good of the whole community.[1] If community is opposed to institution, then it is an option for community *against* the institution. If theory is opposed to praxis, then it is an option for praxis *against* theory. If ethical-political action is opposed to aesthetic experience, then it is an option for ethical-political action *against* aesthetic experience—or the reverse. If private is opposed to public, then it is an option for the public arena *against* domestic life. If truth is opposed to meaning, then it is an option for meaning *against* truth.

All of these, indeed, represent *mis*interpretations of the option for the poor. If liberation theologians, for instance, emphasize one of the poles in each dichotomy, they do not do so to the exclusion of the other pole—even if, as already noted, liberation theology is influenced by and interpreted through those dichotomies when it is read in a North American context, and even if liberation theologians have, like all of us, been influenced by the ambiguous tendencies of modern anthropologies and modern notions of praxis.

As its grateful heirs and dialogue partners, U.S. Hispanic theologians have appropriated many of the key insights of liberation theology, especially its methodological insights. We also acknowledge the need to strike out on our own with the hope of, eventually, contributing to the very development of those fundamental insights. Yet we know that we are not really on our own, since the dialogue and friendship between Latin American and U.S. Hispanic theologians are stronger and more fruitful than ever. As I have already mentioned, both groups are turning increasingly to popular religion as a source for theology. By choosing this *locus theologicus* as particularly definitive of our communities' praxis, we implicitly set for ourselves the task of reexamining the theological categories that have emerged from other *loci*. In the preceding chapters, I have attempted to reexamine the notions of the person, community, praxis, reason, truth, pluralism, etc. Yet the starting point of liberation theology—indeed, of all liberation theologies—has always been the preferential option for the poor. This notion specifies, for liberation theologians, the concrete historical meaning of liberating praxis. Liberating praxis is itself possible only in the context of an identification with the poor.

---

1. If, as Alasdair MacIntyre avers, what defines individualism is not so much an emphasis on the individual but an assumptive dichotomy between the individual and the community (see chapter 3, note 44), then it can be argued that those critics of Latin American liberation theology who see in the preferential option for the poor (or "for" any group) an option *against* the common good are, at bottom, individualists.

In this chapter, I will suggest that, taking Latino popular Catholicism as a *locus theologicus*, U.S. Hispanic theology (and, thus, the preceding analysis of its anthropological and epistemological warrants) presupposes, implies, and demands—both ethically and rationally—a preferential option for the poor. This option is itself, however, understood in a new light when interpreted within the context of U.S. Hispanic popular Catholicism. How, then, might this foundational notion be interpreted from the perspective of U.S. Hispanic popular Catholicism, in the light of the anthropological and theological perspectives underlying popular Catholicism? Moreover, how would a reformulation of the option for the poor—together with the reformulations of the other categories discussed in the previous chapters—influence the character and development of U.S. Hispanic theology?

The Preferential Option for the Poor: Rationale and Implications

In responding to the question of why Christians are called to make a preferential option for the poor, Gustavo Gutiérrez has argued for the scriptural basis of this historical option:

> The entire Bible, beginning with the story of Cain and Abel, mirrors God's predilection for the weak and abused of human history. This preference brings out the gratuitous or unmerited character of God's love. The same revelation is given in the evangelical Beatitudes, for they tell us with the utmost simplicity that God's predilection for the poor, the hungry, and the suffering is based on God's unmerited goodness to us.[2]

The Peruvian priest thus suggests that, if one reads the Scriptures from the perspective of the poor, one discovers two overarching and mutually implicit themes, 1) the universality and gratuity of God's love, and 2) God's preferential option for the poor:

> God's preferential option for the poor . . . cannot be understood apart from the absolute freedom and gratuitousness of God's love. . . . Universality and preference mark the proclamation of the kingdom. God addresses a message of life to every human being without exception, while at the same time God shows preference for the poor and the oppressed.[3]

Though these two themes appear, at first glance, to be mutually contradictory, they are, in fact, mutually implicit. If 1) God's love is universal

---

2. Gutiérrez, *A Theology of Liberation*, p. xxvii.
3. Gutiérrez, *The God of Life*, p. 116.

and gratuitous (i.e., given freely to all of us equally), and 2) God's love is made manifest in history, and 3) that history includes injustice, conflict, and division, then 4) God's love *must* take sides with the victims of that injustice, conflict, and division. Consequently, the grounds for this option are not in the poor themselves but in God:

> God has a preferential love for the poor not because they are necessarily better than others, morally or religiously, but simply because they are poor and living in an inhuman situation that is contrary to God's will. The ultimate basis for the privileged position of the poor is not in the poor themselves but in God, in the gratuitousness and universality of God's agapeic love.[4]

The logic of this theological argument can be illustrated by an example from family life. As the parent of a nine-year-old daughter and a four-year-old son, I have at times had to deal with disagreements and fights between them. Since my daughter is much bigger than my son, she has the decided advantage in these fights. When I have found her fighting with her brother, how should I have responded? I could have chosen to remain neutral: I might then have informed them that, since I love both of them equally, I would not take sides in their conflict. Instead, however, I have chosen to become involved by separating my daughter and her brother. In that context, 1) my love was universal and gratuitous (I love both of my children equally), 2) my universal love had to be made manifest concretely, in a historical situation, 3) that situation involved injustice and conflict (one wrestler was bigger than the other), therefore 4) I had to "take the side" of my son by separating the children.

To have remained neutral would have meant to have implicitly sided with the bigger child—since, by my inaction, I would have implicitly condoned the status quo, i.e., the ongoing battery. Had I remained neutral, therefore, my daughter would have been thrilled. Indeed, she might even have encouraged my neutrality by warning me that these little everyday fights are none of my business; as a parent, I should remain "above" such petty squabbles. In the face of my neutrality, however, my four-year-old son would have felt abandoned and even hated. Since I decided to "take his side," however, my son felt affirmed and loved. On the other hand, now my daughter herself felt that I had abandoned her because I had taken the side of her brother. She suspected that I did not love her as much as I love him. If I really loved them both equally, she argued, I would not have taken sides.[5]

---

4. Gustavo Gutiérrez, *On Job* (Maryknoll, NY: Orbis, 1987), p. 94.

5. The illustration and conclusions would still hold if the "conflict" between my daughter and son were not open and physical but only tacit, e.g., if my son were excluded from full participation in the life of the family while the daughter

In this short illustration, it becomes clear that, if God loves us all equally, then God *must* make a preferential (not exclusive) option for the poor. It is precisely *because* God loves us all equally that God loves the poor preferentially.[6] If God did not love the poor preferentially, then, by virtue of God's neutrality, God would implicitly be loving the wealthy preferentially—by implicitly condoning the unjust status quo from which the wealthy benefit. To say that God's love is universal is not to say that God's love is neutral; indeed, it is to say the very opposite. Only if God is identified preferentially with the poor, then, is God's love truly universal.

Implicit here, as well as in the writings of other Latin American liberation theologians, is an assertion that, if God is present preferentially among the poor, we can only know God if we place ourselves there also. The option for the poor is, then, the most important *epistemological precondition for Christian faith*: to know God we must first opt for the poor. The experience of the poor forces us, in Jon Sobrino's words, to be "honest about the real."[7] If God is revealed in history, the victims of that history are the defenders of God's transcendence, for it is their suffering which prevents us from simply identifying God with the status quo or the existing social system. It was my four-year-old son's suffering which, in the face of my neutrality, would have implicitly identified me with his sister's position in the fight. At that point, my love would no longer be "universal." The Native Americans, African Americans, Hispanic Americans, women, the homeless, the unemployed, etc. are the privileged bearers of the *transcendent* God because their historical suffering and struggles are the only obstacle to the assumptive identification of U.S. society with the Reign of God, or "the New Jerusalem." To turn a deaf ear to the cries of the poor is implicitly to identify God's voice with that of the status quo and, hence, its established power structures. To hide their suffering and struggles is thus to make faith in a transcendent God impossible.

---

had a privileged position in the family. Even if that exclusion, or ostracism, were a consequence of the son's own behavior (the individualist argument), the parent's love, precisely because it is "universal and gratuitous," will turn preferentially toward the child—in this case, the son—who is in the greatest need. Was this not, after all, a (the?) central theme in the parable of the prodigal son (Lk 15:11–32)? "But while he [the younger son] was yet at a distance, his father saw him and had compassion, and ran and embraced him and kissed him. . . . But he [the elder son] was angry . . . " (vss. 20, 28). He was angry because he believed that his father was showing a preference for the younger brother—and that his younger brother did not deserve it.

6. Precisely *because* the elder son did not think that the younger son deserved or merited the father's love, the father's willingness to run to this latter and lavish attention upon him is the proof, and the logical consequence of the unmerited and universal character of the father's love.

7. Jon Sobrino, *Spirituality of Liberation* (Maryknoll, NY: Orbis, 1988), pp. 14–17.

The bloated belly of the hungry child and the tears of her mother stand in the way of any attempt to identify the history of conquest, or the history of "progress" with salvation history. They are the defenders of God's mystery and transcendence against the idolatrous tendency to identify God with human wealth and power. The preferential option for the poor is, thus, more than an ethical-political imperative derived from our Christian faith; it is, on the contrary, the first *precondition* for authentic Christian faith. If God is the Absolute Other, then that God is revealed first among those persons who themselves are excluded and marginalized, i.e., those who are most "other" to our society.

The preferential option for the poor is thus defensible not only ethically but also logically and rationally. *If* God is transcendent, that is, if God is "outside" human social structures, *then* God will be revealed—logically, *must* be revealed—among those who themselves are "outside" the social structures, that is, among those persons who do not benefit from the the current social, political, and economic arrangements and who are thus "useless" to those structures. As Enrique Dussel writes: "*In* the system the only possible *locus* of God's epiphany is those who are non-system, what is other than the system, the poor. Jesus' identification with the poor (Mt. 25) is not a metaphor; it is a logic. God, the other absolute, is revealed in the flesh (the system) by what is other than the system, the poor."[8]

The option for the poor also forces us to be honest about reality by forcing us to recognize the intrinsically relational, or communal character of human persons and human action. In other words, the choice before all of us, wealthy and poor alike, is not whether to be with the poor, but whether to do so *self-consciously* and *intentionally*; like it or not, we are already with the poor, and the poor are already with us. Every day, all of us—whether poor or wealthy, underprivileged or privileged—experience the consequences of poverty and oppression. For the privileged, those consequences take many forms: a paralyzing fear of other persons, constant anxiety about protecting one's possessions against the "threat" represented by the poor, the need to enclose and seclude oneself behind increasingly high walls and expensive alarm systems, the psychological problems, broken relationships, and various forms of addiction caused by this obsessive, ever-present, stressful fear and anxiety, etc., etc. The need to enslave *others* inevitably produces a generalized fear and anxiety which, in the end, enslave us *all*.

The intentional option for the poor forces us to recognize the reality that the poor are *already* with us, already present in our lives. As Martin Luther King insisted, as long as there is one black person who is in chains,

---

8. Enrique Dussel, "An Ethics of Liberation: Fundamental Hypotheses," in *The Ethics of Liberation: The Liberation of Ethics*, ed. Dietmar Mieth and Jacques Pohier (Edinburgh: T. & T. Clark, 1984), 57.

we are all in chains. If community is the source of the individual self, then the suffering and struggles of the poor are present in our every breath and our every action. Conversely, all that we are and do impacts the lives of the poor. The very refusal to act impacts the lives of the poor. We can never truly escape the poor.

Thus, the option for the poor is already implicit in an organic anthropology that views human persons and human praxis as inherently relational. Likewise, only within an individualistic anthropology can the option for the poor be interpreted as, fundamentally, 1) a voluntary act of the will that contradicts the individual's "instinctive" and, thus, "rational" self-interest, or 2) an option *against* the wealthy and powerful. The option for the poor is not simply an act of the will but also *an active recognition of that which we already are through no choice of our own.* My action is never simply mine; before I ever choose or opt I have already been chosen. This option is not, then, some "leap" beyond reason and self-interest but, on the contrary, a leap *into* rationality and authentic self-interest, a leap into the truth. To love the poor preferentially is to make an *intentional* choice to be that which we already *are* through no choice of our own: individual persons defined by our *a priori* relationships to others, to humanity, to the universe, and, ultimately, to the Triune (i.e., intrinsically relational) God.

If to be a human person is to be intrinsically related to others, what is *irrational*, then, is the *failure* to acknowledge that reality. Such a failure is not only ethically wrong; it is also fundamentally stupid and ignorant since it represents an incorrect interpretation of "the real." It thus appears as irrational only from outside, to the "rational" observer. Only when one indeed opts for the poor does the utter rationality of that option disclose itself. Thus, the option for the poor implies, at the same time, a *transformation* and a *disclosure* of our lives, at the same time a transformation of our relationships (praxis) and a disclosure of truth (theory).

Here again, U.S. Hispanic popular Catholicism has a great deal to contribute to our understanding of the preferential option for the poor. In the narratives, symbols, and rituals of popular Catholicism, the universality and gratuity of God's love are made manifest, above all, in the least significant persons and materials. If, in U.S. Hispanic popular Catholicism, everyday materials in their particularity mediate and reveal a universal, spiritual reality, those materials *most* capable of doing so—and thus implemented in rituals—are precisely the *most* common and *least* significant: e.g., wood, plaster, flower petals, candle wax, cloth, clay, bread. If God can love even clay, then God can love gold and silver. Likewise, the Jesus who is loved and prayed to is, above all, the abandoned and crucified Jesus. If—and only if—God can love even the crucified criminal, then God can love the ruler.

The Mary revered on Good Friday is the abandoned *Madre Dolorosa* and *la Soledad*. In the feast of Guadalupe, the Mary who reveals God's love is a dark-skinned mestiza who identifies herself as the mother of the indigenous man Juan Diego, an outcast and, in his own words, a nobody, "the people's dung." God loves him preferentially because, if God can love even "the people's dung," then God can love anything and anyone, i.e., God's love is universal.

As I suggested in chapter 3, within an anthropology that views the person as inherently related to others, there can be no greater lowliness, humiliation, or dehumanization than the abandonment experienced by Jesus on the cross or *la soledad* experienced by Mary. To be alone is to be the *least* significant, literally a no-body. *This* is the particularity which, in popular Catholicism, is the epiphany of the universal God. This, indeed, is the meaning of God's preferential option for the poor. God's universal, gratuitous love is revealed above all, not in just any particular object, person, or group, but especially in and among the least of these: not in gold but in clay and wood, not on a throne but on the cross, not in thunder but in flowers, not in pure white skin but in "impure" mestizo skin, not in the Spanish bishop but in Juan Diego.

This preferential option for the poor, or identification with the least significant, reveals 1) a God who is identified with the poor, who in turn reveals 2) the injustice and idolatry of those who, seeking God elsewhere, deny the poor the dignity bestowed on them by God. This has important implications for the development of a truly pluralistic, multicultural society, academy, and church. First, the option for the poor compels us North Americans to confront the historical fact that, whatever our pretensions or aspirations, we do not live in a truly pluralistic, multicultural society. Secondly, the option for the poor unmasks the great inequalities of power that beset our society and that, thus, must be taken into consideration in any discussion of pluralism. Thirdly—and perhaps most importantly—the option for the poor requires us to begin any discussion of pluralism, multiculturalism, or intercultural dialogue with the acknowledgment that, before there can be a genuine dialogue or conversation among different social groups (racial, cultural, gender, class, etc.), these must be recognized as equal partners in the dialogue.

There can be no true pluralism of equal positions, or dialogue between conversation partners, in a situation where one of the positions or "partners" has power over the other. A master cannot have a dialogue with a slave. The Southern plantation was certainly "pluralistic" in the sense that different cultures and races were represented, and there was plenty of intercultural "dialogue" between the white masters and black slaves. No one, however, would cite the plantation as an example of a pluralistic, multicultural society—or an example of intercultural dialogue. As a teacher, to cite another example, I have always tried to create a classroom environment in which my students will see themselves not merely as pupils but also as my co-equal colleagues in the educational enterprise. I have gradually learned, however, that, however "enlightened" this intention, my ability to create such an environment is inevitably hampered by one simple fact: at the end of each semester, I will have to give each student a grade. The concrete, historical situation *de facto* precludes the possibility of genuine collaboration between teacher and students as co-equal partners—regardless of the teacher's intentions. Nor would I be having an authentic intercultural dialogue if I, as a white teacher, were engaged in a classroom discussion with an African American student. However noble my intentions, the structural inequality of the historical context makes it impossible for me to truly carry out those intentions.

No authentic dialogue is possible between teachers and students, masters and slaves, men and women, rich and poor, Anglo and Hispanic—unless and until the asymmetrical power relationships are corrected. Otherwise, the most visible, influential, and powerful voice in the dialogue will continue to be that of the wealthy, white, male Anglo—*de facto*. This is true however noble the intentions of the individual wealthy, white, male Anglo. What makes true dialogue impossible is not his personal intentions, but his particular socio-historical situation, that is, the role he plays within an unequal social structure.

In a historical context of asymmetrical, or unequal relationships, what the master thinks or says will always *ipso facto* be more true, more ethical, and more rational than what the slave thinks or says; what the teacher thinks or says will always be more true, more ethical, and more rational than what the student thinks or says. In such a context, Juan Diego's words will always be depreciated and those of the Spanish bishop will always be considered divine—even if the bishop is a good person, with an open heart and mind, and the best of intentions.

From the perspective of the poor, pluralism is not the *foundation* of a truly free society—as it is for modern liberal individualism—but the *consequence* of authentic liberation, the consequence of the option for the poor. As long as certain cultures and races remain socially, politically, and economically marginalized, there can be no true cultural and racial pluralism. Thus, the possibility of universal dialogue, tolerance, and understanding is predicated upon a preferential identification with one concrete, historical, flesh-and-blood, *particular* person: the poor person. Far from precluding the possibility of taking a stand for one particular position over others—e.g., for the poor and against the wealthy—pluralism *demands* that we take such a stand. Authentic pluralism is a far cry from universal, uncritical tolerance; it is, indeed, its very opposite.

This understanding of pluralism differs markedly from the pluralism of the modern liberal individualist. The starting point of authentic pluralism is not the autonomous, socially unsituated self, confronted with an unlimited choice among a multiplicity of options in a marketplace of ideas where all experiences and opinions are, in themselves, equally valid and where none can make any prior claim on his or her loyalty. The starting point of authentic pluralism is, instead, the scarred hands, weathered face, and sun-parched olive skin of the elderly Mexican woman . . . of Our Lady of Guadalupe . . . of the crucified Jesus.

It is from their perspective that the intrinsically relational character of the person is revealed. It is, paradoxically, in the faces of those persons most alienated, most abandoned, most excluded that the intrinsic bonds that unite us *all* show forth—as that which is denied by such injustice. That is precisely why our society continues to alienate, abandon, and exclude the poor—because, face-to-face with the poor, one is forced to confront our intrinsically relational reality. What their concrete, flesh-and-blood bodies reveal about God and about all of us—that we are constitutively related to each other and, therefore, responsible to and for each other—is so threatening that those bodies must be isolated, hidden from view in barrios, ghettoes, reservations, hospitals, etc. If all else fails, those bodies will be destroyed—through all the forms of suffering and death that characterize life in the isolated inner city and rural areas to which the poor are relegated.

A U.S. Hispanic anthropology which views the person as intrinsically and, by definition, related to the rest of creation becomes accessible not directly but only indirectly, as mediated by its very opposite, that is, as paradoxically revealed in the midst of human alienation, abandonment, and dehumanization, in the poor person's everyday struggle against injustice. The preferential option for the poor enables us to recognize our essential relatedness to others by compelling us to confront the painful consequences of our *failure* to recognize that relatedness. When we recognize the *in*justice of those consequences, we get our first glimpse of what true justice is.

If I, as an exile, have experienced the separation from my family, my community, my native country, and my history as profoundly painful, it is because that experience threatens, and thus evokes a truth deeper and more fundamental than that of separation, namely, the truth of community. The experience of exile, or "abandonment," has nurtured my conviction that we do not exist in isolation from each other, and my commitment to struggle for a society in which this fundamental truth is affirmed and realized.

If the churches of the poor are so often vital sources of life and hope, this is because only those who confront and resist death and hopelessness can truly know that these are not Ultimate Reality. When that which is essential to us as human beings is taken from us *and* we recognize that as an injustice, we are implicitly acknowledging that, indeed, it *is* essential. When we are treated as mere objects *and* experience this as an injustice, we are implicitly affirming our intrinsic intersubjectivity and relatedness as essential to our very humanity.

If we experience such attacks as unjust, it is because we have some implicit, underlying sense of our own dignity, or value, as persons who are sacraments of our Creator. Thus, it is through an identification with the poor that we all come to recognize ourselves as implicated in their struggles and intrinsically related to them in their suffering. Paradoxically, it is the face of the marginalized person which, by revealing the injustice of that marginalization, reveals our common complicity in the injustice and, thus, our intrinsic relation to that person, as children of a common God. This was the experience of Martín de Porres, Bartolomé de Las Casas, Camilo Torres, Oscar Romero, Cesar Chávez, Francis of Assisi, Mahatma Gandhi, Martin Luther King, Jr., Dietrich Bonhoeffer, Franz Jaegerstatter, Dorothy Day, and many other men and women whose recognition of the intrinsic value of each person, and our organic relationship to each other, was born of their encounter with those persons whose dignity and worth, and intrinsic relationship to the rest of society, are continually denied.[9]

Moreover, in the unjust suffering of their brothers and sisters, the poor recognize the injustice of their own suffering. This was the experience of the elderly Mexican woman reaching to kiss the crucified Jesus' feet: in the unjust suffering of the crucified Jesus she recognized her own unjust suffering. This was the experience of the men and women kneeling alongside Mary, *la Soledad*, at the celebration of the *Pésames* on Good Friday: in the injustice of her loneliness at Jesus' tomb, they recognized the injustice of their own loneliness. This was the experience of Juan Diego: in the injustice of the Spanish bishop's rejection of *la Morenita*, he was able to recognize the injustice of his own rejection—which he had formerly simply accepted as a matter of course. This is the experience of the Mexican people who, during the *Posadas*, accompany Joseph and Mary as they walk from house to house in search of shelter—and are repeatedly turned away: in the rejection and homelessness experienced by Joseph and Mary, the people recognize their own rejection and homelessness.

It is the corporate, shared character of suffering, undertaken in mutual solidarity, that distinguishes suffering from mere debilitating sadness and makes possible our common struggle *against* suffering: "If it is experienced as a personal disgrace, an illness is exhausting and engenders self-centeredness and alienation. Seen as part of the pain of all the poor, it allows for rebellion in the face of pain."[10] That solidarity in the midst of suffering is what reveals to us the ultimate powerlessness of suffering: our common life, manifested in our relationships of solidarity, overcomes all attempts to destroy that life. Suffering shared is suffering already in retreat.

---

9. It is this identification of "otherness" with the concrete, historical otherness of a particular person, the poor person, that is inadequately addressed in postmodern evocations of otherness. Even Emmanuel Levinas, whose incarnational understanding of otherness, in the "face-to-face" encounter, has been influential among some Latin American theologians, has himself been suspected of a Eurocentric ambiguity on this point. See, e,g., Enrique Dussel, *Método para una filosofía de la liberación* (Salamanca: Sígueme, 1974), pp. 176–81; idem, *Para una ética de la liberación latinoamericana*, 2 vols. (Buenos Aires: Siglo Veintiuno, 1973) 2:89–92, 156–62.

10. Francísco Moreno Rejón, *Salvar la vida de los pobres: aportes a la teología moral* (Lima: CEP, 1986), p. 156.

Justo González recalls how, in the Lope de Vega play, *Fuenteovejuna*, solidarity in common, unjust suffering led to a town's liberation from tyrannical rule. After the despotic ruler of Fuenteovejuna was assassinated, the citizens refused to accuse any one individual of the murder. Instead, they assumed corporate responsibility. When asked who had committed the deed, they responded in unison: "Fuenteovejuna, my lord." González explains their response: "they are not simply trying to cover up for one another. What has happened is that through their suffering and final uprising, such solidarity has arisen that they do believe that it was the town, and not any individuals in it, that killed the commander."[11] Human solidarity in the face of suffering is the beginning of liberation. Lived as an end in itself—indeed, as the highest end—that solidarity of and with the poor becomes a seedbed of hope in the face of despair.

In Jesus Christ's own cry of abandonment, and his intractable hope against all hope, we hear our own cry and discover our own hope. The revelation that death does not have the last word, that death is not Ultimate Reality, takes place on the cross when Jesus' death is revealed as the unjust execution of an innocent man. The revelation of Jesus as Son of God takes place not in the resurrection but on the cross. The Roman centurion's confession, "Truly, this was God's Son," takes place at the foot of the cross, as a response to Jesus' cry of abandonment, "My God, my God, why have you abandoned me?" (Mk 15:34), and to Jesus' death, "And Jesus uttered a loud cry and breathed his last" (Mk 15:37). At the foot of the cross, not even the centurion can continue to deny reality.

By forcing us to confront its opposite, the cross discloses to us the true dignity of *all* persons and, consequently, the victory of life over death. Jesus' is not a passive resignation to death and abandonment, but, on the contrary, a struggle against death and abandonment: "My God, my God, *why . . .?*" "And Jesus uttered a loud cry" . . . not a cry of despair but a cry of stubborn, unyielding hope, a cry that refuses to accept abandonment as a *fait accompli.* Jesus did not passively accept his death; he resisted it to the bitter end, crying out to the heavens with his last breath. In that resistance, in that heart-rending acknowledgment that God had unjustly abandoned him, Jesus is revealed as Son of God. It is in the confrontation with death that life is revealed, and in the confrontation with abandonment that our inherently relational humanity is revealed. It is the unjustly abandoned person who knows most clearly who God is and, therefore, who we human beings are.

On the cross, life conquers death. On the cross, the inherent dignity of human life survives all attempts to destroy it. On the cross, then, Jesus is already resurrected: " 'In the death struggle of the creature, at the opposite pole from freedom, freedom . . . shines out irresistibly as the thwarted destiny of matter. . . .' The suffering creature, its mask distorted by pain,

---

11. González, *Mañana*, pp. 28–9.

gives expression, now as a subject, to the suffering and calls the pain into question."[12] A Hispanic woman, María, explains: "At times I say, 'My God, why do I have to suffer so much? Do I merit such suffering? I am not that bad of a person.'"[13] "My God, my God *why . . .?*" . . . "I am not that bad of a person": here we already encounter the resurrection, for here we encounter human life resisting and overcoming all attempts to reduce that life to a mere thing, a mere passive, inert object.

Any talk of human solidarity, community, freedom, or peace that is removed from the concrete reality of the cross, human abandonment, alienation, oppression, and disunity will inevitably be ahistorical, disembodied and, as such, will perpetuate rather than ameliorate the alienation. Any talk of pluralism and multiculturalism not born out of a particular commitment to a particular people in a particular social location, namely, the poor, will likewise be ahistorical, disembodied and will, thus, perpetuate cultural marginalization and exclusion. A necessary precondition of authentic community is a preferential identification with *particular* poor persons, whose perspective—precisely as particular—is not merely "one among many equally-valid others," but, since it is the one presently excluded from the community, is the one without which no authentic community is possible. In other words, the particularity of the poor is the most accurate perspective from which to view the community as a whole—and from which to "opt for" *all* persons. That perspective is, thus, relevant and true not only to the poor themselves, but to the entire community or society. To opt for *this* particularity is to opt for the whole.

What, however, is "this" particularity? Who, in fact, are "the poor?" Gustavo Gutiérrez proffers a three-fold definition of poverty. *Material poverty* "refers first of all to those who live in a social situation characterized by a lack of the goods of this world and even by misery and indigence. Even further, it refers to a marginated social group, with connotations of oppression and lack of liberty" (e.g., "Blessed are you poor"; Lk 6:20).[14] *Spiritual poverty* refers to the attitude of "spiritual childhood," in which one is "totally at the disposition of the Lord" (e.g., "Blessed are the poor in spirit"; Mt 5:1).[15] Finally, in its deepest Christian sense, poverty refers to the act of solidarity with the materially poor, an act *undertaken voluntarily as a protest against the evil of material poverty.* All three dimensions of poverty are intrinsically interrelated. The option for the 1) materially poor reveals a deeper form of human poverty, demanding thereby that we acknowledge our common 2) spiritual poverty before

---

12. Russell A. Berman, *Modern Culture and Critical Theory: Art, Politics, and the Legacy of the Frankfurt School* (Madison, WI: University of Wisconsin, 1989), pp. 20, 26.

13. Quoted in Isasi-Díaz and Tarango, *Hispanic Women*, p. 36.

14. Gutiérrez, *A Theology of Liberation*, p. 170.

15. Ibid., p. 169.

God, our radical dependence on God. Yet, only by 3) identifying with the poor voluntarily, as a *protest* against the injustice of poverty, can we avoid the dangers of romanticizing material poverty or of reducing spiritual poverty to a merely "interior detachment" which would legitimate wealth and power by justifying our retention of these possessions as long as we remain "spiritually detached" from them:

> Material poverty is a scandalous condition. Spiritual poverty is an attitude of openness to God and spiritual childhood. . . . We turn now to a third meaning of the term: poverty as a commitment of solidarity and protest. We have laid aside the first two meanings. The first is subtly deceptive; the second partial and insufficient. In the first place, if *material poverty* is something to be rejected, as the Bible vigorously insists, then a witness of poverty cannot make of it a Christian ideal. . . . On the other hand, our analysis of the Biblical texts concerning *spiritual poverty* has helped us to see that it is not directly or in the first instance an interior detachment from the goods of this world, a spiritual attitude which becomes authentic by in-carnating itself in material poverty. Spiritual poverty is something more complete and profound. It is above all total availability to the Lord. Its relationship to the use or ownership of economic goods is inescapable, but secondary and partial. . . . How are we therefore to understand the evangelical meaning of the witness of a real, ma-terial, concrete poverty? *Lumen gentium* invites us to look for the deepest meaning of Christian poverty in *Christ.* . . . The taking on of the servile and sinful human condition, as foretold in Second Isaiah, is presented by Paul as an act of voluntary impoverishment . . . But he [Christ] does not take on the human sinful condition and its consequences to idealize it. It is rather because of love for and solidarity with others who suffer in it. It is to redeem them from their sin and to enrich them with his poverty. It is to struggle against human selfishness and everything that divides persons and allows that there be rich and poor, possessors and dispossessed, oppressors and oppressed. . . . Christian poverty has meaning only as a com-mitment of solidarity with the poor, with those who suffer misery and injustice. The commitment is to witness to the evil which has resulted from sin and is a breach of communion. It is not a question of idealizing poverty, but rather of taking it on as it is—an evil—to protest against it and to struggle to abolish it.[16]

It is this last, most radical and most Christian sense of poverty, which defines the preferential option for the poor as a commitment of volun-tary solidarity with the poor that witnesses to and struggles against the

---

16. Gutiérrez, *A Theology of Liberation*, pp. 171–72.

evil of poverty. In this sense, insists the Peruvian theologian, "even the poor must make the option for the poor (I know many poor persons making the option to be rich)."[17]

When Gutiérrez speaks of material poverty, he is emphasizing the socio-economic dimension of poverty. Yet, in his most recent writings, he has increasingly insisted that material poverty is not limited to the socio-economic, but includes cultural, racial, and gender dimensions:

> . . . the turbulent situation in Latin America has caused many to place an almost exclusive emphasis on the social and economic aspect of poverty (this was a departure from the original insight). I am indeed convinced that it is still necessary to call attention to this dimension of poverty if we are to do more than touch the surface of the real situation of the poor, but I also insist that we must be attentive to other aspects of poverty as well. . . . In this whole matter I have found it very helpful to enter into dialogue with theologies developed in settings different from our own. Through direct contacts with Christian groups in other countries and continents (as well as through meetings with those who are trying to reflect theologically in those contexts) I have learned much about situations different from the Latin American. At the same time, I have gained a better understanding and appreciation of aspects of our people that had been clear in theory but had little or no consequence in practice. As a result, I have come to see with new eyes our racial and cultural world, and the discrimination against women.[18]

Thus, while the complexity of material poverty was by no means ignored in his earlier writings, Gutiérrez's ongoing discussions with U.S. Hispanics, African Americans, Native Americans, and feminists have contributed to a more explicit broadening of his understanding of material poverty to include these other dimensions:

> Poverty is certainly a social and economic issue, but it has much more than a social and economic dimension. In the final analysis, poverty means death: unjust death; early death; death due to illness, hunger, repression; physical death; and cultural death. When a language or race is despised, we are killing the people who speak this language or belong to this race. When we discriminate against women in society, we are killing them. Not recognizing a person's

17. Gustavo Gutiérrez, "Church of the Poor," in *Born of the Poor: The Latin American Church Since Medellín*, ed. Edward L. Cleary, O.P. (Notre Dame, IN: University of Notre Dame Press, 1990), 16. See also idem, *A Theology of Liberation*, p. xxvi.

18. Gutiérrez, *A Theology of Liberation*, pp. xxi–xxiii.

full human rights is one way to kill a person, to cause a cultural death. Anthropologists are accustomed to say "Culture is life." When we do not value a culture, we are killing the people who belong to it. . . . To be poor is a very complex condition. To be poor is to be a human person, to make friends, to have free time, to play, but also to be poor is to be insignificant. To be poor is to be nameless. To be poor is to be irrelevant to our society and our church. We mean this kind of poor—*really* poor—when we say "preferential option for the poor. . . . My most important experience in the last ten to twelve years has been of the complexity of the world of the poor. Personally, I was not as conscious of this complexity twenty years ago as I am today."[19]

U.S. Hispanic theologians have emphasized the cultural and racial aspects of this complex world of the poor. In his groundbreaking work, *Galilean Journey*, for example, Virgilio Elizondo has demonstrated that an important aspect of Jesus' poverty was his Galilean roots. Not only was Jesus the son of a carpenter, but he was from Nazareth, from the borderlands, hardly the center of civilized life. Coming from an area where different cultures, races, religions, and languages constantly mixed, Galileans were impure "half-breeds"—in a word, mestizos:

> At the time of Jesus, Galilee was peopled by Phoenicians, Syrians, Arabs, Greeks, Orientals, and Jews. . . . A natural, ongoing biological and cultural mestizaje was taking place. The Jews were scorned by the Gentiles, and the Galileean Jews were regarded with patronizing contempt by the "pure-minded" Jews of Jerusalem. The natural mestizaje of Galilee was a sign of impurity and a cause for rejection. . . . From the time of Solomon the land of Galilee had come to be known as the land of Cabul, which in itself meant "like nothing" or "very displeasing." The connotation remained and the inhabitants of the region came to be looked down on and considered good for nothing. . . . In the wisdom of God, it is precisely here in this impure, culturally mixed, freedom-loving, rebellious region that God made the historical beginning of his visible reign on earth. One cannot follow the way of the Lord without appreciating the scandalous way of Jesus the Galilean.[20]

The power of U.S. Hispanic popular Catholicism derives precisely from the fact that, in its narratives, symbols, and rituals, God is identified with the half-breed, the racially and culturally marginalized. Jesus is a Galilean, and Mary is *la Morenita*.

---

19. Gutiérrez, "Church of the Poor," 15–18.
20. Elizondo, *Galilean Journey*, pp. 51–54.

Mujerista theologians have underscored the role of gender as a form of poverty intrinsically related to culture, race, and class.[21] Latinas are marginalized even within the U.S. Hispanic community itself. Consequently, the option for the poor must itself include a preferential option for women. Again, an option for this particularity is the only adequate way of opting for the whole; an option for Latinas is the only adequate way of opting for the U.S. Hispanic community since, unless Latinas participate as full subjects, or genuine "others," in the community, we cannot claim to have an authentic community, i.e., we cannot honestly say *"nosotros."*

If community extends beyond this time and place to past and future generations, the poor also include those persons and groups who, in a dominant culture that denies the transgenerational character of community, are excluded from participation in the present because their concerns are identified with the past and the future: these poor are, especially, the elderly and the youth. Where the "dangerous memories of suffering" are forgotten, the elderly, who bear those memories, will be cast aside.[22] Where the hope in a future of genuine peace and freedom, which can come only through justice, gives way to cynicism and despair, the youth, who bear that hope, will be ignored. The two are intrinsically related: the memories of our ancestors' struggles in the past are what give birth to our hope in the future. Today we struggle for a more just future because we refuse to believe that those past struggles were without meaning or purpose. We are the stewards of the lives and struggles of our parents and grandparents. Those lives and struggles will bear fruit today and tomorrow . . . unless we forget. To turn our backs on the past is, thus, to turn our backs on the future; to forget *"nuestros ancianos"* and *"nuestros antepasados"* is to ignore our children, born and unborn.[23] The loss of the traditions that bind us to the past implies a loss of the hope which binds us to the future.

We live in a U.S. society, however, for whom the present is divorced from the past and the future. It is no accident, then, that this society systematically depreciates and discards its elderly, while abandoning its youth to violence, poverty, and self-hatred. The continuing destruction of the social and natural environment which we will bequeath to our children is a sign of our society's disregard for them and their future. Ironically, the same society which idolizes "youth" as an ideal tolerates and perpetuates the ongoing destruction of its concrete, flesh-and-blood youths.

---

21. See, especially, Isasi-Díaz and Tarango, *Hispanic Women*; Isasi-Díaz, *En la Lucha*; Aquino, *Our Cry for Life*; and Rodríguez, *Our Lady of Guadalupe*.

22. On the notion of "dangerous memories of suffering," see Metz, *Faith in History and Society*, pp. 88–118, 184–204.

23. The Mexican tradition of visiting the graves of deceased loved ones on *"el día de los muertos"* (All-Souls Day) reflects this sense that, as long as we remember them, the dead remain with us as a part of our present-day community.

Gleaming, modern, technologically sophisticated health spas exist side by side with dilapidated public schools and parks; obsessed with "youthfulness" we ignore our youths. Millions of dollars are spent on plastic surgery, liposuction, and body sculpting while millions of children continue to suffer from malnutrition and inadequate health care.

It is, likewise, no accident that we U.S. Hispanics revere our elderly and our children; for they are the bearers of a community that spans many generations. They remind us that our responsibility is not just to the present—or, more precisely, to a present divorced from past and future. The elderly and the youth remind us that, if we forget the past and ignore the future, we will destroy the present. Yes, we do live in the present; but the present always includes the past and the future. The preferential option for the poor must thus include a preferential option for the elderly and the youth as privileged bearers of God in the present.[24]

Since, as indicated in chapter 4, human praxis is mediated by poiesis, human relationships are mediated by material relationships. Consequently, all the abovementioned forms of marginalization are mediated by economic marginalization. Unless we recognize this fact, cultural, racial, gender, and intergenerational openness will simply mask and, indeed, legitimate the continued oppression of U.S. Hispanics. Above all, the preferential option for the poor must involve a preferential option for *the materially poor* in all the above groups. Again, it is no accident that what all marginalized groups have in common is a disproportionate amount of material poverty. Liberation theology's emphasis on socioeconomic poverty should thus be retrieved in the light of the U.S. Hispanic experience of cultural, racial, gender, and intergenerational oppression, as that which mediates these latter forms of poverty. (Indeed, in his more recent writings, Gutiérrez refers to these as themselves forms of *material* poverty.)[25]

Without such poietic or socio-economic mediation, the preferential option for "Hispanics" will reflect the same dangerous dichotomy between culture (as the "private" realm of ambiguity, affect, symbol, story, etc.) and economics (as the "public" realm of theoretical rationality, productivity, etc.) that serves the dominant culture's interests and perpetuates the dehumanization of U.S. Hispanics. As we have seen, cultural openness too easily becomes an instrument whereby the autonomous individual can appropriate, or rather expropriate, the symbols and values of another culture as mere salve for the psychic wounds inflicted by the dominant culture. The result is that Latino symbols and values are stripped from their context in the history of an oppressed community, used by the dominant culture to prop up its own walking wounded, thereby sustaining,

---

24. On the liberation of the youth, see Dussel, *Philosophy of Liberation*, pp. 87–95.

25. See notes 14–16 above.

perpetuating and, indeed, bolstering social structures and practices that continue to marginalize Latinos and Latinas. U.S. Hispanic popular Catholicism has its own history, which furnishes the horizon within which it can be adequately interpreted: ". . . the symbol is not totally equivocal, for it only leaves open a *determinate* span of valid meanings. Moreover, though in the abstract it does not have a prior or fixed, universally univocal determination, nevertheless, it becomes 'dis-ambiguized' in the concrete situation and context."[26] When this concrete context is ignored, rape will be mistaken for "an abundance of love."

Putting Theology in Its Proper Place: A Domestic, Urban Theology of Accompaniment

The concrete context of Latino popular Catholicism, precisely as "concrete," also has a spatial, geographical dimension; it is practiced some-*where*. Thus, the preferential option for the poor—specifically, for the popular Catholicism of the U.S. Hispanic poor—includes an option for particular places as the preferred loci (in the most literal sense) of theology: those *places* where the poor live, whether by choice or by coercion.

The *locus*, or "place," of theology should not be understood in a purely metaphorical sense. The very notions of "social location" and "experience" themselves remain, after all, mere theoretical categories—as does "praxis." If we take seriously the concrete particularity of human praxis and, therefore, the option for the poor, we must also take seriously the concrete particularity of the place where theology is done. If we do this, we are left with only one conclusion, a conclusion which modern theologians and scholars, whether liberal or conservative, have largely evaded, namely, that in its fundamental sense, the *locus* of theology is the *physical, spatial, geographical place* of theological reflection. To walk with Jesus and with the poor is to walk *where* Jesus walks and *where* the poor walk.[27]

A U.S. Hispanic understanding of the preferential option for the poor that takes seriously particularity and embodiment would thus seek to articulate the significance of place, or space, for theological reflection. In a society where barriers, spatial separation, isolation, and distance are chief means of exclusion and oppression, a theology from the perspective of

---

26. Scannone, "Un Nuevo Punto," 42.
27. This assertion does not deny the possibility of the theologian's self-transcendence, for thought is never completely determined by its physical location. Indeed, as we have already seen, the exact opposite is the case: *unless* theological thought is rooted in a particular, physical, historical place, it *cannot* be communicated to other particular, physical, historical places. What makes all communication, and hence self-transcendence possible is precisely particular, concrete embodiment.

the poor cannot ignore the importance of physical location, or space, as a theological category.

As suggested in chapter 5, U.S. Hispanic popular Catholicism is located at the crossroads, or the intersection of domestic life and public life, moving freely between them. Located in the main plaza, at the intersection of the "private" life of religious faith and the "public" life of the city, San Fernando breaches the artificial barriers that, in U.S. society, have isolated one from the other. This isolation has been more than merely metaphorical; it has been, in the most literal sense, concrete, physical, spatial, geographical. The lives of Hispanics in the United States, however, are identified with *the home* and, increasingly, with *the city*. *The church* is, in turn, the place where these meet. These have become the spatial, geographical axes of our lives.

Consequently, these should also be spatial, geographical axes of a U.S. Hispanic theology. The preferential option for the poor thus implies a preferential option for the home, the city, and, the crossroads where home and city meet, the church. Because it is an option for particular flesh-and-blood persons, it will also be an option for particular *places*, the places where the poor live, die, and struggle for survival. To "opt for the poor" is thus to place ourselves *there*, to *accompany* the poor person in his or her life, death, and struggle for survival.

A U.S. Hispanic theology will thus be preferentially (again, not exclusively) a *domestic, urban theology of accompaniment*. Such a theology would, in turn, underscore three dimensions of the option for the poor: 1) the affective dimension, as enfleshed in particular relationships; 2) the spatial, geographical dimension, as represented by the unity of home and city; 3) the dimension of interiority, as reflected in the theologian's own, personal appropriation of the option for the poor; and 4) the spiritual dimension, as incarnated in the faith of the poor, which transgresses all spatial, geographical barriers. Such a theology would, therefore, underscore the importance of those particular persons for whom the home and the city have too often functioned, not as places where their lives (praxis) are enjoyed and valued as ends in themselves, but as places of isolation from full participation in social life. To place ourselves in the home and the city is thus to accompany, above all, the women, children, the elderly, and the economically, or materially impoverished in our U.S. Hispanic communities.

As concrete persons, the poor are encountered, first and foremost, in the home, in the arena of interpersonal, domestic life: in our family relationships and our friendships. They are encountered first, as the women who, by being exclusively identified with domestic life, have been denied their full humanity. Though, as we have seen, human life is always both domestic and public, women have been denied any "public" significance in a society where human praxis, or action, is *defined as* public, social, political, and economic productivity.

Thus the preferential option for the poor must include a preferential option for the home as a privileged *locus theologicus*. This is not to idealize home life or to suggest that women "belong in the home" any more than to suggest that we theologians should place ourselves among the poor is to idealize the urban barrio or to suggest that the poor "belong in the barrio." The home and (as I will argue below) the urban barrio and ghetto are privileged places for theology because these are the principal places where the poor—especially women, children, the elderly, and the economically poor—live, die, and struggle for survival. Indeed, to make the home a privileged place for theology is to insist that it be so not only for women but especially for men.[28]

This is not to suggest that men can presume to speak on behalf of women, but, on the contrary, to insist that we men *place ourselves in the home*, accompany those women who have always been there, especially in their struggle to breach the oppressive spatial, geographical barriers which have for so long kept women in the home and men outside. Furthermore, such a process of accompaniment will make more difficult that idealization of "family life" and the home which has so often masked the ways in which home life has merely replicated economic, productive relationships, and has, thus, prevented the home from becoming a place where life is truly valued as an end in itself. Idealization and romanticization thrive on distance and separation; by definition, we can only romanticize that which we do not truly know. If knowledge is grounded in praxis, and praxis presupposes empathic fusion, or affect, then the only way to prevent the romanticization of the home is to place ourselves there. The home will no longer be romanticized only when men become the *compañeros* of women in the life of the home.

Moreover, when the home is valued as a privileged place for theology (by both women and men), and interpersonal intimacy is recognized as an essential dimension and a defining characteristic of *all* human action (for both women and men), the concrete lives of women will be recognized as the praxis of human *subjects* rather than the *objects* of male, adult, public action (in both the home and the marketplace). For, when women are identified exclusively with domestic life, and "domestic" intimacy is itself marginalized vis-à-vis the Real World of political struggle and economic production, women themselves will inevitably be marginalized. It will then come as no surprise that the highest rates of poverty in the United States are found among women and their children.

An option for the home as a privileged place for theology would also imply a new appreciation of the affective, aesthetic dimension of the option for the poor. We are called, above all, to *love* poor persons. And this

---

28. Though many women theologians have seen in the "private" life of the home a rich resource for theological reflection, a privileged *locus theologicus* (e.g., Aquino and Isasi-Díaz), few men have as yet done so.

love includes not only the "public" ethical-political struggle for justice but also "private" interpersonal, intimate relationships. The affective love of family becomes the paradigm for *all* human action and, especially, for the love of the poor.

It is important to note, however, that, while the affect (e.g., love, compassion) which characterizes U.S. Hispanic relationships includes feelings, this is not an *irrational* affect. The Spanish word for "to feel" is *sentir*, which does not have the same connotation as in the English. Reflecting the modern affect-intellect dichotomy, the English "to feel" connotes an exclusively emotional response, over against the verb "to know," which connotes an intellectual response. In Spanish, however, the verb *sentir* connotes, not feelings *per se*, but an experiential form of knowledge, or perception, involving the whole person: "it does not concern a sentimental 'feeling' ['*sentir*'], but one which is sapiential and ethical, that is, of the 'heart.'"[29] To *sentir* with the poor person is to be one with her or him affectively and ethico-politically, and, thus, to know her or him. To *sentir* God's presence is to be *affectively* united to God, to *do* God's will, and thus to *know* God.[30]

It is this affective dimension of human praxis, and the option for the poor, that safeguards the *unitive* character of the action. Though ethical-political praxis always mediates aesthetic praxis, the former also implies separation and individuation—as Vasconcelos so clearly saw. Ethical-political action involves at least two separate, distinct persons; it involves at least two "others," or two subjects who relate to each other. Aesthetic action, then, is what makes this relationship a distinctively *human* relationship, wherein the two distinct persons become one *as whole persons*, while nevertheless retaining their distinctness (a possibility not available to mere material objects). This unity is mediated by (i.e., does not extinguish) the concrete particularity of each person. As we saw earlier, the affective union, in fact, enhances the particularity and individuality of each person.

There is no such thing as an option for "the poor," only an option for poor *persons*. Human praxis is always inter*personal*; it is always an interaction between or among particular, concrete human beings. In order to "do" good (ethical-political praxis) with and for the collective poor, one must be able to "feel" empathy with and for particular poor persons. Only by loving the poor can one know (theory) the poor, and only by loving particular poor persons can one love "the poor." As Vasconcelos

---

29. Scannone, "Un Nuevo Punto," 32.

30. Lupe, one of the women whose stories are recounted by Ada María Isasi-Díaz and Yolanda Tarango, explains community in this way: "I feel very connected. . . . I consider myself a part of a lot of people, particularly women; part of many women who went before me, like my grandmother. . . ." Another woman, Olivia, speaks of *feeling* the presence of God. Isasi-Díaz and Tarango, *Hispanic Women*, pp. 50–51.

pointed out, authentic community and relationship involves an empathic, affective union of concrete, embodied others—it is impossible to have an empathic union with an abstract concept. What distinguishes the subject-subject, or person-person relationship from the subject-object, or person-thing relationship is precisely the aesthetic, affective character of the former. Affect is mediated by the body, by physical presence. (Even the memory of a now-absent beloved is a memory of physical presence, and is experienced as physical presence.)[31]

As characterized by the affective character of familial relationships, the option for the poor implies, therefore, an option to love concrete, particular poor persons *as members of our family*. The human intimacy and friendship that characterize family life are an essential element of the option for the poor, for these are the "useless" and "unproductive" forms of human interaction in which are reflected an affirmation of the intrinsic value of the life of the other person, the poor person, as an end in itself. Only if the struggle for social transformation and justice does not obviate, but mediates empathy, or compassion, can that struggle represent an authentic option for poor persons in their historical concreteness. Where the option for the poor is simply reduced to an option for social justice, the poor will inevitably be reduced to an abstract concept or a manipulable object. Once again, the universal is mediated by the particular; universal love is mediated by particular love, and the most particular love is familial love. It is, therefore, impossible to make an authentic option for the poor in the absence of everyday relationships with concrete poor persons. The foundation of the preferential option for the poor is the aesthetic, affective praxis of friendship with poor persons.

The paradigmatic relationships of love, intimacy, and friendship are those of domestic life, the life of the home. Indeed, the gospel defines the poor person as our "brother," our "sister," and our "neighbor"—all terms derived from the domestic sphere. These particular domestic relationships are thus universalized as the paradigms of *all* human relationships. What we *feel* for our brother, sister, and neighbor we must feel for all persons, especially poor persons. The everyday struggle for survival, the simple, seemingly insignificant acts of familial affection and care through which we affirm our life-giving relationships with our brothers, sisters, and neighbors become, in the gospel, the norm for all human praxis. God is revealed first and preferentially not in grand political projects of liberation and transformation, but in the "insignificant," everyday, common struggle for survival—though this latter is always intrinsically related to

---

31. This is reflected in the Spanish word *recordar* (to remember), whose etymological roots are in the Latin word *cor* (heart). In English, one remembers with the mind (*memoria*), in Spanish one remembers with the heart. The palpable presence of our forebears is also reflected in the practice of calling out *¡Presente!* as the names of the dead are announced in litanies.

the larger political and economic struggle. The most basic form of resistance against those forces which seek to destroy one's life, to reduce it to a mere instrument of production, is the affirmation of the intrinsic value of one's relationships and, therefore, of one's life.

Thus, to make the home a privileged place for theology is to make affect, or familial love and compassion, an intrinsic aspect of the preferential option for the poor, which is, in turn, to make particular love of concrete, particular poor persons the *sine qua non* of the option for the poor: for one can only "feel with" a flesh-and-blood person. Particular friendships are a *sine qua non* of any authentic option for the poor.

As I have argued, the affirmation of everyday particularity and embodiment as essential to intersubjective praxis is implicit in the popular religious understanding of Jesus and Mary. These are our *family*, together with Joseph and the communion of saints: "in Hispanic popular faith-experience, God's unique efficacious mediator (Jesus) and God's 'family' (Mary and the saints) become . . . very real and personal family members for the living faith of Hispanics. . . ."[32] The community's relationships with them are always personal and particular, and thus intimate and embodied—otherwise we could not truly love them as we love our own family.[33]

To love God is to love this particular person, Jesus of Nazareth; God can no more be loved in the abstract than human beings can. To love Jesus of Nazareth is to physically *walk with him* on the way to Calvary, or to kiss his feet nailed to the cross; Jesus can no more be accompanied in the abstract than human beings can. To sing to Mary is to sing to this particular Mary. To accompany her is to walk beside her in the *Posadas* as she seeks a room for shelter. To accompany *la Soledad* is to physically kneel beside her and feel her loneliness with her; it is to identify our sorrows with hers. To pray to God for our loved ones is to physically pin their photographs to this particular crucifix, thereby establishing the particular, concrete relationship which will make com-passion (not just feeling, but "feeling *with*") possible. It is in and through the concrete particular that the universal is encountered. We can only truly know that which—like our family relationships—is particular and embodied. Because what we cannot know in the particular we cannot feel—and what we cannot feel we cannot know.

The ability to establish personal relationships with particular poor persons—a precondition for the preferential option for "the poor"—is today threatened by the increasing separation of the home from the city. Geographical distance and spatial isolation are becoming increasingly effective means of preventing the very contact with concrete poor persons which, I have argued, is the *sine qua non* of Christian faith and theology. U.S. society is becoming increasingly segregated and polarized into

---

32. García and Espín, "Lilies of the Field," 81.
33. Ibid.

"chocolate cities and vanilla suburbs." Largely white, middle and upper class, Anglo suburbs are becoming the economic and political "center" of our nation, the place to which people can flee from the city:

> we are becoming more separated geographically. Increasingly the poor are stuck in poor neighborhoods in cities surrounded by more afflu- ent suburbs. The better schools, the safer neighborhoods and the jobs are in the suburbs and the poor people are stuck in the cities. . . . If we continue to spread apart geographically according to income, we will find it extremely difficult to provide real opportunity for our poor citizens. Left behind in deteriorating neighborhoods by those who are able to leave and take good schools and jobs with them, the poor may never get back into the mainstream of the American economy and so- ciety. But most Americans living in affluent neighborhoods probably are not ready to deal with dispersal of the poor.[34]

In the wake of "white flight," the city becomes economically, politically, and culturally peripheral, marginalized vis-à-vis the center of U.S. self- identity, the suburbs:

> Dramatic new patterns of segregation have emerged as whites have moved to the suburbs surrounding the declining cities, many of which have majority black and Latino populations. The nation . . . is mov- ing steadily toward a national politics that will be dominated by the suburban vote. The suburbs allow white, middle-class voters to meet their own communities' needs by taxing themselves for direct ser- vices (e.g., schools, libraries, police), while denying resources to the increasingly poor and nonwhite cities.[35]

The polarization of city and suburbs is the geographical manifestation of the polarization of public and domestic, or private life. Life in the sub- urbs is perceived as tranquil compared to the "chaos" of the city. Life in the suburbs is private and secluded, as opposed to the publicness and openness of the city. Cities have sidewalks that are open to the general public. Suburbs eliminate sidewalks, replacing their public openness with the private enclosure of cul-de-sacs. In some suburban neighborhoods,

---

34. Warren R. Copeland, "Poverty in America: Causes, cures . . .," *Chicago Tribune*, January 10, 1995, sec. 1, p. 13.

35. Michael Omi and Howard Winant, "The Los Angeles 'Race Riot' and Contemporary U.S. Politics," in *Reading Rodney King, Reading Urban Uprising*, ed. Robert Gooding-Williams (New York: Routledge, 1993) 102. See also Thomas L. Dumm, "The New Enclosures: Racism in the Normalized Community," in ibid.; Thomas Byrne Edsall and Mary Edsall, *Chain Reaction: The Impact of Race, Rights, and Taxes on American Politics* (New York: Norton, 1991). Increasingly, whites are fleeing even inner-ring suburbs, which become identified with the city's "problems" as blacks and Latinos move into some of these older suburbs.

homeowners are even discouraged from placing their address numbers on their houses, under the assumption that anyone who does not already know to which house he or she is going does not belong on the neighborhood streets anyway. The city square is replaced by the suburban mall as the symbol of civic life. The difference is that, in the enclosed mall, everyone looks alike, talks alike, and behaves the same way. The city is dirty and messy, whereas the suburbs are clean and tidy. Life in the suburbs is perceived as human (praxis, "family values"); life in the city as inhuman (poiesis, "the Rat Race").

Thus, in order to be a complete, successful human person, one must be able to *use* the "inhuman," productive life of the city—and, therefore, the city's "inhuman," productive residents—to make the money necessary to purchase a suburban home far removed from the "urban jungle." The suburban home (i.e., the ability to live away from the city) thus becomes the principal symbol of one's full humanity. In the process, the (suburban) home is idealized, or romanticized, and the city is vilified.

It is its perceived inhumanity which makes the city the center, not of human praxis, now identified with suburban life, but of poiesis: the place where the suburbanite goes to make money, which he or she can use to purchase the more "humane" life of the suburbs. (Indeed, as jobs and employers themselves increasingly flee to the suburbs, the suburbanite is less likely to venture into the "urban jungle" at all.) Like the city itself, those persons who actually live in the city will be perceived as dirty, messy, chaotic, inhuman, violent, and mere instruments of economic production. The segregation of economically poor African Americans and U.S. Hispanics in inner city ghettoes and barrios thus reinforces their dehumanization at the hands of an increasingly suburban dominant culture. For all intents and purposes, the only connection remaining between private, suburban life and public, urban life is the one-and-a-half hour commute. Any contact with "those people" who live in the city will be deemed bearable only if it occurs in the context of instrumental, or productive relationships, wherein the poor are merely employees or workers, and, therefore, only if the nature and extent of the contact remains under the suburbanite's control, i.e., only as long as one knows one can return to a home in the suburbs.

The idealization of the suburban home and the concomitant vilification of the city thus has a further implication: the vilification of the urban home and its inhabitants.[36] Once again, one cannot make a preferential

---

36. A further consequence is the vilification of the poor persons *within the suburban home itself*, especially women and children (independent of race, culture, or class). The dichotomy between home and city thus obscures both the humanity of city life and the inhumanity of suburban home life; it obscures the affective, aesthetic character of urban life-as-praxis, on the one hand, and the ways in which the productive, instrumental relationships of the marketplace influence suburban family relationships, on the other.

option for the poor without making an option for the physical place where the poor live: conversely, to abandon the city is to abandon the persons who live in the city. Hence, the result of these demographic shifts is the increasing geographical polarization of the U.S. population and the increasing disempowerment of economically poor U.S. Hispanics, African Americans, and other historically marginalized groups. These continue to live primarily in the inner city, precisely the area of least political and economic significance, and the area most peripheral to the dominant culture, which is itself increasingly defined by suburban life. This geographical, spatial separation makes genuine interaction virtually impossible, especially since the separation also increases mutual fear. The fear, in turn, reinforces the separation. In the end, the isolation of "minorities" in the inner city becomes not only a byproduct of the suburbanization of society, but the very *raison d'être* of the suburb. The suburb is a safe haven from the chaos of the city and, in order to be preserved as such, must maintain the separation.

The poor, therefore, must remain geographically confined. The spatial border must be respected. As a society, we are happy to help and serve the poor, as long as we don't have to walk *with* them where they walk, that is, as long as we can minister *to* them from our safe enclosures. The poor can then remain passive objects of our actions, rather than friends, *compañeros* and *compañeras* with whom we interact. As long as we can be sure that we will not have to live with them, and thus have interpersonal relationships with them, we will try to help "the poor"—but, again, only from a controllable, geographical distance.

For this reason, current attempts, in cities like Chicago, to de-localize poverty by encouraging the development of "scattered site" public housing are meeting with tremendous resistance. It is not poverty that concerns the suburbs, but scattered poverty . . . not violence, but scattered violence . . . not black persons, but scattered black persons . . . not Hispanics but scattered Hispanics. Poor persons will be tolerated as long as they can be confined and isolated—in the ghetto, the barrio, the urban home, or the prison. Violence will likewise be tolerated as long as it can be confined and isolated in these places.[37] The suburbs are, then, a fundamental geographical obstacle to the option for the poor, for they make "place," or "space," an instrument of exclusion and oppression. In the

---

37. What spurred the flight to the suburbs during the 1980s was not increased crime, since crime rates have, in fact, remained essentially level over the past fifteen years (and have, in some cases, actually decreased), but rather the *randomness* of crime. As long as crime remained localized and contained, it remained "their" problem. As long as, as a society, we believed that we could avoid crime simply by avoiding certain neighborhoods at certain times, we felt we could remain in control of our lives. We don't object to murder as long as we can know and control who gets murdered, and where or when they get murdered.

1990s, the city has become a plantation managed from the "master's house" in the suburbs.

If a preferential option for poor persons is an epistemological precondition for Christian theological reflection, and if our society is so radically divided racially, culturally, and economically between suburban and urban spaces, a Christian theology in the United States today (and *a fortiori*, a Christian theology from the perspective of U.S. Hispanics) must be preferentially an urban theology. To opt for the poor is thus to breach the serene, controlled, suburban enclosure, where the intrusion of "undesirable elements" is prohibited, by opting for the randomness and openness of urban life, where one risks coming face-to-face with poor persons.

Yet the violence, chaos, and insecurity resulting from geographical separation are not limited to urban spaces. Native Americans on reservations and the Appalachian poor also know the oppressive power of geographical separation, isolation, and confinement. For Latinos and Latinas, this form of oppression is also associated in an especially profound way with the borderlands. For a Mexican, transgressing the border is as dangerous as breaching the suburban enclosure.[38] Indeed, what both have in common is their significance as geographical, spatial instruments of exclusion.[39]

If the poor are excluded culturally, politically, and economically, they are also excluded geographically. A theology grounded in an option for the poor will thus be a theology that is, somehow, born amidst the violence, insecurity, unpredictability, messiness, randomness, and chaos of those *geographical spaces* which function as the most basic and fundamental instruments of exclusion. More specifically, it will be a theology born in the everyday *struggle* for survival in the midst of that chaos (as Ada María Isasi-Díaz writes, *"en la lucha"*). For *this* is the concrete, everyday life of the poor, who cannot so easily isolate the home from the vicissitudes of the city: the poor live not on cul-de-sacs but on thoroughfares, not in the malls but in the public square.

When the theologian places him or herself in this particular place (the ghetto, the barrio, the public square) he or she soon discovers that the randomness and chaos of "the city" are not abstractions, but are the common lot of poor *persons*: random illness, random death, random gunfire, random searches, random employment and unemployment, random health care, etc., etc. To abandon the poor to these instruments of death while the privileged few escape into geographical isolation is to condone

---

38. It is an indication of the comparative values which the dominant U.S. culture places on human life (praxis) and commodities (poiesis) that the North American Free Trade Agreement (NAFTA), which opens up the borders to *commodities*, is passed virtually simultaneously with California's Proposition 187, which seeks to close those same borders to *human beings*. The commodity produced by a Mexican worker is thus more free than the worker himself or herself; the product is liberated and the person enslaved.

39. On the role of geographical place in the marginalization of U.S. Hispanics, see Elizondo, *Galilean Journey*, pp. 54–55.

and perpetrate genocide—for the children who are being abandoned to inner city violence are, of course, predominantly poor African American and Latino children.

When one reads the Scriptures in the geographical context of the city, one discovers, however, that the place where randomness and chaos reign is the place which Jesus defines as the Reign of God. If the central symbol of Jesus' life and ministry was the Reign of God, that Reign is itself always pictured by Jesus as unpredictable, random, messy, and chaotic—like inner city life. For the random and chaotic character of God's Reign implies the destruction of all boundaries which would circumscribe, confine, and thus limit God's action in the world. That randomness and chaos is what safeguards the universality of God's love against those who would want to limit its scope. An essential element of God's own identification with the poor is, thus, the transgression of the spatial, geographical boundaries which separate rich and poor in order to walk with the poor where they walk and live with the poor where they live. The violation of these physical, geographical barriers is a virtually absolute precondition for loving the poor.

Not even our love and concern for our nuclear family can be allowed to stand in the way of our responsibility to breach those barriers. When Jesus dared to breach spatial barriers by communing with "unclean spirits" he was pursued by his family (Mk 3; Mt 12; Lk 8), who were concerned about him and feared that he was in danger. Yet, when he was advised by some bystanders that his family was "outside" waiting for him, his response was unwavering: "Who are my mother and my brothers? And looking around on those who sat about him, he said 'Here are my mother and my brothers! Whoever does the will of God is my brother, and sister, and mother' " (Mk 3: 33–35). His brother, his sister, his mother are those who walk with Jesus among the unclean, not those who stay outside.[40]

The Jesus of the gospels relativizes the nuclear family in order to insist that the most intimate, most particular, and most personal of relationships, our family relationships, must extend beyond the nuclear family and characterize *all* our relationships. The authentic community is inclusive not exclusive; it is, of its essence, open to "the other" as a unique human person. The family is not merely a collection of self-sufficient, autonomous individuals, but the birthplace of our very personhood; the person is not the "building block" of the family but its unique mediation. Likewise, the larger human community is not merely a collection of self-sufficient, autonomous families, but the network of social relationships

---

40. On the relativization of the nuclear family, see also Lk 9:59–62, 11:27–28, 12:51–53, 14:26. Justo González makes the perceptive observation that, for Latinas and Latinos, the extended family functions as a bridge between the nuclear family and the larger community, thus blurring and attenuating the difference; see his *Santa Biblia: The Bible Through Hispanic Eyes* (Nashville: Abingdon, forthcoming).

which gives birth to our families; the family is not the "building block" of the human community but its unique mediation. When any family turns its home into a barricade which isolates its members from other families and from the larger human community, it thereby denies its intrinsic and constitutive connection to that larger community. This is the radical significance of Jesus' own relativization of family values: he does so not to relativize human relationships but, on the contrary, to insist that these must not be circumscribed by and limited to the home. The true home is one that opens up to the public square.

Numerous other times in the gospels, Jesus is portrayed as the one who transgresses spatial, geographical barriers and boundaries: e.g., in the parable of the rich man and Lazarus, a central symbol is the gate which separates the rich man, inside the gate, from the poor Lazarus, who is prostrate *outside* the gate (Lk 16:19–31); in the famous parable of the man who gives a banquet to which none of the invited guests come, the man instructs his servant to "go *outside* to the streets and bring back [*inside*] those whom you happen to meet, so that they may dine (Mt 22:2–14)." Invitations to the Reign of God are extended randomly, to whomever happens to be walking by, or standing around, or passing through. To limit that randomness, to impose an order on God's Reign, to seek personal security for ourselves and our families by building fences, barriers, or cul-de-sacs is, like the rich man, to exclude ourselves from the Reign of God. We must be willing to walk out through the gate, out into the streets, for that is where we will find Lazarus.

In other parables, the Reign of God is compared to seed that is "*scattered* upon the *earth*" (Mk 4:26–29)—again, what is underscored is the random, or chaotic character of God's grace, which is scattered freely about—or God's Reign is compared to a mustard seed planted in a garden (Lk 13:18–19). As John Dominic Crossan has observed, the mustard plant is little more than a weed: "the point . . . [of the mustard seed parable] is not just that the mustard plant starts as a proverbially small seed and grows into a shrub of three or four feet, or even higher, it is that it tends to take over where it is not wanted, that it tends to get out of control, that it tends to attract birds within cultivated areas where they are not particularly desired. And that, said Jesus, was what the Kingdom was like . . ."[41] That is, for the dominant U.S. culture, what the poor are like. To say that God's grace has no boundaries or limits is to say that it is experienced as random, chaotic, and undesirable, especially by those who live "within cultivated areas." What is terrifying, subversive, and thus encounters resistance is not the seed, but the *scattered* seed, not public housing, but *scattered site* public housing. To say that God is preferentially identified with the least significant persons is to say that God will be found

41. John Dominic Crossan, *The Historical Jesus: The Life of a Mediterranean Peasant* (San Francisco: Harper, 1991), pp. 278–79.

in the least significant places, the least cultivated places, not between well-trimmed hedges but among the scattered seeds and rampant weeds.

Jesus' life represented a threat to all who would limit and impose an order, including a spatial and geographical order, on God's Reign. He was not crucified so much for what he *did* as for *where* he *was*; he "walked with" the wrong people and in the wrong places. That was enough to get him beaten up, enough to get him crucified. In Jesus' world, everyone had his or her proper place. Justice was defined as ensuring that every person stay in the place appropriate to him or her. To accompany the poor and the outcasts was to transgress the established and accepted boundaries which separate "us" from "them."[42] Consequently, by walking with the poor, by accompanying the outcasts, Jesus put himself in the "wrong" place, and he was crucified as a result. He should have stayed in his proper place. To walk with Jesus is thus to walk with the wrong persons in the wrong places. To note that Jesus was not a political revolutionary is both to state the obvious and to miss the point; the fundamental political act is the act of transgressing boundaries, the act of walking and living with the outcast where he or she walks and lives.

God's grace is associated not with barriers and gates but with bridges and thoroughfares, not with order but with disorder, not with well-established rules of behavior but with randomness, not with predictability but with unpredictability, not with "staying in one's proper place" but with "spilling over" into inappropriate places, not with the isolation of the suburban cul-de-sac but with the uncontrolled intercourse of the urban sidewalk. Dare we suggest, consequently, that God's grace is associated not with the "closed and deadened spaces of the suburbs" but with the "messy and open qualities of heterogeneous urban spaces?"[43] And, therefore, with those persons who live and walk in those spaces? If that is true, the preferential option for the poor is, not only an option for particular persons, but also a preferential option for a particular place. If one takes seriously the concreteness and particularity of human praxis, and if one wants to walk with the poor, he or she must be willing to walk *where* poor persons walk.

---

42. Marcus Borg observes that the "image of God as gracious . . . is implicit in one of the most striking features of Jesus' ministry, namely the meals which he shared with 'sinners,'—that is, outcasts. Given that sharing a meal in first-century Palestine signified acceptance of one's table companions, Jesus' behavior signified his acceptance of them. . . . Implicit in the action is an understanding of God as gracious and compassionate, embracing even the outcasts, those whose mode of life placed them outside the boundaries of respectability and acceptance established by conventional wisdom. . . . These boundaries . . . were negated by the Jesus movement." Marcus J. Borg, *Jesus: A New Vision: Spirit, Culture, and the Life of Discipleship* (San Francisco: Harper Collins, 1987), pp. 101–2, 131.

43. Dumm, "The New Enclosures: Racism in the Normalized Community," 192.

For Latinos and Latinas, geographical place is intimately linked to our self-identity: as exiles and mestizos/as, we are, by definition, persons who have no place to call home, persons who live "in between." To be a U.S. Hispanic is to be a mestizo/a and an exile, a bridge across cultural, racial, and geographical boundaries. It is to be a mustard shrub which wends its way through cultivated areas—unwanted and undocumented. To be a bridge or a mustard shrub is, by definition, to transgress boundaries.

Latinos and Latinas know the crucial importance of transgressing borders and boundaries in order to walk with others; as exiles, we have experienced the destruction and dehumanization of the border—whether that of the Rio Grande or that of the Caribbean Sea. My earliest memories are of that airplane suspended in between Havana and Miami. All U.S. Hispanics know the importance of geographical place . . . because we have none. We live on the border, on the boundary—and, therefore, at the crossroads, at the intersection . . . neither here nor there but always both/and. Abandoned in an alien land, we have known the cruelty and injustice of abandonment.[44] Thus, we have known the liberating power of *acompañamiento*, which transgresses boundaries.

Our mestizaje and exile are symbols of our identification with a Jesus who also transgressed boundaries. The public character of so much of our popular religion, especially pilgrimages and processions such as that of Good Friday, reflects our refusal to have our lives, identities, and, above all, our God circumscribed and limited by the spatial boundaries which U.S. society has erected. This transgression of boundaries—even if only temporary—is already an act of subversion and, thus, of liberation:

> Processions, and above all pilgrimages are a "road" through profane space towards the centrality of the consecrated space *par excellence*, the shrine of the Virgin of Guadalupe, those of Copacabana, the Christ of "Gran Poder" or Esquipulas. As long as the religious practice lasts, for a short time there is some control over the space of "transition" [i.e., the boundary, or border], which may be hostile but is now controlled by the people.[45]

Like Jesus', our very existence represents a threat to all boundaries, borders, and barriers. We, therefore, suffer the same consequences. When U.S. Hispanics walk with Jesus, we are walking with someone who was him-

---

44. As noted in chapter 1, even in the case of Latin American immigrants or exiles who "choose" to come to the United States, that decision is itself necessitated, to a great extent, by a history of U.S. intervention in Latin America. To the extent that this is true, the experiences of immigration and exile are also experiences of abandonment; because Latin America had earlier been abandoned by the U.S., Latin Americans must now "choose" to emigrate.

45. Enrique Dussel, "Popular Religion as Oppression and Liberation: Hypotheses on its Past and Present in Latin America," in *Popular Religion*, eds. Greinacher and Mette, 89.

self a mestizo and an exile, a no-body from no-where. A Galilean, he lived at a crossroads . . . neither here nor there, but both/and."[46] In the same way the Mexican immigrants are rejected as "wetbacks" in this country and as "*pochos*" in Mexico, the expectant Mary and Joseph could find no room to lay their heads. If the dominant culture in the U.S. erects borders and gates to exclude the "unclean," or "undesirables," Jesus enters their homes and goes "outside to the streets" to bring them to dinner, to break bread with, or accompany (*ad-cum-panis*) them. If the dominant culture fears the unruly and uncontrollable mustard shrub, which does not respect the cultivated garden's boundaries, Jesus compares the mustard shrub to the Reign of God. The preferential option for the poor is thus a preferential option for this particular, physical place: that place which, for the dominant culture, is no-where—because no-body lives there.

As paradigmatic for the option for the poor, the particular, embodied, and affective character of the life of the home, now extended to include urban life itself, is thus reflected in the theme of *acompañamiento* so prevalent in U.S. Hispanic popular Catholicism. Consequently, this theme can be retrieved by U.S. Hispanic theology as a rich resource for expanding and deepening our understanding of the preferential option for the poor. If, for Latinos and Latinas, the home is the paradigmatic locus of all human life (familial, urban, and religious) the paradigm for that life is the *the act of accompaniment*, or "*acompañamiento*."

To be among family is to be accompanied by others; and, as we have already seen, to be accompanied by others is to be a person. The fundamental importance of this theme is made explicit at the end of the Guadalupe story. Surrounded by co-workers on their way to build the temple at Tepeyac, Juan Diego pays his uncle a visit. Here, the final affirmation of Juan Diego's full humanity and dignity is placed on the lips of his uncle, who expresses surprise at seeing Juan Diego "so well-accompanied and honored [in the Spanish translation, *muy acompañado y muy honrado*]."[47] To be a human being is to be in relationship with others, and to be in relationship with others is to be "*acompañado*."[48]

---

46. Elizondo, *Galilean Journey*, pp. 54–56.

47. Siller, *Para comprender el mensaje de María de Guadalupe*, p. 93.

48. The importance of accompaniment for U.S. Hispanics is poignantly conveyed in the following anecdote recounted by Virgilio Elizondo. The story concerns *una viejita* (the term, though literally translated as "a little old lady," connotes *cariño* and respect), whose namelessness itself indicates her insignificance in the eyes of the world. As so many Roman Catholic churches in recent years, her church had been remodeled. As part of the renovation, all the statues had been taken out of the church, save a lone crucifix behind the altar. Upon entering the renovated church and surveying the scene, she became sad and dejected. She explained: "Sé que Jesús tiene que estar en el centro de la iglesia, pero eso no quiere decir que tiene que estar solo." (I know that Jesus has to be in the center of the church, but that doesn't mean that he has to be alone.) Another anecdote tells of a woman who, when asked why Our Lady of Guadalupe was so impor-

By definition, the act of accompaniment "suggests going with another on an equal basis" and, thus, implies the transgression of discriminatory barriers.[49] Only in and through the concrete *act* of accompaniment do we love others as "others," as equals, and are we, in turn, loved by them. As action, or praxis, accompaniment includes not only "being" with another, or feeling with another, but also "doing" with another.

In the *Posadas*, the community walks with Joseph and Mary from house to house. In this process of accompaniment, the people seek some family, some home, which will not exclude them; they seek a home which will be open to the homeless of the city. Before he had even been born, Jesus was already challenging spatial barriers. To walk with Joseph and Mary is thus to challenge those same barriers today. It is this active sense of accompaniment which is conveyed so powerfully, above all, by the San Fernando community's Holy Thursday procession with Jesus to Gethsemane, during which the people repeatedly sing the refrain "*Caminemos, con Jesús*," that is, "let us walk with Jesus."

To accompany another person is to *walk with* him or her. It is, above all, by walking with others that we relate to them and love them. This notion now further specifies the act of accompaniment: the paradigmatic form of human action is not simply that of "being with" another but, rather, the act of "walking with" the other. To be in relationship with others and, therefore, to be a human person is to walk with others. The notion of "walking with" incorporates both the ethical-political and the aesthetic dimensions of human praxis.

It is, first of all, a concrete, physical, historical act. The act of walking implies directionality: one walks in a particular direction. That directionality implies, in turn, an ethical-political content: implicit in the act of walking are the questions, "In which direction?" "How is the direction determined?" and "Who determines the direction?" These are ethical-political questions. If, as I will suggest below, the act of accompaniment necessarily implies equality, the possibility of accompanying the poor does not exist unless and until the poor themselves are equal participants in dialogue and interaction through which these questions are answered.

Consequently, the act of accompaniment is never the act of autonomous individuals; it is by definition a walking "with." Human interpersonal action is never simply a "doing" but is also always, at the same time, a "being with" and an "interacting with." It is a communal action: "let *us* walk *with* Jesus." Therefore, it is never simply ethical-political activity "moving" in a particular historical direction (e.g., toward a more just society), but it is also the ethical-political interaction between and among

---

tant to her, responded: "Se quedó con nosotros " (She stayed with us.); Elizondo, *Mosaic of God*.

49. William Morris, ed., *The American Heritage Dictionary of the English Language* (New York: Houghton Mifflin, 1975), p. 8.

those persons walking together, and the aesthetic interaction that unites the persons, or others, in the process. This unity implies both empathy, as the fullest sense of "being with" another, and concrete, distinct individuality, as the precondition for *inter*action, or walking *with*. By definition, only distinct persons can *inter*relate. Thus, when we walk together, our common personhood is affirmed: we become *compañeros* and *compañeras*.

The struggle for social justice will, in the long run, simply perpetuate the dehumanization of poor persons if not undertaken *together with* poor persons. Unless social transformation is rooted in an everyday accompaniment of the poor, that is, in the everyday act of walking with, living with, breaking bread with particular poor persons in the concreteness of the poor persons' everyday struggle for survival, the transformation of social structures will, in the long run, simply perpetuate the oppression of the poor. This, unfortunately, has been the legacy of so many well-intentioned attempts to "opt for the poor." In the absence of the particular friendships that require, as a precondition, *physical and affective presence*, the option for the poor inevitably turns the concrete, particular lives of poor persons into an abstract generality (e.g., "the poor," "the people," "the proletariat"). Without the empathy (aesthetic praxis) that can be mediated only by the historical act of accompaniment, human ethical-political praxis inevitably degenerates into poiesis.

If affective, aesthetic union with the poor is the most profound way of knowing the poor as persons, and if this affective, aesthetic union can only take place between and among concrete, particular persons, then one *cannot* know the poor or perceive reality from the perspective of the poor unless he or she is literally and physically walking with particular poor persons.[50] This is not the *only* way of being together with the poor, or of perceiving reality from the perspective of the poor, but it is certainly the *sine qua non* of *walking* with the poor, which is, in turn, the *sine qua non* of the preferential option for the poor. As such, this active, concrete, and particular relationship with the poor is the preferential form which the option for the poor must take: "Option means a free decision to choose to exist in the world of the poor. Option is to be committed to the poor and to try to be present in their world. Option is to try to share one's life with them, to have friends among them, and to be

---

50. Gustavo Gutiérrez makes this point with regard to Bartolomé de Las Casas: "Making the viewpoint of the Indian one's own requires actually approaching, drawing near, concrete persons. . . . [Las Casas] does more than merely adopt the viewpoint of another. That would have been too abstract for him. He regards that other as a brother or sister in the gospel sense of the word, the neighbor we are to love. Unless we are willing to go this far, we shall not understand Las Casas' sense of what we call 'otherness' today—sensitivity for a person's right to be different" (*Las Casas*, p. 90).

committed to their social class, race, and culture. Option is actually to live with the poor."[51]

Yet to walk with the poor demands more than putting oneself in the geographical place of the poor. That is a necessary, but not a sufficient condition for loving and knowing the poor; embodiment, or physicality, is a necessary, but not a sufficient condition for empathy and relationship. The call to accompany Jesus and the poor is also a call to interiority, self-appropriation, and self-reflection (though not the reflection of an autonomous self).[52] This call to develop one's *interior* life—as an intrinsic dimension of the option for the poor—emerges from our organic anthropology. If, in fact, a person's identity mediates and, therefore, expresses in some unique way the identity of those communities which have given birth to the person, then his or her relationships with other persons imply not only a contact with those others in the "external" world but also a contact with them *within* him or herself, as those other persons have become a constitutive part of his or her personal identity.

Walking with, or accompanying another person implies more than physical *movement* (e.g., "walking").[53] For one to identify with other members of one's family means more than simply living with them in the external world; it also means living with them as internalized constituents of one's own personal identity.[54] The option for the poor requires more

---

51. Gutiérrez, "Church of the Poor," 16–17.

52. I use the term "interiority" to refer to the theologian's—or any person's—process of asking and responding to three basic questions: "What am I doing when I am knowing? Why is doing that knowing? What do I know when I do it?" (Lonergan, *Method in Theology*, p. 83). The willingness and ability to address these questions honestly is the measure of one's willingness and ability to understand how *one's own* social location influences one's understanding of "the poor." On the notions of interiority and self-appropriation, see especially ibid., pp. 6–7, 13–16, 83–85; Stephen Happel and James J. Walter, *Conversion and Discipleship* (Philadelphia: Fortress, 1986), p. 150; Carla Mae Streeter, OP, "Glossary of Lonerganian Terminology," *Communication and Lonergan*, ed. Farrell and Soukup, 322–23.

53. As noted in chapter 4, "modern notions of praxis all tend either to connote or explicitly invoke *movement*" (Lamb, "Praxis," 785). This reduction of human action to mere physical movement is already implied in the modern understanding of praxis as production, or transformation: in order to produce or transform the external environment, one must physically act *upon* or *manipulate* it. The modern temptation would thus be to reduce the option for the poor to a *merely physical* accompaniment, and to understand the act of accompaniment itself in exclusively physical terms.

54. Anyone who has ever sworn, in vain, that he or she "will never raise my own children the way my parents raised me" knows how foolhardy and, indeed, dangerous it is to assume that, once we have left our childhood home behind, we have also left our parents behind. The surest way to perpetuate past injustices and sins is by ignoring how those have become a part of our own identity.

than just a physical presence with poor people; it also means recognizing and appreciating how "who *I* am" influences my understanding of "who *the poor* are." It means, conversely, recognizing and appreciating the ways in which, through that physical presence, I am being changed *by* the poor. It means recognizing how my own identity as a privileged theologian is intrinsically related to and perpetuates the suffering of the poor, those outside my own formative communities as well as other Latinos and Latinas, especially those ancestors whose struggles have given and continue to give me birth. This interiority—or sensitivity to the *a priori* presence of the poor as intrinsic to my own identity—thus creates that spirit of humility without which it is impossible to relate to the poor person as "other." Without such humility, one will—with the best intentions—once again turn the poor into mere instruments of one's own projected designs and ambitions. The preferential option for the poor thus has an extensive, socio-historical dimension (correlative to the ethical-political dimension of praxis) and an intensive, spiritual dimension (correlative to the aesthetic dimension of praxis).[55] The physical face of the other, the poor person, is what reveals his or her intrinsic relationship to me and, in so doing, reveals to me my own deepest identity, an identity rooted in God.

Finally, in U.S. Hispanic popular Catholicism, the act of walking with others is always a fundamentally religious, sacramental act: "Caminemos con Jesús." Interestingly, the refrain calls for the community, not to "follow" Jesus, but to walk "with," or alongside him. Jesus is not ahead of us, or above us, but in our very midst, in the very midst of our relationships with each other. Indeed, Jesus is the one who draws us together, the one with whom and for whom we come together.

If, in U.S. Hispanic popular Catholicism, the human person and, especially, human interaction are sacraments of God, that sacramentality is made manifest and explicit in the act of walking together with Jesus. In the act of accompaniment, Jesus' eucharistic presence (*ad-cum-panis*) becomes fully identified with the community's everyday life; the eucharist, the breaking of the bread, is taken from the altar into our homes, into the streets, into the city.

Consequently, if the option for the poor has a necessary, aesthetic dimension and, as Vasconcelos maintains, the highest form of aesthetic union is mystical union, a necessary dimension of the option for the poor implies a personal, interior *spiritual* life. Here, however, the person is not the autonomous individual, the interior life is not separate from "exterior" social life, and the spiritual life is not separate from physical life. On the contrary, a central thesis of this book has been that, in the context of U.S. Hispanic popular Catholicism, these dichotomies are

---

55. See my "*Nosotros*: Toward a U.S. Hispanic Anthropology," *Listening* 27:1 (Winter, 1992): 55–69.

artificial, since the spiritual is always mediated by the sacramental concrete.[56] Accompanying the poor implies a spirituality because that act is, above all, a sacramental act.

If we are called to recognize the ways in which "walking with the poor" changes us internally, as persons, so too are we called to recognize how our identification with the faith of the poor—how the sacramental act of walking with Jesus on Good Friday—effects changes in our own religious faith. In other words, a theology grounded in U.S. Hispanic popular Catholicism, in the preferential option for the poor, presupposes and demands a *spirituality* born in and nurtured by the concrete, historical process of accompaniment.[57]

We can now return to our starting point: San Fernando as an axis of U.S. Hispanic popular Catholicism, the place which, literally in between the home and the urban public square, serves as the crossroads of these two worlds. The spirituality of San Fernando, as manifested in the cathedral's popular religious celebrations, is lived out in a particular place, the church, which is itself an extension of the home and the city. In U.S. Hispanic popular Catholicism the church, as a place of worship, derives its significance precisely from its position in between the home and the city. To worship *there* is thus to know a God for whom there are no barriers, borders, or boundaries. It is to know a Mestizo/a, an Exile, an Immigrant who transcends all divisive barriers, whether based on economic class, gender, race, culture, age . . . or geographical place. Consequently, this is a God who is at home at the crossroads, in Galilee, on the border, on the *balsa*, on the airplane.

To know this God is to be transformed, body *and* soul. U.S. Hispanic popular Catholicism is much more than an anthropological or cultural curiosity; it is a life of faith. If we identify with the poor, if we "walk with the poor," we will be transformed by the truth of that faith, not only as theologians but as Christians and human beings.[58] As theologians, we cannot truly love the poor unless we love the God whom the poor themselves love. That God will transform and liberate us all—if we will but walk

---

56. For this reason, I have left the discussion of interiority and spirituality to the end; not because these are any less important—indeed, they are fundamental—but because they are mediated by the foregoing considerations which specify the concrete historicity of that interiority and spirituality.

57. On U.S. Hispanic spirituality, see especially Orlando Espín, "The God of the Vanquished: Foundations of a Latino Spirituality," *Listening* 27:1 (Winter, 1992): 70–83. On a Latin American spirituality of liberation, see especially Gustavo Gutiérrez, *We Drink from Our Own Wells: The Spiritual Journey of a People* (Maryknoll, NY: Orbis, 1984); Jon Sobrino, *Spirituality of Liberation* (Maryknoll, NY: Orbis, 1988).

58. A powerful testament to the personal, spiritual, and theological transformation that takes place as we accompany, or walk with poor persons is provided in the following reflections of a Dominican missionary priest, Brian Pierce: "I

together. The preferential option for the poor implies an identification not only with the socio-historical situation of the poor but also with this liberating God, the God of the poor. We encounter this God outside, in the "external" world, but also inside, in our interior life. Indeed, as I have argued, these are intrinsically related dimensions of a single, sacramental, historical struggle.

The preferential option for the poor is not only an ethical-political option, or an aesthetic option, or a rational option—though it is all of these too; it is, fundamentally, a spiritual option. Through this commitment Jesus transforms not only social structures, not only our hearts and minds, but also our very souls. In the cry "*Caminemos con Jesús*," we proclaim *Jesus* as the source of our community, our solidarity, and, therefore, our liberation. All the nuances, complexities, and ambiguities of our theological analyses of U.S. Hispanic popular Catholicism must ultimately return to this single, simple, fundamental fact. "*Caminante, no hay camino*" . . . "*Caminemos con Jesús*." That place which, for others, is nowhere is for us the Way. Those persons who, for others, are irrational and simple-minded are for us the privileged witnesses to the Truth. Those who, for others, are no-bodies are for us the bearers of Life. As we walk together with Jesus, it is together with him that we find our liberation. ¡*Caminemos con Jesús*!

---

remember standing for hours as a young Dominican theology student in Lima, Peru, on Good Friday, holding the large crucifix, along with another brother, as hundreds and hundreds of mourners approached to adore and kiss the feet of the crucified Christ. The women wept as if their only son had just been gunned down by a death squad. It overwhelmed me. Three days later, on Easter Sunday, there was just a scattering of folks to celebrate the Resurrection. 'They are obsessed with suffering,' I screamed in my heart, trying to understand it all. 'Where is the hope? Where is the promise of new life?' I knew that I had seen and experienced every day a deep hopefulness in the people, but I could not make a theological connection between that lived hopefulness and what I perceived as an overemphasis on the crucifixion of Jesus. Little by little, the scales have fallen from my eyes, thanks to the patient accompaniment of the people. It is only now that I can see the failure of Jesus as a source of hope. There is no contradiction between the bloodied statue of Jesus in the church and faith in the Resurrection. . . . God, like us, is on a pilgrim journey. The resurrection is experienced not as final victory, but in the recognition of the close presence of the living God who chooses to walk with and suffer alongside the poor. Resurrection is joyful and faithful reassurance here and now." Brian J. Pierce, "The Cross and the Crib: Hope From the Underside," *America*, April 2, 1994, 13–14. In the process of accompaniment, Brian Pierce was converted to the living God ("the scales have fallen from my eyes"); the Dominican priest had now experienced the resurrection not as an end product ("final victory") but as the process of accompaniment itself.

Bibliography

Altizer, Thomas J. J. et al., eds. *Destruction and Theology*. New York : Crossroad, 1982.

Aponte, Edwin David. "Coritos as Active Symbol in Latino Protestant Popular Religion." *Journal of Hispanic/Latino Theology*, 2:3 (February, 1995): 57–66.

Aquino, María Pilar. *Our Cry for Life: Feminist Theology from Latin America*. Maryknoll, NY: Orbis, 1993.

Arac, Jonathan, ed. *Postmodernism and Politics*. Minneapolis: University of Minnesota Press, 1986.

Arendt, Hannah. *The Human Condition*. Chicago: University of Chicago Press, 1958.

Aristotle. *Nicomachean Ethics*. New York and London: Garland, 1987.

———. *Politics*. Cambridge and New York: Cambridge University Press, 1988.

Axelos, Kostas. *Alienation, Praxis, and Technē in the Thought of Karl Marx*. Austin, TX: University of Texas Press, 1976.

de Beer, Gabriella. *José Vasconcelos and His World*. New York: Las Américas, 1966.

Bell, Catherine. *Ritual Theory, Ritual Practice*. New York: Oxford University Press, 1992.

Bellah, Robert N. et al. *The Good Society*. New York: Alfred A. Knopf, 1991.

———. *Habits of the Heart: Individualism and Commitment in American Life*. New York: Harper and Row, 1985.

Benhabib, Seyla. "Epistemologies of Postmodernism: A Rejoinder to Jean-François Lyotard." *New German Critique* 33 (Fall, 1984): 103–26.

Berman, Russell A. *Modern Culture and Critical Theory: Art, Politics, and the Legacy of the Frankfurt School*. Madison, WI: University of Wisconsin, 1989.

Bernstein, Richard. *Beyond Objectivism and Relativism: Science, Hermeneutics, and Praxis*. Philadelphia: University of Pennsylvania Press, 1985.

———. *Praxis and Action: Contemporary Philosophies of Human Activity*. Philadelphia: University of Pennsylvania Press, 1971.

Blake, William. *The Complete Poems*. Ed. W. H. Stevenson. London: Longman, 1989.

Boff, Clodovis. *Theology and Praxis: Epistemological Foundations*. Maryknoll, NY: Orbis, 1987.

Boff, Leonardo. "Theological Characteristics of a Grassroots Church," in *The Challenge of Basic Christian Communities*. Ed. Sergio Torres and John Eagleson. Maryknoll, NY: Orbis, 1981.

———. *Trinity and Society*. Maryknoll, NY: Orbis, 1988.

Borg, Marcus J. *Jesus: A New Vision: Spirit, Culture, and the Life of Discipleship*. San Francisco: Harper Collins, 1987.

Borrat, Hector. "Liberation Theology in Latin America." *Dialog* 13 (Summer, 1974): 172–76.

Buber, Martin. *I and Thou.* New York: Scribner's/MacMillan, 1970.

Bulnes, Francisco. *El Verdadero Díaz y la revolución.* México, DF: Editora Nacional, 1967.

Büntig, Aldo et al. *Catolicismo popular.* Quito: IPLA, 1970.

Camps, Victoria. *Virtudes públicas.* Madrid: Espasa Calpe, 1990.

Candelaria, Michael. *Popular Religion and Liberation.* Albany, NY: SUNY Press, 1990.

Carter, Stephen L. *The Culture of Disbelief: How American Law and Politics Trivialize Religious Devotion.* New York: Basic Books, 1993.

Chopp, Rebecca. *The Praxis of Suffering: An Interpretation of Liberation and Political Theologies.* Maryknoll, NY: Orbis, 1986.

Comte, Auguste. *Auguste Comte and Positivism: The Essential Writings.* Chicago: University of Chicago Press, 1983.

———. *A Discourse on the Positive Spirit.* London: Reeves, 1903.

Conferencia Episcopal de Latinoamérica (CELAM). *Medellín conclusiones: La Iglesia en la actual transformación de América Latina a la luz del Concilio.* 14a edición. Bogotá: Secretariado General del CELAM, 1987.

———. *Puebla: La Evangelización en el Presente y en el Futuro de América Latina.* México: Librería Parroquial de Clavería, 1991.

Copeland, Warren R. "Poverty in America: Causes, cures . . ." *Chicago Tribune,* January 10, 1995.

Crossan, John Dominic. *The Historical Jesus: The Life of a Mediterranean Peasant.* San Francisco: Harper, 1991.

Crowley, Brian Lee. *The Self, The Individual, and the Community.* Oxford: Clarendon Press, 1987.

Davis, F. James. *Who is Black? One Nation's Definition.* University Park, PA: Pennsylvania State University Press, 1991.

Dealy, Glen Caudill. *The Public Man: An Interpretation of Latin American and Other Catholic Countries.* Amherst, MA: University of Massachusetts Press, 1977.

Deck, Allan Figueroa. Introduction. In *Frontiers of Hispanic Theology in the United States.* Ed. Allan Figueroa Deck. Maryknoll, NY: Orbis, 1992.

———. *The New Wave: Hispanic Ministry and the Evangelization of Cultures.* New York: Paulist, 1989.

Descartes, René. *Philosophical Essays of Descartes,* vol. 1, *Discourse on Method,* part 4. New York: Bobbs-Merrill, 1960.

Deústua, Alejandro. *Estética aplicada: Lo bello en el arte: la arquitectura (apuntes y extractos).* Lima: Compañía de Impresiones y Publicidad, 1932.

———. *Estética aplicada: Lo bello en el arte: Escultura, pintura, música (apuntes y extractos).* Lima: Imprenta Americana, 1935.

———. *Estética aplicada: Lo bello en la naturaleza (apuntes).* Lima: Rivas Berrio, 1929.

———. *Estética general.* Lima: Imprenta E. Rávago, 1923.

Douglas, Mary. *Purity and Danger.* London: Routledge and Kegan Paul, 1966.

Drake, Stillman. *Discoveries and Opinions of Galileo.* New York: Doubleday Anchor Books, 1957.

Dumm, Thomas L. "The New Enclosures: Racism in the Normalized Community." In *Reading Rodney King, Reading Urban Uprising.* Ed. Robert Gooding-Williams. New York: Routledge, 1993.

Dunne, Joseph. *Back to the Rough Ground: 'Phronesis' and 'Techne' in Modern Philosophy and in Aristotle.* Notre Dame, IN: University of Notre Dame Press, 1993.

Dussel, Enrique. *El Encubrimiento del Indio: Hacia el Origen del Mito de la Modernidad.* México, DF: Editorial Cambio XXI, 1992.

———. "An Ethics of Liberation: Fundamental Hypotheses." In *The Ethics of Liberation: The Liberation of Ethics.* Ed. Dietmar Mieth and Jacques Pohier. Edinburgh: T. & T. Clark, 1984.

———. *Filosofía de la producción.* Bogotá: Editorial Nueva América, 1984.

———. *Método para una filosofía de la liberación.* Salamanca: Sígueme, 1974.

———. *Para una ética de la liberación latinoamericana,* 2 vols. Buenos Aires: Siglo Veintiuno, 1973.

———. *Philosophy of Liberation.* Maryknoll, NY: Orbis, 1985.

———. "Popular Religion as Oppression and Liberation: Hypotheses on its Past and Present in Latin America." In *Popular Religion.* Ed. Norbert Greinacher and Norbert Mette. Edinburgh: T. and T. Clark, 1986.

Eagleton, Terry. *The Ideology of the Aesthetic.* Oxford: Basil Blackwell, 1990.

The Economist. "America's New Lifestyle is Just Hard Work." Reprinted in *The Chicago Tribune,* November 1, 1994.

Edsall, Thomas Byrne and Mary Edsall. *Chain Reaction: The Impact of Race, Rights, and Taxes on American Politics.* New York: Norton, 1991.

Eliade, Mircea. *Images and Symbols.* New York: Sheed and Ward, 1969.

Eliade, Mircea, and David Tracy, eds. *What is Religion? An Enquiry for Christian Theology.* Edinburgh: T. & T. Clark, 1980.

Elizondo, Virgilio. *The Future is Mestizo: Life Where Cultures Meet.* Bloomington, IN: Meyer-Stone, 1988.

———. *Galilean Journey: The Mexican-American Promise.* Maryknoll, NY: Orbis, 1983.

———. *La Morenita: Evangelizer of the Americas.* San Antonio, TX: Mexican American Cultural Center, 1980.

———. *Mestizaje: The Dialectic of Cultural Birth and the Gospel.* San Antonio, TX: Mexican American Cultural Center, 1978.

———. "Popular Religion as Support of Identity: A Pastoral-Psychological Case-Study Based on the Mexican American Experience in the U.S.A." In *Popular Religion.* Ed. Norbert Greinacher and Norbert Mette. Edinburgh: T. & T. Clark, 1986.

———. *The Third Creation: A Woman Clothed with the Sun.* Maryknoll, NY: Orbis, forthcoming.

Elizondo, Virgilio, Timothy Matovina, and the People of San Fernando, *Mestizo God.* To be published as part of the Lilly-funded study of San Fernando Cathedral.

Espín, Orlando O. "The God of the Vanquished: Foundations of a Latino Spirituality." *Listening: Journal of Religion and Culture* 27:1 (Winter, 1992): 70–83.

———. "Grace and Humanness: A Hispanic Perspective." In *We Are a People! Initiatives in Hispanic American Theology.* Ed. Roberto S. Goizueta. Minneapolis: Fortress Press, 1992.

————. "Pentecostalism and Popular Catholicism: Preservers of Hispanic Catholic Tradition?," Presidential Address at the Fourth Annual Colloquium of the Academy of Catholic Hispanic Theologians of the United States (San Diego, 1992). Text in: *ACHTUS Newsletter* 4 (1993).

————. "Popular Catholicism: Alienation or Hope?" In *Aliens in the Promised Land*. Ed. Ada María Isasi-Díaz and Fernando Segovia. Minneapolis: Fortress Press, 1995.

————. "Popular Catholicism among Latinos." In *Hispanic Catholic Culture in the U.S.: Issues and Concerns*. Ed. Jay P. Dolan and Allan Figueroa Deck. Notre Dame, IN: University of Notre Dame Press, 1994.

————. "Popular Religion as an Epistemology (of Suffering)." In *Journal of Hispanic/Latino Theology* 2:2 (Nov., 1994): 55–78.

————. "Religiosidad popular: un aporte para su definición y hermenéutica." *Estudios Sociales* 58 (1984): 41–56.

————. "Tradition and Popular Religion: An Understanding of the *Sensus Fidelium*." In *Frontiers of Hispanic Theology in the United States*. Ed. Allan Figueroa Deck. Maryknoll, NY: Orbis, 1992.

Espín, Orlando O. and Sixto J. García. " 'Lilies of the Field': A Hispanic Theology of Providence and Human Responsibility." In *Proceedings of The Catholic Theological Society of America* 44 (1989): 70–90.

Falla, Ricardo. *Esa muerte que nos hace vivir: estudio de la religión popular*. San Salvador: UCA, 1984.

Fatula, Mary Ann. *The Triune God of Christian Faith*. Collegeville, MN: The Liturgical Press, 1990.

Ferreira dos Santos, Mário Dias. *Filosofias da afirmação e da negação*. São Paulo: Logos, 1965.

Foster, Hal. "(Post)Modern Polemics." *New German Critique* 33 (Fall, 1984): 67–78.

Fox, Matthew. *The Coming of the Cosmic Christ*. San Francisco: Harper and Row, 1988.

Francis, Mark R. "Building Bridges between Liturgy, Devotionalism, and Popular Religion." *Assembly* 20:2 (April, 1994): 636–38.

Friedemann, C. J. *Religiosidad popular entre Medellín y Puebla: Antecedentes y desarrollo*. Santiago de Chile: Pontificia Universidad Católica, 1990.

Gadamer, Hans-Georg. "Hermeneutics and Social Science." *Cultural Hermeneutics* 2 (1975): 307–16.

Galilea, Segundo. *Religiosidad popular y pastoral*. Madrid: Ediciones Cristiandad, 1979.

————. "The Theology of Liberation and the Place of Folk Religion." In *What is Religion? An Inquiry for Christian Theology*. Ed. Mircea Eliade and David Tracy. Edinburgh: T. and T. Clark, 1980.

García, Sixto J. "A Hispanic Approach to Trinitarian Theology: The Dynamics of Celebration, Reflection, and Praxis." In *We Are a People! Initiatives in Hispanic American Theology*. Ed. Roberto S. Goizueta. Minneapolis: Fortress, 1992.

García, Sixto J., and Orlando O. Espín. "Hispanic-American Theology." In *Proceedings of the Catholic Theological Society of America* 42 (1987): 114–119.

Gates, Henry Louis, Jr., ed. *"Race," Writing, and Difference*. Chicago: University of Chicago Press, 1985.

Geertz, Clifford. *The Interpretation of Cultures*. New York: Basic Books, 1973.

Giddens, Anthony. *Positivism and Sociology*. London: Heinemann, 1974.

Goizueta, Roberto S. *Liberation, Method and Dialogue: Enrique Dussel and North American Theological Discourse*. Atlanta: Scholars Press, 1988.

———. "*Nosotros*: Toward a U.S. Hispanic Anthropology." *Listening: Journal of Religion and Culture* 27:1 (Winter, 1992): 55–69.

———. "U.S. Hispanic Theology and the Challenge of Pluralism." In *Frontiers of Hispanic Theology in the United States*, ed. Allan Figueroa Deck. Maryknoll, NY: Orbis, 1992.

González, Justo. "Hispanics in the United States." In *Listening: Journal of Religion and Culture* 27: 1 (Winter, 1992): 7–16.

———. *Mañana: Christian Theology from a Hispanic Perspective*. Nashville: Abingdon Press, 1990.

———. "Metamodern Aliens in Postmodern Jerusalem." In *Aliens in the Promised Land*. Ed. Ada María Isasi-Díaz and Fernando Segovia, Minneapolis: Fortress Press, 1995.

———. *Santa Biblia: The Bible Through Hispanic Eyes*. Nashville: Abingdon, forthcoming.

da Graça Aranha, José Pereira. *A esthetica da vida*. Rio de Janeiro, 1920.

Graham, Lawrence S. "Latin America: Illusion or Reality? A Case for a New Analytic Framework for the Region." In *Politics and Social Change in Latin America: The Distinct Tradition*. Ed. Howard J. Wiarda. Amherst, MA: University of Massachusetts Press, 1974.

Griffin, David Ray. *God and Religion in the Postmodern World*. Albany, NY: SUNY Press, 1989.

Guerrero, Andrés. *A Chicano Theology*. Maryknoll, NY: Orbis, 1987.

Gutiérrez, Gustavo. "Church of the Poor." In *Born of the Poor: The Latin American Church Since Medellín*. Ed. Edward L. Cleary, O.P. Notre Dame, IN: University of Notre Dame Press, 1990.

———. *The God of Life*. Maryknoll, NY: Orbis, 1991.

———. *Las Casas: In Search of the Poor of Jesus Christ*. Maryknoll, NY: Orbis, 1993.

———. "Liberation Praxis and Christian Faith." In *Frontiers of Theology in Latin America*. Ed. Rosino Gibellini. Maryknoll, NY: Orbis, 1979.

———. *On Job*. Maryknoll, NY: Orbis, 1987.

———. *A Theology of Liberation*. Revised Edition with a New Introduction. Maryknoll, NY: Orbis, 1988.

———. *We Drink from Our Own Wells: The Spiritual Journey of a People*. Maryknoll, NY: Orbis, 1984.

Haber, Honi Fern. *Beyond Postmodern Politics: Lyotard, Rorty, Foucault*. New York: Routledge, 1994.

Habermas, Jürgen. *Legitimation Crisis*. Boston: Beacon, 1975.

———. "Modernity Versus Post-Modernity." *New German Critique* 22 (Winter, 1981): 3–14.

———. *The Theory of Communicative Action*. Boston: Beacon Press, 1984.

———. *Theory and Practice*. London: Heinemann, 1974.

Haddox, John H. *Vasconcelos of Mexico: Philosopher and Prophet*. Austin, TX: University of Texas Press, 1967.

Haight, Roger. *Dynamics of Theology*. New York: Paulist Press, 1990.

Hanchard, Michael. "Identity, Meaning, and the African-American." *Social Text* 24 (1990)

Haney, Kathleen M. *Intersubjectivity Revisited: Phenomenology and the Other*. Athens, OH: Ohio University Press, 1994.

Happel, Stephen, and James J. Walter. *Conversion and Discipleship*. Philadelphia: Fortress, 1986.

Hegel, G. W. F. *Phenomenology of Mind*. Trans. J. B. Baille. London: George Allen and Unwin, 1964.

Huyssen, Andreas. *After the Great Divide: Modernism, Mass Culture, Postmodernism*. Bloomington, IN: Indiana University Press, 1986.

Irarrazaval, Diego. "Religión popular." In *Mysterium Liberationis: Conceptos fundamentales de la teología de la liberación*, vol. 2. Madrid: Editorial Trotta, 1990.

Isasi-Díaz, Ada María. *En la Lucha/In the Struggle: Elaborating a Mujerista Theology*. Minneapolis: Fortress Press, 1993.

———. "A Hispanic Garden in a Foreign Land." In *Inheriting our Mothers' Gardens: Feminist Theology in Third World Perspective*. Ed. Letty M. Russell, Kwok Pui-lan, Ada María Isasi-Díaz, and Katie Geneva Cannon. Louisville: Westminster Press, 1988.

Isasi-Díaz, Ada María, and Yolanda Tarango. *Hispanic Women: Prophetic Voice in the Church*. Minneapolis: Fortress, 1992.

Jameson, Fredric. *Postmodernism, or The Cultural Logic of Late Capitalism*. Durham, NC: Duke University Press, 1991.

Kavanaugh, John Francis. *Following Christ in a Consumer Society: The Spirituality of Cultural Resistance*. Maryknoll, NY: Orbis, 1981.

Kress, Robert. "Theological Method: Praxis and Liberation." *Communio* 6 (Spring, 1979): 113–34.

LaCugna, Catherine Mowry. *God for Us: The Trinity and Christian Life*. San Francisco: Harper, 1991.

Lafaye, Jacques. *Quetzalcóatl and Guadalupe: The Formation of Mexican National Consciousness, 1531–1813*. Chicago: University of Chicago Press, 1976.

Lamb, Matthew. "Praxis." In *The New Dictionary of Theology*. Ed. Joseph Komonchak et al. Wilmington, DE: Michael Glazier, 1987.

———. *Solidarity with Victims*. New York: Crossroad, 1982.

Lévi-Strauss, Claude. *The Naked Man*. New York: Harper and Row, 1981.

Lobkowicz, Nicholas. *Theory and Practice: History of a Concept from Aristotle to Marx*. Notre Dame, IN: University of Notre Dame Press, 1967.

Loesberg, Jonathan. *Aestheticism and Deconstruction: Pater, Derrida, and De Man*. Princeton, NJ: Princeton University Press, 1991.

Lonergan, Bernard. *Insight: A Study of Human Understanding*. San Francisco: Harper and Row, 1957.

———. *Method in Theology*. New York: Crossroad/Seabury, 1972.

———. "The Ongoing Genesis of Methods." In *Studies in Religion* 6:4 (1976–77): 341–55.

Lyotard, Jean-François. *The Differend: Phrases in Dispute*. Minneapolis: University of Minnesota Press, 1988.

———. *Just Gaming*. Minneapolis: University of Minnesota Press, 1984.

———. *The Postmodern Condition: A Report on Knowledge*. Minneapolis: University of Minnesota Press, 1984.

Machado, Antonio. *Selected Poems*. Translated with an Introduction by Alan S. Trueblood. Cambridge, MA: Harvard University Press, 1982.

MacIntyre, Alasdair. "Durkheim's Call to Order." *The New York Review of Books*, March 7, 1974.

————. *Whose Justice? Which Rationality?* Notre Dame, IN: University of Notre Dame Press, 1988.

Maldonado, Luis. *Génesis del catolicismo popular*. Madrid: Ediciones Cristiandad, 1979.

————. *Introducción a la religiosidad popular*. Santander: Sal Terrae, 1985.

Martí, José. "Nuestra América." In *José Martí: Sus mejores páginas*. Ed. Raimundo Lazo. México: Editorial Porrúa, 1978.

Martin, James Alfred, Jr. *Beauty and Holiness: The Dialogue Between Aesthetics and Religion*. Princeton, NJ: Princeton University Press, 1990.

Marx, Karl. "Economic and Philosophic Manuscripts of 1844." In *The Marx-Engels Reader*. Ed. Robert C. Tucker. New York: W. W. Norton and Company, 1978.

————. *Writings of the Young Marx on Philosophy and Society*. Ed. Loyd Easton and Kurt Guddat. Garden City, NY: Doubleday, 1967.

McCoy, John A. "Popular Religion in Latin America." *America*, December 31, 1988.

McGovern, Arthur. *Marxism: An American Christian Perspective*. Maryknoll, NY: Orbis, 1980.

————. *Liberation Theology and Its Critics*. Maryknoll, NY: Orbis, 1989.

Mendus, Susan. "Strangers and Brothers: Liberalism, Socialism and the Concept of Autonomy." In *Liberalism, Citizenship and Autonomy*. Ed. David Milligan and William Watts Miller. Aldershot, England: Avebury, 1992.

Merod, Jim. *The Political Responsibility of the Critic*. Ithaca: Cornell University Press, 1987.

Merton, Thomas. *New Seeds of Contemplation*. New York: New Directions, 1961.

Metz, Johann Baptist. *Faith in History and Society: Toward a Practical Fundamental Theology*. New York: Seabury/Crossroad, 1980.

Meynell, Hugo. "Philosophy After Philosophy." In *Communication and Lonergan: Common Ground for Forging the New Age*. Ed. Thomas J. Farrell and Paul A. Soukup. Kansas City: Sheed and Ward, 1993.

————. "On Truth, Method, and Gadamer." In *Communication and Lonergan: Common Ground for Forging the New Age*. Ed. Thomas J. Farrell and Paul A. Soukup. Kansas City: Sheed and Ward, 1993.

Milligan, David, and William Watts Miller, eds. *Liberalism, Citizenship and Autonomy*. Aldershot, England: Avebury, 1992.

Moreno Rejón, Francisco. *Salvar la vida de los pobres: aportes a la teología moral*. Lima: CEP, 1986.

Norman, Richard. "Citizenship, Politics and Autonomy." In *Liberalism, Citizenship and Autonomy*. Ed. David Milligan and William Watts Miller. Aldershot, England: Avebury, 1992.

Ollman, Bertell. *Alienation: Marx's Conception of Man in Capitalist Society*. Cambridge: Cambridge University Press, 1971.

Omi, Michael, and Howard Winant. "The Los Angeles 'Race Riot' and Contemporary U.S. Politics." In *Reading Rodney King, Reading Urban Uprising*. Ed. Robert Gooding-Williams. New York: Routledge, 1993.

Paz, Octavio. *El laberinto de la soledad*. México, DF: Fondo de Cultural Económica, 1973.

Peukert, Helmut. *Science, Action, and Fundamental Theology: Toward a Theology of Communicative Action*. Cambridge, MA: MIT Press, 1984.

Pierce, Brian J. "The Cross and the Crib: Hope From the Underside." *America*, April 2, 1994.

Rahner, Karl. "The Theology of the Symbol." In *Theological Investigations*, vol. 4. Baltimore: Helicon Press, 1966.

Ricard, Robert. *The Spiritual Conquest of Mexico*. Berkeley: University of California Press, 1966.

Richard, Pablo, and Diego Irarrazaval. *Religión y Política en América Central: hacia una nueva interpretación de la religiosidad popular*. San José, Costa Rica: DEI, 1981.

Ricoeur, Paul. *The Symbolism of Evil*. Boston: Beacon, 1967.

Rodríguez, Jeanette. *Our Lady of Guadalupe: Faith and Empowerment among Mexican American Women*. Austin, TX: University of Texas Press, 1994.

Rodriguez, Richard. "When Did Americans Ever Embrace Family Values?" *Chicago Tribune*, January 5, 1995, sec. 1, p. 23.

Romero, C. Gilbert. *Hispanic Devotional Piety: Tracing the Biblical Roots*. Maryknoll, NY: Orbis, 1991.

Ross, Andrew, ed. *Universal Abandon? The Politics of Postmodernism*. Minneapolis: University of Minnesota Press, 1988.

Rotenstreich, Nathan. *Alienation: The Concept and Its Reception*. Leiden: E. J. Brill, 1989.

Rouner, Leroy S., ed. *Civil Religion and Political Theology*. Notre Dame, IN: University of Notre Dame Press, 1986.

Sandel, Michael. *Liberalism and the Limits of Justice*. London: Cambridge University Press, 1982.

Scannone, Juan Carlos. "Enfoques teológico-pastorales latinoamericanos de la religiosidad popular." *Stromata* 40 (1984): 261–74.

———. "Filosofía primera e intersubjetividad: El a priori de la comunidad de comunicación y el nosotros ético-histórico." *Stromata* 42 (1986): 367–86.

———. "Un nuevo punto de partida en la filosofía latinoamericana." *Stromata* 36 (1980): 25–47.

———. "Religión, lenguaje y sabiduría de los pueblos: Aporte filosófico a la problemática." *Stromata* 34 (1978): 27–42.

Schmitz, Kenneth. "Is Liberalism Good Enough?" In *Liberalism and the Good*. Ed. R. Bruce Douglass, Gerald M. Mara, and Henry S. Richardson. New York: Routledge, 1990.

Schreiter, Robert J. *Constructing Local Theologies*. Maryknoll, NY: Orbis, 1985.

Segundo, Juan Luis. *Faith and Ideologies*. Maryknoll, NY: Orbis, 1984.

———. *Our Idea of God*. Maryknoll, NY: Orbis, 1974.

———. *The Liberation of Theology*. Maryknoll, NY: Orbis, 1976.

Seladoc, Equipo. *Religiosidad popular*. Salamanca: Sígueme, 1976.

Siller Acuña, Clodomiro L. "Anotaciones y comentarios al *Nican Mopohua*." *Estudios Indígenas* 8:2 (1981): 217–74.

———. *Flor y canto del Tepeyac: Historia de las apariciones de Santa María de Guadalupe, texto y comentario*. Xalapa, Veracruz, México: Servir, 1981.

————. *Para comprender el mensaje de María de Guadalupe.* Buenos Aires: Editorial Guadalupe, 1989.

Smith, Jonathan Z. *To Take Place: Toward Theory in Ritual.* Chicago: University of Chicago Press, 1987.

Sobrino, Jon. *Spirituality of Liberation.* Maryknoll, NY: Orbis, 1988.

Stephanson, Anders. "Interview with Cornel West." In *Universal Abandon? The Politics of Postmodernism.* Ed. Andrew Ross. Minneapolis: University of Minnesota Press, 1988.

Streeter, Carla Mae, O. P. "Glossary of Lonerganian Terminology." In *Communication and Lonergan.* Ed. Thomas J. Farrell, and Paul A. Soukup. Kansas City: Sheed and Ward, 1993.

Sullivan, William M. "Bringing the Good Back In." In *Liberalism and the Good.* Ed. R. Bruce Douglass, Gerald M. Mara, and Henry S. Richardson. New York: Routledge, 1990.

Taylor, Mark Kline. *Remembering Esperanza.* Maryknoll, NY: Orbis, 1990.

Terán, Oscar. *En busca de la ideología argentina.* Buenos Aires: Catálogos Editora, 1986.

Thompson, Jon. *Fiction, Crime, and Empire: Clues to Modernity and Postmodernism.* Urbana and Chicago: University of Illinois Press, 1993.

Tönnies, Ferdinand. *Community and Society.* East Lansing, MI: Michigan State University Press, 1957.

Toulmin, Stephen. *Cosmopolis: The Hidden Agenda of Modernity.* New York: The Free Press, 1990.

Tracy, David. *The Analogical Imagination: Christian Theology and the Culture of Pluralism.* New York: Crossroad, 1981.

————. *Plurality and Ambiguity: Hermeneutics, Religion, Hope.* San Francisco: Harper and Row, 1987.

Turner, Victor. *Dramas, Fields and Metaphors: Symbolic Action in Human Society.* Ithaca: Cornell University Press, 1974.

————. *The Ritual Process: Structure and Anti-Structure.* Ithaca: Cornell University Press, 1977.

Vasconcelos, José. *Obras Completas,* 4 vols. México, DF: Libreros Mexicanos Unidos, 1958–61.

Vidal, Jaime. "Popular Religion among Hispanics in the General Area of the Archdiocese of Newark." In *Presencia Nueva: A Study of Hispanics in the Archdiocese of Newark.* Newark: Archdiocesan Office of Research and Planning, 1988.

Villaseñor, Victor. *Rain of Gold.* New York: Dell, 1991.

Voegelin, Eric. *The Ecumenic Age. Order and History,* vol. 4. Baton Rouge, LA: Louisiana State University Press, 1974.

von Balthasar, Hans Urs. *The Glory of the Lord: A Theological Aesthetics.* 7 Vols. San Francisco: Ignatius Press, 1982–1991.

————. *Theo-Drama: Theological Dramatic Theory.* 5 Vols. San Francisco: Ignatius Press, 1982–1992.

Wachtel, Paul. *The Poverty of Affluence.* New York: Free Press, 1983.

Weber, Max. *The Protestant Ethic and the Spirit of Capitalism.* New York: Scribner's, 1956.

Woodward, R. L. *Positivism in Latin America, 1850–1900*. Lexington, MA: Heath, 1971.

Zea, Leopoldo. *Apogeo y decadencia del positivismo en México*. México, DF: El Colegio de México, 1944.

———. *Dos etapas del pensamiento en Hispanoamérica: del romanticismo al positivismo*. México, DF: Colegio de México, 1949.

Index